HERBS AND SPICES OF THE WORLD

HERBS AND SPICES

Schiffer Publishing Ltd
Box E Exton, Pennsylvania 19341

OF THE WORLD

BY HERMIE KRANZDORF

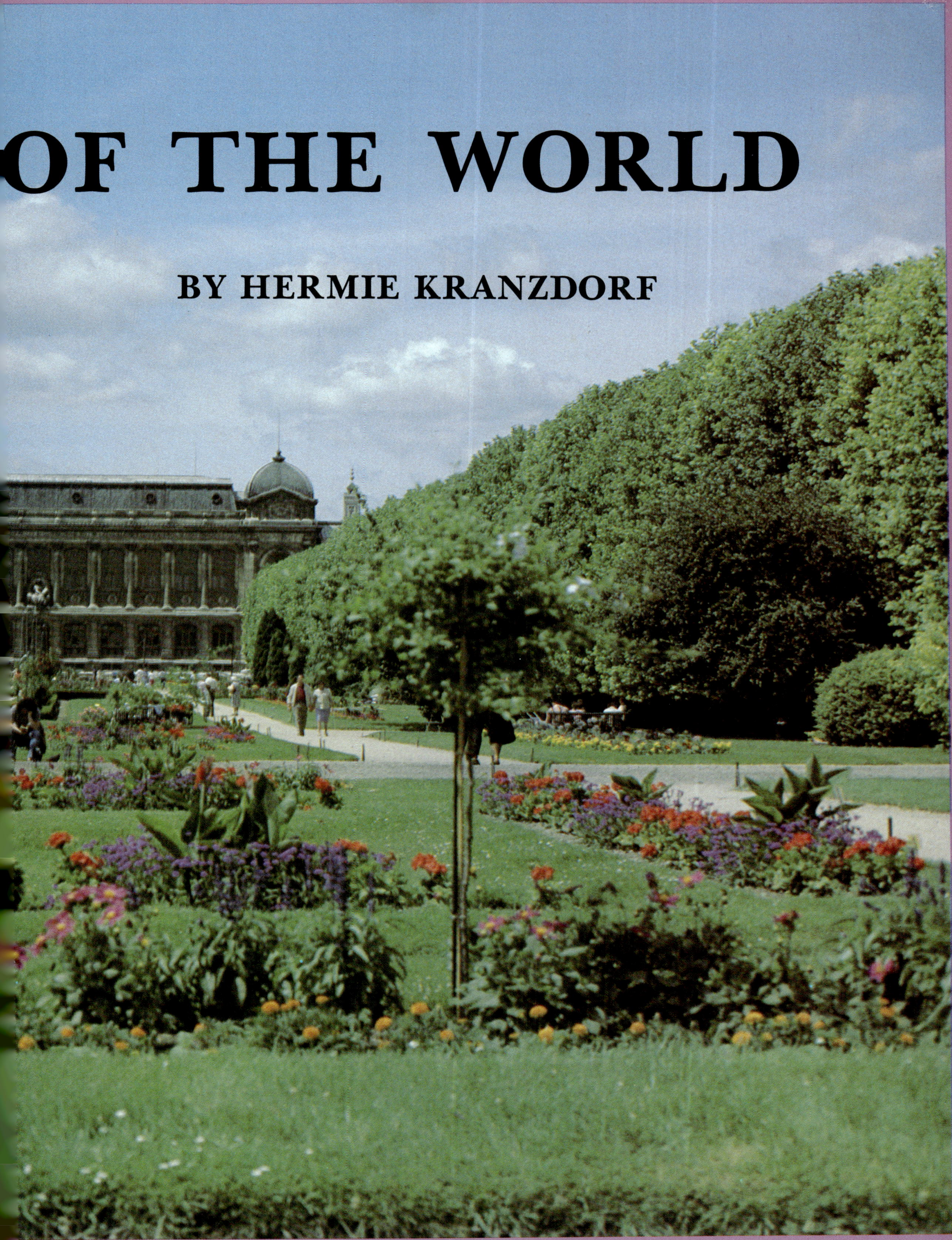

With love to three,
for Norman, Betty and Mike

Other books by this author:
Cooking For The '80's
Co-Author of:
Chef Tell Tell's All

The following material was reprinted from copywritten publication with permission: Pear Custard Tart, by Hermie Kranzdorf, page 182, *International Association of Cooking Schools Cookbook,* Irena Chalmers Cookbooks, Inc. and color picture, page 184 courtesy Argo and Kingsford corn starch, Best Foods.

Photography: Norman M. Kranzdorf

Library of Congress Catalog Number: 83—61647.

Printed in the United States of America.
ISBN: 0-916838-84-6
Published by Schiffer Publishing Ltd., Box E, Exton, Pennsylvania 19341

CONTENTS

ACKNOWLEDGMENTS

It is difficult to know how to thank someone for their help after sharing most of a lifetime together. The list has no beginning and certainly, no end. So to my chief photographer, editor, critic, world travelling companion and food taster, who has borne the brunt of my constant experimenting, a special thank you for your patience and sage advice in helping with this book. For all the early mornings and uncomfortably long trips to visit some out of the way herb garden or food market, weighted down with camera equipment, it was a job well done.

I want to thank the library staff of the Pennsylvania Horticultural Society for their cooperation in affording me easy access to their large and excellent collection of books.

And for a fascinating glimpse of how herbs and spices were used in the past, I want to thank Mr. Walter Johnson of the Rosenbach Museum who allowed me the privilage of researching many of their rare and priceless old cookbooks.

A thank you, also, to Mrs. Walter Howard who let me visit her magnificent herb garden and patiently answered many of my questions. To Judy Street of Apple-Pie Farms for her kindness and to Mary Opiela and to my mother for proofreading, a thank you as well.

OUTDOOR MARKET, INDIA

HISTORY

Since the dawn of history, herbs and spices have been used by man for two primary purposes; to flavor his food and to cure his ills. Folklore and superstition flourished and grew about the magical qualities of many of these plants, for man's religious beliefs were hopelessly intertwined with their usage. Disease was believed to come from the influence of the gods and had to combatted by strong magic, often with a large dose of mysticism and a little bit of astrology thrown in for good measure. No doubt Stone-Age man was often experimented on by his mate, for this so-called "magic" was just an awareness, often by trial and error of the natural healing properties of growing things, much of which is valid to this day.

Thousands of years ago, civilizations grew and flourished in Egypt, China, India and Mesapotamia. They began to collect herbs and spices and record their usage. An interesting version of the creation of the earth appears on an Assyrian stone tablet carved over 5000 years ago. That scripture relates that the gods, being duly impressed with the difficulty of their prodigious task, assembled for a meeting before beginning the creation. While discussing their problem they sipped sesame seed wine.

Writings on ancient Papyrii found in Egyptian tombs describe how herbs and spices were used by this highly developed civilization in the making of perfumes, cosmetics and dyes, in oil offerings to the gods, incense and embalming ointments and last but not least, to season their food. Our Egyptian forefathers were known to have issued a daily ration of garlic and onions to the slave-builders of the pyramids to keep them healthy. The famous Ebbers Papyrus, written in 1500 B.C. (discovered in 1874 by the German George Ebbers) tells us much about this early Egyptian knowledge of herbs and spices.

Herbs and spices are mentioned frequently in the Old Testament. We learn that Joseph was sold by his brothers into slavery for twenty pieces of silver to a passing caravan of spice traders on their way to Egypt. And the Queen of Sheba, along

HERB SECTION AT JARDIN DE PLANTES, PARIS, FRANCE

with her many charms, also brought several kinds of spices to King Solomon for good measure.

Artifacts of ancient Chinese and Indian civilizations have not survived to any great extent. What records we do have indicate that the use of herbs and spices was at least as great in the Orient as it was in Egypt. The Chinese Emperor Shen Nung who lived about 2700 B.C., called the 'divine cultivator', is credited with writing about herbs. Part of his text supposedly survived long enough to be copied by others, but since there was no written language at the time, this story is difficult to prove. The treatise was probably compiled about the first century A.D. Herbs and spices were mentioned to some degree in early Indian religious texts, mostly for their medicinal usage.

A brisk spice trade flourished between the East and the principal cities of the Mediterranean long before the birth of Christ. Caravans of Arabian traders developed overland 'incense routes' through the deserts. Interestingly enough, it is said that camels were not used on these routes until about 1000 B.C. It must have been a long, hot walk before then.

The conquests of Alexander the Great opened and established many trade routes between the Greeks and the lands they conquered. Along with the spread of Greek civilization, we have the beginning of man's attempt to document and record the scientific knowledge of his times. The Greek scholar, Theophrastes (372-287 B.C.) is called the 'father of botany', for his enquiry into the study of plants was a basic effort at their complete classification.

Hippocrates (460 B.C.) wrote a treatise on the use of herbs and spices in which he emphasized the importance of diet and hygiene in preventing man's ills, as opposed to the influence of the supernatural. Small groups of ancient Greeks, knowledgeable about the use of drugs, harvested, gathered and sold the roots of medicinal plants to pharmacologists. These men and women were known as 'rhizomatists' or 'root gatherers' and our present day apothecaries are descendants of these early foragers.

With the decline of Greek influence, the Holy Roman Empire came to power. The Romans used herbs and spices to an even greater extent than did their predecessors. Conquering garrisons of Roman soldiers brought seeds and plants with them, spreading their growth and use throughout the known world. Dioscorides, a Greek educated Roman physician in Nero's army, wrote 'De Materia Medica' during the first century, A.D. in which he described over 600 medicinal plants, their uses and healing virtues. For over 1500 years this book remained the prime authority in its field.

The period of the Dark Ages (641 - 1069 A.D.) was grim for herbs and spices as well as for the general populace. Much of man's system of agriculture was killed off by the repeated invasions of Southern Europe. Only the monastery gardens flourished and survived. St. Gall in Switzerland, run by the Benedictine monks and St. Benedict at Monte Cassino are prime examples of the wisdom and foresight of these monks. Physic and kitchen gardens were maintained by the Sacristan, a monk whose job it was to provide the monastery with herbs for medicinal as well as culinary purposes.

Pharmacies as we know them today were still a long way off in the future. By the fifteenth century, all large European households had 'still rooms' for the production of medicinals for their own needs. In each household, individual books of recipes were cherished and handed down through the generations with great care and secrecy. The invention of the printing press allowed books such as the great herbals, heretofore copied patiently by hand by the monks, to reach the general public. With the spread of the printed word, the popularity and usage of these herbals was greatly enlarged.

Herbs and spices were used during the Middle Ages (and even before) for their disinfectant and antiseptic qualities. Sweet smelling herbs such as chamomile and marjoram were popular for their aroma as well as their germ-killing properties. Called 'strewing herbs', they were placed or 'strewn' on the floors of castles, churches and households to deodorize the rooms and hide the ever present dank and evil smells. Surprisingly, this custom survives today in a rather unique way. At weddings, flower girls still 'strew' flower petals along the path that the bride is to walk.

Man, for one reason or another, has often associated foul odors with the presence of evil spirits. Since early times, incense has been burned so that the sweet smelling smoke would rise to appease the gods. With the lack of sanitation, it also appeased those who burned it, I am sure. Pleasant smelling herbs such as thyme and rosemary were often burned as were many spices, such as fenugreek and the classical myrrh and frankincense.

Fragrant herbs wrapped in a cloth, called 'tussie mussies' or nosegays, were carried by our forefathers to be sniffed as they walked outdoors, because fresh air was thought to be harmful. Pommanders were originally aggregations of spices and herbs in a container which were either worn on the person or hung and used to deodorize rooms. Pommander balls were later made by filling or sticking apples and oranges with sweet smelling spices such as cloves. We still see these balls featured as a popular gift item at holiday times.

In 1498, Vasco de Gama rounded the Cape of Good Hope and ended the long dependence of man on overland spice routes. The virtual monopoly of the Moslems declined as sea routes were opened and flourished. Spain and Portugal came to power as the 'Age of Exploration' began. America was discovered while explorers were hunting for a spice route to the East.

Once the sea routes were opened, special guilds came into being to control and monopolize this new trade. In 1600, the East India Company was founded in London. This was followed two years later by the Dutch East India Company as first England, then Holland, took over from the Spanish and Portuguese and began to monopolize the spice trade. In 1447, the first food ordinance in history which prohibited the adulteration of spices, was passed in England.

Man has always cultivated growing things for his own pleasure and profit but not necessarily to increase his knowledge. In 1545, a garden was planted to supply the faculty of the University of Padua with herbs to be used for teaching purposes. Thus, 'Orto Botanico' was the first herb garden in the world planted primarily for study.

Formal gardens began to reach new heights in popularity everywhere. They were cultivated and grown in patterns based on set geometric shapes. Knot gardens, though formidable to maintain, flourished as well. In seventeenth century Italy and France, 'Parterre' gardens were the fashion. Planted to resemble formal embroidery, these gardens were ornamental only, meant to be looked at, not to be used.

From the dawn of time, both the lack of proper refrigeration and storage has caused much of man's foodstuffs to become inedible. Herbs and spices were often used to disguise the rancid quality of food. Renaissance man's diet contained some very unusual mixtures by today's standards. The first known cookbook, "De Re Coquinaria" is credited to a Roman named Apicius, who wrote it during the first or second century A.D. Although Apicius was known to be an excellent cook, this book was probably a conglomeration of works by earlier Greek and Roman writers.

By the fourteenth century, cookbooks utilizing herbs and spices became very popular. Two early and well known books often mentioned are the English "Form of Curry" and the French "Menanger de Paris". By 1652 we have a popular book by Francois-Pierre de la Varenne, a famous chef in the service of the Marquis d'Uxelles, who replaced some of the heavily spiced and seasoned foods of the times with lighter fare—a process that seems to repeat itself with every generation of new cookbook writers.

Many great herbals were written between the late fifteenth to the seventeenth century. Authors such as John Gerald, William Turner, John Parkinson and Nicholas Culpepper produced lasting works. Many of these writers professed faith in what was called the "Doctrine of Signatures". This doctrine stated that 'the cure is found with the cause'. Each and every plant was named after and used to cure a specific part of the body. This relationship between body and plant could be determined in one of several ways: the color—red flowers were thought to be blood purifiers; texture—soft leaves ease pain; aroma—an evil smell is a fumigant; habitat, etc. Interestingly enough, some of these theories have a basis in truth. For example, willow trees grow and flourish in damp areas where rheumatism abounds (habitat). In 1763, the decocted cellulose bark of the willow tree was used to treat rheumatism. We now know that this willow bark contains salicylic acid—a forerunner of our modern day aspirin.

Astrology was also brought into the Doctrine of Signatures, stating that each part of the body had its own sign and was ruled by one of the planets. In order to cure someone, a physician had to know both the planet ruling the patient's body and the sign of the herb he wished to use. Culpepper's very popular herbal (1789) was based on theories which combined herbalism with astrology.

One brief but relevant word on magic before we complete our history. The ancients believed that there were certain auspicious times of the day, as well as days of the year, for the gathering of herbs and spices. Magic was thought to be more powerful at these specific times, therefore making the herb more valuable. Midsummer Eve (June 22) was thought to be the best day for harvest. And the most appropriate time of the day was considered to be early morning, once the sun was up and the dew had dried from the plants. As it turns out, June 22 is indeed a good day, as many herbs have reached their peak growth by then. And in the warmth of the morning, the volatile oils found in the leaves are in their most concentrated form. Harvesting then will indeed yield the best flavored herbs.

During the last century, the world spice trade has for the most part become decentralized, with no one country dominating the marketplace. The production of medicinals no longer relies primarily on herbs and spices as it once did, for drugs are now synthesized chemically, as well as most ingredients found in dyes, perfumes and cosmetics.

But herbs and spices have not yet been and hopefully never will be replaced for their use in cooking. There is no substitute for the unique flavors they lend to enhance the food we eat. So next June 22, shine only, I hope to see all of you out there along with me, gathering and harvesting a supply of those wonderfully enchanting and enticing flavors that are as near as your own backyard.

MATS FOR DRYING RED PEPPERS, NEPAL

CLASSIFICATION

WHAT ARE HERBS AND SPICES

Defining what is an herb or what is a spice is not an easy matter, for there are bound to be exceptions to every rule. Webster's dictionary defines an herb as 'a flowering plant whose stem above the ground does not become woody or persistent', which eliminates such commom herbs as rosemary and bay laurel. Webster's says that a spice is 'any of a class of pungent or aromatic substances of vegetable origin', an unclear definition at best. Botanists and herbalists have for centuries uttered equally confusing statements, which have included in their definitions just about any vegetation found growing on this earth.

Since this book is about culinary herbs and spices, the best definition for our purposes is a rather a broad one. To us, an herb is a foliage (or green) plant grown in a temperate climate which is used to flavor foods. When the plant is grown in a tropical region, it is then considered to be a spice. Spices usually consist of seeds, hulls and bark but not foliage.

With the passage of time, the number of herbs and spices—especially herbs, used for culinary purposes, appears to be on the decline. We certainly use fewer than did our forefathers. Botanists tell us that there are about 2500 recognizable species of edible herbs, but the great

OUTDOOR MARKET AT LAKE DAL, KASHMIR, INDIA

majority of these are now neglected. In the time of Hippocrates, 400 different herbs were commonly used throughout the world. This number had dwindled remarkably to about 28 in the nineteenth century. We now use less than 15 culinary herbs on a regular basis in this country.

Much of this decline is really not due to the fact that we use fewer herbs but rather to a reclassification of what constitutes an herb as opposed to a vegetable. In earlier times, all green plants were lumped together in the same category. It was not until the seventeenth century that any distinction was made between them. Herbs were then divided into three categories; sweet or flavoring herbs, potherbs or vegetables and medicinal herbs. Potherbs are now considered to be those plants whose leaves and stems are used for actual food, such as celery and Florence fennel. Sweet herbs are those plants whose leaves, seeds or roots (for example, parsley, anise seed and ginger root) are used to flavor foods. And of course, medicinal herbs are for medicinals.

Spices do not fit into any botanically describable family, but now are considered to be any one of the various tropical plant parts used to flavor foods. They can be categorized by the part of the plant from which they come, such as flower buds, fruits, underground stems or roots, bark and seeds.

CLASSIFICATION SYSTEM

During the eighteenth century, a set of standards was developed by which plants could be classified throughout the world. This system of classification, founded by the Swedish botanist Carolus Linneaus, remains in use today. Latin was adopted as the universal language and each plant was given a two-part Latin name. The first word of the name specifies the genus of the plant and the second word indicates the species.

Once you understand some of the basic words used, you can learn a great deal about the history of the plant by knowing its full Latin name. The Latin word 'officinale' or 'officinalus' means 'of the shop'. If the word officinale follows the species name, it means that this particular plant had been sold by apothecaries. 'Sativus' means that it was a cultivated plant as opposed to one found growing only in the wild. 'Tinctura' indicates its use as a dye and 'fragrans' or 'odorata' mean that the plant has a sweet scent. The word 'vulgare' or 'vulgaris' describes the species as being the common or ordinary variety of that particular genus.

Many times you will see this double Latin name followed by a letter. The letter denotes the name of the botanist who first discovered the species (for example, L. stands for Linneaus). Hybrids are indicated by the letter 'x' following the Latin name. The abbreviation 'var' following the name denotes a variation which occurs within a particular species.

Many of today's popular culinary herbs can be classified as belonging to one of three major plant families. The largest of these is Compositae, which is the sunflower or daisy family and contains more than 100 genera. This family can be recognized by its flowerheads made up of closely clustered florets with ray-like petals. Their hard, dry fruits are called achenes. Examples of Compositae would be the chamomile, marigold and tansy plants.

The second largest family is the Labiatae or mint family, which contains the most aromatic of the herbs, such as marjoram, basil and lemon balm. Labiatae have square stems and irregular two-lipped flowers with four stamens. They are fertilized mainly by bees and insects and their fruit is small and contains four seeds.

The third largest is the Umbelliferae, the parsley or carrot family. They have umbels, or umbrella-like clusters of flowers on round, hollow flower stalks. All herbs and spices whose seeds (really fruits) are used for flavoring come from this family. Examples of Umbelliferae would be anise, caraway and dill.

ANNUALS, BIENNIALS AND PERENNIALS

All herbs and spices, actually all growing plants, can be classified as annuals, biennials or perennials. An annual is a plant that completes its life cycle, from seed to harvest, in one growing season.

A biennial is a plant which takes two years to finish its life cycle because only one part of its growth is completed during the first year. The top of the plant dies back to the ground but its underground root system remains alive. The plant will flower as well as produce seeds during its second and last growing season.

A perennial plant has a life cycle of more than two years. Once it reaches maturity, it will produce flowers and seeds every year for many years. In temperate climates, only the root system of the plant stays alive during the winter, while in tropical climates, the entire plant can remain green all year round.

GROWTH

HOW SEEDS GROW

Once a seed is planted, whether in a frame, a pot, or in the ground outdoors, the growing process is exactly the same. The first step is the opening of the seed coat, which can take from one day to several weeks, depending on the particular germination time of the type of seed planted. At the bottom of the seed a tiny root appears, whose purpose is to secure initial anchorage into the ground or potting medium. From the top of the seed a shoot next appears and heads directly towards a light source. Energy for this first growth comes from the food stored within the seed itself and not from any outside source.

As the root begins to develop, minute one-celled root hairs start to take in water and salts from the soil in the form of a solution. Once the top shoot, which is white in color, breaks through and is above ground, it begins to turn green. For with the presence of light, photosynthesis can then occur.

Growth of the plant continues basically by the extension of these two primary (root and shoot) structures. Specialization begins to take place as two kinds of plant organs develop. One set of organs is concerned with reproduction and become the seed-containing fruits and the flowers. The other set is vegetative, or those which are concerned with the growth and maintenance of the plant. They develop and become the roots, stems and leaves.

In time, the roots become more and more anchored into the growing medium. It is their job to absorb water as well as nutrients from the soil. The plant stem has a two-fold function. It acts as a support for the leaves, fruits and flowers and as a pathway for the absorption of food.

Specialization can go even further and in some interesting directions. Some plants develop large underground stems called rhizomes or tubers (such as ginger root), or even bulbs or corms (saffron) which are used for food storage. Plants with large taproot systems, such as horseradish and members of the parsley family, store food in their large edible roots.

The plant leaves also have a two-fold function. They are necessary for the processes of photosynthesis and transpiration. A simple way to explain photosynthesis is to remember that plants take in both carbon dioxide and water from the soil. Energy from sunlight is trapped in the leaves of the plants by a green pigment called chlorophyll. This chlorophyll acts as a catalyst and enables the plant to convert the carbon dioxide and water into glucose (or food) and to release oxygen into the air. The process of transpiration is the giving off of waste materials formed in the plant through pores in the surface of the leaves.

GROWING HERBS

I live in the Mid-Atlantic or northeastern part of the United States and as much as I would like to grow all of the many herbs and spices I use for cooking, it is just not possible in this temperate climate. Spices need tropical conditions, lots of rainfall and a hot daily temperature to flourish and grow. A few can be grown successfully indoors, preferably in a greenhouse, but not all. So for the most part, I raise my own herbs and buy most of my spices.

I do not grow herbs, or anything else for that matter, commercially. I raise enough to take care of my own needs—those of a small family. One or two plants of each variety of herb (with a few exceptions such as basil and chervil) is more than enough to give me an ample supply of fresh herbs all summer long, with enough left over to preserve for the winter.

Most of us, including myself, begin the project of growing herbs by buying a few plants at a local nursery. When buying herb plants, try to select full, sturdy looking ones which seem to have a fairly well developed root growth. Spindly looking specimens do not always do well. Do not, no matter how you are tempted, plant the herbs in your garden until the frost is over and the soil has begun to warm. The month of May works well in my area. Check the maps found in most seed catalogues, or with your local State Extension Service as to the best time for planting in your area. It is better to start things a week or two late rather than have them harmed by frost.

There are two main elements that are absolutely necessary for growing herbs successfully in your own garden. First, it is essential that the soil have good drainage, which means that the soil is able to absorb a normal amount of rainfall without having the water run off too quickly. If the roots remain too dry, or conversely, too wet, the plants will not do well. The second requirement is ample sunshine, about seven hours a day for herbs which call for full sun and three to four hours for those which grow best in partial shade. Of course, there are exceptions to every rule, so check for the best growing conditions for individual herbs before planting.

Some tender plants need protection against the wind. Herb gardens planted next to walls or alongside a house do very well. Even hedging or a thick garden fence (not just poles) also help to break the force of the wind. If, in the listings following the individual plants, the 'Conditions Preferred' indicate shelter, it means the above.

If you are planting your herbs in a new area in the garden, it is a good idea to dig up the soil and turn it well first. This loosening or aerating of the soil will break up any hard clumps and it is better for both the plant and for you. Digging the plant in will be much easier and the root system will be able to function better.

Do not be afraid to shift around some of your herbs if they are not doing well. This season or next, you can try them in a different part of the garden. The drainage may be better, or the sunlight a little less strong. When all else fails, shifting often works for the more difficult to grow herbs.

Herbs are, for the most part, very easy to grow. The natural habitat for many of them is the hilly and barren countryside surrounding the Mediterranean Sea. There, the plants are exposed to a great deal of sun and wind. They grow and flourish in very rocky and sandy soil.

To adapt to the difficult conditions in this area, many of the herbs have developed characteristics which afford them natural protection from the elements. Some have very narrow leaves which prevent large amounts of evaporation or water loss by the plant. Others have sharp protective tips to keep them from being eaten by grazing animals. Herbs that grow in this harsh and hostile climate tend to develop extremely strong flavors. They form a thick protective layer of volatile oils to act as a shield from the strong Mediterranean sun. Herbs grown in other parts of the world will have distinctive strength and flavor differences because of the variables in soil and climatic conditions.

PLANTING HERBS

Let us assume that the best location has been selected and the ground has been properly prepared. Your newly purchased herbs are sitting in their pots waiting to be planted—now what? Begin, naturally enough, by digging a hole just a

SOLAR HOUSE AT LONGWOOD GARDENS, KENNETT SQUARE, PENNSYLVANIA

little larger than the container in which the plant was purchased. If the soil is very dry, pour a cup or two of water into the hole and allow it to drain completely.

Remove the plant from its clay or plastic pot (if it is in a peat or dissolvable container, this is not necessary) by tapping the sides of the pot gently while holding it almost upside down. Never pull the plant out by the top, as you may end up with all leaves and no root. You may need to spread the roots out a little by hand if they seem very tangled. Place the bottom of the plant in the hole and cover about two-thirds full with soil. Then fill the hole with water and let it drain. Fill to the top with the remaining soil and tamp down by pressing firmly all around the plant. I like to water again once everything is planted. The best time to do your planting is when the sun is not too hot. Late afternoon is an especially good time for digging in nursery stock.

Tender herbs can be either brought indoors for the winter, or left outdoors if some care is taken. For the most part, I prefer to take my chances by leaving them outdoors with a covering of some kind. A thick layer of mulch (leaves and grass clippings) or straw is excellent. Even a sheet of heavy plastic will do the job if you leave a few air holes. I remove the cover towards the end of March or the beginning of April. With a little luck, most of my herbs will have survived. If the winter has been particularly harsh, a few will die off and have to be replaced. I find that I do better on the average by leaving things in place outdoors rather than bringing my herbs inside.

PLANTING SEEDS

Once purchased, it is always tempting to plant an entire packet of seeds—I hate to see anything go to waste. Many packages contain up to one hundred seeds or more. Other than growing a lifetime supply of just one herb, I'd also have no room left for anything else in my garden. Each year I try to win the battle of self-restraint by not starting all of each kind of seed. I do, however, plant more than the amount of seeds that I think I will need, for I have found through the years that often some of them do not take. It is better to discard or give away a few seedlings than to have to start all over again. This way I usually end up with enough plants for my family plus a few to share.

If it has been a warm spring and I am late in getting started, I sow the seeds directly into the ground in the area where the herb is to remain.

HILLTOP HERB FARM, CLEVELAND, TEXAS

Seeds should be planted at a depth of about twice the size of the diameter of the particular seed. This can be very tricky with tiny seeds as they can be easily washed away by a strong rainfall. If nothing comes up in what should be the correct amount of time, start again. When watering new seedlings, be careful to use just a fine mist until they have taken.

If it has been a long, cool spring and I am anxious to get an early start, I begin my seeds indoors. I prefer to use those little peat pots that can be set directly into the ground so that the seedlings do not have to be disturbed. I keep a box of these flat peat discs around for starting both my herbs and vegetables. The discs should be lined up in plastic trays and watered from the bottom (several times) until they are fully rehydrated, according to the directions. I plant a few seeds in each pot and set the tray for a week or so under a window that does not get direct sunlight. Once they have sprouted, I move the seedlings to a sunny spot until they are large enough to be taken outdoors. If they are to remain indoors for any length of time, thin out the seedlings so that only one or two remain in each pot. Otherwise, separate them when planting outdoors.

Just like plants which are kept indoors for the winter, seedlings that are started indoors cannot be taken directly outside and should first be 'hardened off'. This means that the plants should be brought outside each day for increasing amounts of time and then brought back inside by nightfall for a week or so, before they are permanently planted outdoors.

GROWING HERBS INDOORS

Many herbs can be grown indoors successfully if you have no outside garden area. They will need lots of light and a window with southern exposure is always best. Plant 'grow' lights can be used in addition, if you have the room for them. Just remember that it takes about two hours of artificial light to equal one hour of natural sunlight. As most indoor plants do not like changes or drafts, try to keep them where the temperature will be fairly even.

Good drainage is essential for herbs whether they are indoors or out. Pots which have drainage holes in the bottom should be used. Block the hole with some stones or a piece of a broken clay pot on the inside before filling with soil. This will allow any extra water to drain out easily while the soil remains in place. I like to set these pots into saucers filled with small stones or gravel. The stones raise the plant just enough so that the bottom of the pot never sits in a saucer full of water and allows the roots to drain adequately.

Most perennial herbs go through a dormant period during the winter the same as if they were outdoors. Do not add any fertilizer during the winter months of December and January and do not water too frequently. You should wait until the plants are really dry before watering. I must say that I am as bad as the next about over-watering my indoor plants during the winter. I get guilt feelings about neglecting them.

If you live in a city where there is a lot of soot and dirt, it is a good idea to wash or wipe off the leaves once in a while to keep them from getting clogged with grime. Remember, plants breathe through their leaves.

PROPAGATION OF PERENNIALS

Many perennial herbs become woody and unweildy after several years and should be replaced if they are to be used for cooking. You can always begin again with another plant but there are several ways to reproduce new plants from the ones you already have. The method of propagation depends on the nature of the plant involved.

Layering

This is the best method for thin stemmed plants which will root by themselves in the soil. Propagation by layering enables you to end up with a plant which is an exact replica of its parent because layering is an asexual reproductive process.

Select a supple branch which has a prominent node. Scrape away a little of the bark and make a partial cut into the stem on an angle below the node on the underside of the branch. Be careful not to cut all the way through the branch, halfway is more than enough. Some experts suggest dipping the cut into a commercial plant hormone powder, while others prefer to leave it alone, this is optional.

Dig a small hole in the ground next to the plant, bend the branch and place the bottom into the hole (cut side down). Fasten the branch down by using a bent wire hanger or a very large hairpin to keep it in place. Fill the hole with soil, tamp it down well and then water. You can place a weight, such as a stone or brick, over the depression as added insurance to keep the branch in place.

The advantage of the layering technique is that the new plant remains attached to its parent for nourishment until it is ready to be cut off and transplanted. Check the plant in about six to eight weeks for root growth. Once an adequate root system has developed, you can cut off the branch completely and the plant is on its own. If you layer the branches late in the summer, you can leave the baby plants attached to the parent over the winter and transplant in the spring.

Mound Layering

Mound layering is used to propagate bush-like perennial herbs such as sage. Build up a mound of soil high around the base of the bush so that the stems are covered as much as possible, with only

SHALIMAR GARDENS, KASHMIR, INDIA

WATERLOO GARDENS, DEVON, PENNSYLVANIA

the tops of the shoots sticking out. Roots should form by themselves at the leaf joints. The only problem with this method is that rain will sometimes wash mounded soil away. This usually happens to me. If so, just replace the soil and start again. Mounding is probably most successful when done in the fall and left in place over the winter months. In the spring, clear away the soil, cut off the branches with the roots attached and plant them.

Division

A plant which grows in the form of a clump (such as chives) and has no central stem can be dug up and divided. A shovel or even a garden fork can be used to dig out the plant. Shake off the extra soil so that you can see the roots and then just divide the clump into halves or quarters, depending upon its size. You can use your hands or the fork to divide the plant, just make sure you leave plenty of roots attached to each piece. Dig a new hole, replant each of the clumps separately and water well.

Root Cuttings

This method is best used for plants that form runners or those which send up new stems from their roots. The classic way to take a root cutting is to cut off a small section of the plant making sure that the piece has some root as well as a bud attached. Use a nursery flat and bury the sections in vermiculite or rooting medium. Water well and keep the flat indoors. Once the cuttings become established and are growing well, harden them off and plant outdoors.

I prefer to use a more simple method that will achieve almost the same results. Instead of the classic method of root cutting described above, I treat the runners as I would small clumps and divide them instead. This saves the work of bringing the plants indoors and then having to harden them off before replanting. If you want only one or two plants as I usually do, try this system.

Stem Cuttings

Cut off a four inch piece of the stem from the top of the plant where there is new growth. Then remove about half of the lower leaves. You can dip the cut end of the stem in hormone powder, if you wish. It is important to keep the cut ends of the stem moist so that they do not dry out, so you can either wrap them in damp paper towels or work quickly. Plant the stems at a 45 degree angle, burying them about halfway in a pot of vermiculite or rooting medium. Bring indoors and keep these plants in the shade for a week or two. Water often.

New growth does not always appear first at the top of the stems, so it pays to check the root system as well. Tug gently on the stems and when you feel some resistance, you know that you are on your way. Harden off and transplant once the roots are about one inch long.

Bulbs and Corms

After they are planted, many bulbs will divide by themselves to form small clusters. Garlic and shallots are prime examples of this. The clusters can be dug up, divided and replanted (as well as harvested). The saffron crocus will form tiny cormlets around the base of the old bulbs. Each of these cormlets can be removed and replanted individually.

HARVEST

PICKING, HARVESTING AND PRESERVING HERBS

For daily use, herbs can and should be picked fresh all summer long. For herbs that grow in a clump, such as chives, nip from the outside of the clump towards the center. No plant should ever be cut completely down to the ground, always remember to leave at least three inches of growth so that the plant has a chance to re-establish itself.

Herbs, such as basil, which grow from a single stem should have the tips of their central stems pinched off regularly during the summer. This will encourage the plant to develop a large leafy side growth and give you a more abundant supply of the herb.

In addition to using them daily, most herbs can be harvested twice and some even three times during the summer months. Usually the last week in June or the first week in July and then again late in August or early September seem to work well in the Northeast. Some years, if I don't have much time, I harvest only once, in mid to late summer. Even with just one harvest, there is usually enough yield to last me through the winter months.

The quality and flavor of herbs depends on the concentration of volatile oils present in the leaves at the time they are picked. This concentration seems to be at its highest level during the morning hours, right after the sun has burned off the dew. To have herbs at their very peak of flavor try to harvest them just before the plant is ready to flower. Although these are excellent rules, I am not always able to follow them myself. One year, I harvested my herbs late on a cloudy afternoon after some of them had come to flower, with no dire results. My winter supply was still better than anything I could buy.

A good general rule to follow for harvesting perennials is to cut them back no more than one-third to one-half of their growth. Annuals should be cut to within three inches of the ground during mid-season. Late in the year, annuals can even be pulled completely out of the ground, although I never do so myself. A few more leaves always seem to appear after harvest time and I manage to have some fresh herbs right up until the frost.

Seeds from herb plants should be harvested while they still are in their natural containers. It is too late if you wait until they fall out of their pods or heads. The best time to cut off seed heads is when they start to turn brown. When shaken, you can just begin to hear the seeds rattle around inside. Roots and stems are best when harvested late in the fall, just as the plants leaves begin to die back. Flowers should be picked for preserving just as they are ready to open.

Herbs to be preserved should be washed before drying and storing. Cleaning some leafy herbs, such as knotted marjoram can be a chore. I find that the easiest way to wash herbs is to do so while they are still attached to their stems. Cut off the stems as instructed and pick off any browned or bad looking leaves. Rinse well, then shake to remove as much moisture as possible. I spread out a large bath towel onto a table and scatter the herbs on top to air dry for an hour or two, turning them once or twice.

At this point, I pack away the herbs which are to be frozen. Leafy herbs, such as tarragon or basil should be packed without their stems. Pick off the leaves and place them directly into freezer containers. And no matter what some experts say, I never blanch herbs which I freeze. They have lasted beautifully for up to two years (I have never had any around for a longer period of time) in my freezer and have retained their full flavor and aroma.

Some people prefer to freeze individual packets of herbs in set amounts, such as in tablespoons. You can do so if you wish. I find it easier to pack one or two large containers of each herb. They take up less room to store and I do not have any trouble in freeing a spoonfull or two as needed. The only herbs which I chop before freezing are chives and dill. The others are better when left whole, and are easiest to chop while still frozen, before they have a chance to thaw.

When you freeze herbs, their best and truest flavor is preserved, but never their color, for they always end up gray and miserable looking. There is a way to disguise their unsightly appearance. For example, when using ugly brown frozen basil, which always looks terrible but tastes wonderful, I add a spoon or two of chopped parsley. Parsley is available fresh all year round and will give whatever you are cooking a nice green color. By using a complimentary fresh herb along with a frozen herb, both color and flavor can be preserved in any recipe.

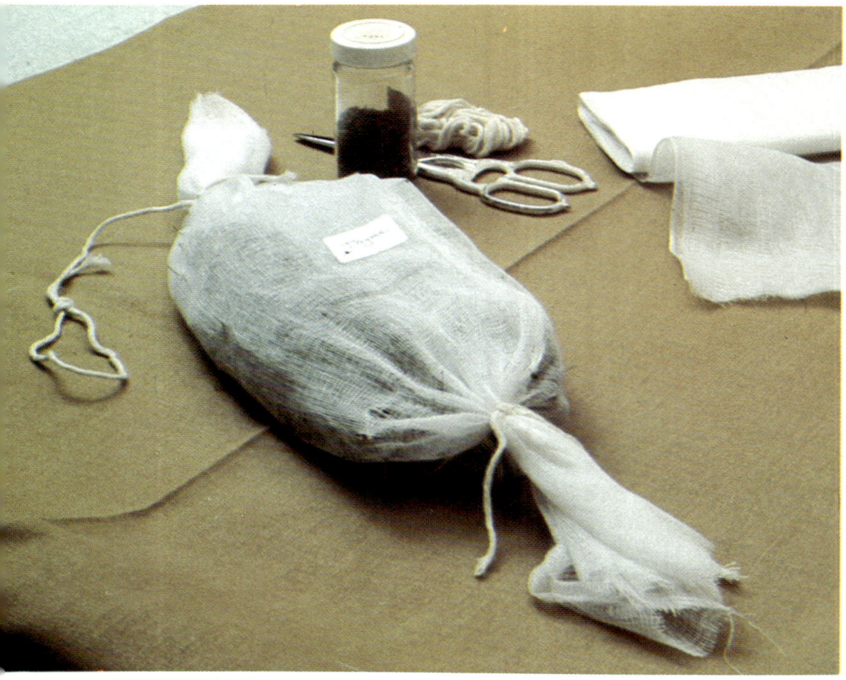

CHEESECLOTH BAG

OREGANO

I find the best way to dry herbs is to hang them while still whole on their stems in cheesecloth bags. This method will keep the herbs dust free and allow for maximum air circulation. To make these bags, cut pieces of cheesecloth the length of the herbs to be wrapped, allowing about ten inches extra in order to have enough cloth to tie off the two ends. Spread open the cheesecloth, place the bundle of herbs in the center, then fold the cloth over the herbs. Tie each end of the cloth together with a piece of string, leaving the top string quite long, about twelve inches or more.

I make it a habit to label each bag at this point. It is not too difficult to mix up which package contains what, especially if you are new at doing this. Tie the long end of the string into a loop and hang the bag in a cool place to dry. Since my kitchen gets no direct sunlight, I often loop the strings over a rod that holds some hanging plants in the window area. If you have an old fashioned coat stand, place it in a shady spot and use it for holding your herbs. I do this at the end of the season when I have lots to dry. By varying the lengths of the string loops, you can fit all your bags over one rod or rack.

Some people object to using cheesecloth, as bits and pieces of herbs will stick to the cloth and may be difficult to remove. I still find it the best

ANOTHER METHOD OF DRYING RED PEPPERS IN NEPAL

DRIED HERBS:

winter savory	golden marjoram	pot marjoram	lemon thyme	thyme	caraway thyme
oregano	rosemary	lemon verbena	lemon balm	basil	curry leaf
chervil	tarragon	fenugreek (mehti)	summer savory	mint	bay laurel

CLOISTERS, NEW YORK

method for drying herbs. If herbs are hung with no protective covering at all, the leaves usually dry and fall off before you have a chance to pack them away. Paper bags are another alternative. However I find that the air does not circulate well in them. Make sure you punch lots of holes in the bag for proper ventilation or else the herbs will turn moldy before they dry properly.

Under normal conditions, it will take a week to ten days for most herbs to dry enough for packing. When you feel them with your fingers through the cheesecloth, they should crackle. When they are dry, open the bags and remove the leaves from the stems. It is much easier to remove these leaves once the herbs are dried than it would be to do so when they are fresh. Dried herbs will retain their flavor longer if the leaves are not finely crushed. Pack into spice jars as whole as possible. For optimum flavor, do not crush the herbs until you are ready to cook with them.

Seedheads can be hung in either cheesecloth or brown paper bags. Which one you choose depends on the size of the seed to be dried. It is impossible to pick tiny seeds out of cheesecloth, so for anything tiny, brown paper bags are preferable. I usually do not allow my plants to flower and therefore dry seeds only occasionally. Most seeds, especially if bought whole and ground when needed, have a good flavor. If you care to dry your own, hang the bags until the seeds rattle around in their pods. This will usually take about two weeks. Then shake the seeds loose and remove them from the bag. Be careful when you pack away seeds that you do not include any bugs which sometimes can hide in the flower pods. It should go without saying, but all seeds and herbs should be stored in jars with tight fitting lids.

There are many commercial drying devices for herbs that you can buy, if you like. Screens work well if you need to dry large quantities of herbs. I do not and therefore find the hanging bag method which I described works quite well for me. Herbs can be dried in a microwave oven, but I have not had much success this way. The flavors seem to be retained best if they are air dried. Never think you are taking a short cut by drying herbs in an oven. It just does not work. The warm oven air will tend to bake your herbs and will remove all of their flavor as well as their color.

Once you have your herbs and spices packed into jars, open them in three or four days to check and see if they are dry enough. If there is any moisture still present, the contents will soon turn moldy and be useless to you. If you do notice some dampness, empty the contents of the jar back into another cheesecloth bag or leave them spread out for a few more days. Check again for dryness, then repack.

This step may sound like a lot of extra work, but it is well worth any time it takes. Once, several years ago, when I first began drying my own herbs, I lost most of them to mold that formed because of extra moisture in the jars. After going through all the trouble of growing, harvesting and packing the herbs, it is a shame to lose them only because you have not given them enough time to dry.

Packing in salt is another method of preservation that will work for some herbs, such as basil and tarragon. Use sea salt or a non-iodized coarse salt. Wash and dry the herbs thoroughly, and in this case, remove the leaves from the stems. Use a large crock or jar and place a fairly thick layer of salt on the bottom. Layer with herbs, then sprinkle salt to cover the herb layer. Repeat until the jar is filled. Press down well and cover the top with a thick layer of salt. Seal and store the jar in a dark place. The herbs can be lifted out and rinsed as they are needed. More color will be retained this way than by freezing, but I find freezing to be much easier and quite satisfactory.

STORAGE

Since heat and light are the natural enemies of herbs and spices, never store them near a heat source or in direct sunlight. Spice cabinets which are hung near a window or over a stove are in the worst possible place. I store most of my herbs and spices in drawers, near but not above my stove. This way they are in a dark, fairly cool place, always within easy reach for cooking.

Some spices are extremely heat and light sensitive and should be kept in a metal or lightproof container for optimum control. Curry powder and paprika are two prime examples. Paprika powder tends to develop bugs and loses its strength very quickly if stored at room temperature. It should be refrigerated. Curry powder should be stored in a lightproof (preferably metal) container.

Herbs that are bought commercially seldom have a shelf life of more than six months. Those preserved at home will maintain their flavor and aroma for a full year, if dried, and even longer, if frozen. Before using any herb or spice for cooking, always check to see if it is still good. The best way to do this is to use your sense of smell. If the herb smells like straw, then it will probably taste like straw as well. Don't even bother to add it to your food, throw it out and substitute something else instead. If you buy dried herbs, always try to buy the smallest possible amount that you can, usually one or two ounces. Buying the large economy size of an herb is not a bargain and unless you have a huge family, you will end up throwing most of this bargain out.

THE PLANTS

Once you have grown your own herbs and spices for cooking, you will be spoiled for life. Whether you use them fresh, frozen or dried, there is a tremendous difference in the flavors and aromas they impart to food. A brief description and history of individual herbs and spices follows, along with growing and storage tips.

Many of the common culinary herbs and spices of the past are no longer popular, nor are they used to any great extent today. They do, however, have a rich and interesting history and no book, such as this, would be complete without at least mentioning some of their names. If you have enough space, you might like to try and grow some of these plants along with the more commonly used ones, as they can be an intriguing and beautiful addition to any garden.

ALLSPICE

Classification: Perennial, tree
Height: 25 to 40 feet
Conditions preferred: Tropics
Part of plant used and storage: Berry, dried
Pimenta dioica
Myrtaceae
Common names: Pimento, Jamaican pepper

Allspice is unique in that it both tastes and smells like a mixture of cloves, cinnamon and nutmeg. I always like to include a few allspice berries in my peppermill for the wonderful aroma that they impart to food. Allspice is the dried fruit of an evergreen tree belonging to the myrtle family. The berries are harvested while they are still green, but once dried they become red-brown in color. Its' Latin name 'pimenta' comes from the Spanish word for pepper, given because the berries do resemble peppercorns.

The fruit is borne by the female tree only, as the male trees have no flowers. The sex of the trees cannot be determined until they are three or four years old. Then the crop of trees is thinned to a ratio of one male to every ten females, proving that there are times when it pays to be female. The female trees begin to bear fruit when they are six years old and continue to flower for more than one hundred years.

This berry is one of the few spices native to the Western Hemisphere and comes mainly from the area around the Caribbean. History reveals that it was used by the Mayan Indians to preserve and embalm the bodies of their leaders, as there is a natural preservative quality inherent in the berry. Allspice was used when sailors packed meats for long sea voyages to help prevent rotting.

Early Central American civilizations used allspice berries as a flavoring for their chocolate drinks. Like vanilla beans, allspice berries were taken to Europe around the seventeenth century by the Spanish explorers when they returned home from their travels.

Today, an excellent quality of berries is raised in Jamaica. Price is determined by both the appearance of the berries and their essential oil (eugenol) content. This essential oil is used commercially in the manufacturing of liqueurs such as Benedictine and Chartreuse, as well as for perfumes and medicines.

ANGELICA

Classification: Biennial
Height: 6 feet
Conditions preferred: Partial shade
Parts of plant used and storage: Stems, fresh and candied; Seeds, dried
Angelica archangelica
Umbelliferae
Common names: Archangel, Wild parsnip

Legend tells us that this herb had the protection of the Archangel Michael, hence its Latin name. In many parts of Europe, angelica will flower on May 8th, which is St. Michael's Day, adding strength to this tale. The plant supposedly had the power to protect people from contagion and during the plagues, was used for this purpose.

Although this plant is a biennial, it will continue to grow for many years if the flowers are clipped off before they bloom. Angelica prefers a cool climate, partial shade and a rich soil. Because it will grow quite large, it needs lots of room.

Since ancient times, angelica has been used as part of a mysterious ritual that takes place in Lapland and Germany. Once a year it is carried in a processional while the marchers sing a song that dates back to pre-Christian times. This song is so old that no living person any longer knows the meaning of the words.

Angelica seeds have long been used for flavoring liqueurs such as gin, Vermouth and Chartreuse. The boiled roots and stems were cooked and eaten much like celery. Today the stems are candied and used as a decoration for cakes and confectionary. Angelica has a very high sugar content and can be cooked with acid fruits such as rhubarb to lessen the amount of sugar needed.

Classification: Annual
Height: 2 feet
Conditions preferred: Full sun
Part of plant used and storage: Fruit (seed), dried

ALLSPICE

BASIL

WHOLE SPICES:

hot red peppers	star anise	cinnamon sticks	saffron threads	fenugreek seeds	sesame seeds
juniper berries	nutmeg	cloves	white cardamom	celery seeds	ground poppy seeds
green peppercorns	black peppercorns	white mustard seed	caraway seeds	cumin seeds	dill seeds
allspice berries	white peppercorns	black mustard seed	fennel seeds	coriander	anise seeds

PURPLE BASIL

BAY LAUREL

GROUND SPICES:

ginger	mace	cardamom	cinnamon	cloves	allspice
coriander	nutmeg	turmeric	cumin	garlic powder	fenugreek
chili powder	paprika	cayenne pepper	black peppercorns	white peppercorns	red pepper flakes
curry powder	five spice powder	mustard powder	garum masala	Szechwan peppercorns	mambosa pepper

Pimpinella anisum
Umbelliferae

Both the seeds and leaves of the anise plant have a licorice-like flavor. Anise is not, however, related to the true licorice plant, but is a member of the parsley family. The small edible crescent shaped seeds (really, the fruits) have a gray-brown color with a slightly greenish cast. Both anise and fennel seeds have a similar flavor because they each contain the same essential oil, anethol.

Anise should be planted where it is going to grow, for it does not like to be moved once established, because of its deep tap root system. An annual plant, anise needs a lot of sunshine and will grow to two feet in height.

Anise was used as one of the flavorings in what is considered to be the forerunner of our modern bridal or wedding cake. During the first century, A.D., the Romans baked a spice cake which they called a 'mustaeceous'. It contained among other things, anise, cumin and fennel seeds. It was wrapped and baked in bay leaves and was customarily served at the end of a large meal or feast to prevent indigestion.

Anise seeds have an interesting history in the United States. In 1619, Virginia passed a law stating that each settler had to bring with him and plant six anise seeds on his land. Anise is widely grown in many temperate as well as warm climates. This plant is native to Egypt, Asia Minor and Greece. It was used as early as 1500 B.C. by the Egyptians as both a seasoning and a medicament.

BASIL

Classification: Annual
Height: 6 inches to 3 feet
Conditions preferred: Full sun, shelter
Part of plant used and storage: Leaves, fresh, frozen and dried
Ocimum basilicum
Labiatae
Common names: Sweet basil, Common basil

Although there are several varieties of this very aromatic herb grown, sweet basil is the most common type used for cooking. A member of the mint family, basil will grow from six to thirty-six inches in height depending on the particular variety. All basil plants like lots of sunshine.

The history of basil dates back about 4000 years. Probably originating in Persia, it was carried by the soldiers of Alexander the Great into Greece and from there to the West. Basil was worshipped in India as being sacred to the Gods Krishna and Vishnu. Tulsi (or Tulasi), the wife of Vishnu was believed to have returned to earth in the form of this plant. A variety called 'sacred basil' is planted around many temples in India.

Forces of both good and evil are thought to be connected with this herb. Considered a symbol of romance in Italy, it was associated with witchcraft in Salem. Ancient Greeks and Romans believed that the herb would not grow unless the plant was cursed while the seeds were being sown. The French expression, 'semur le basilic' meaning to slander or abuse, comes from this legend.

The origin of the plant's familiar name, basil, is unclear. Some say it comes from the Latin word 'basilicus' which was a legendary fire eating dragon. Basil leaves were supposed to be an antidote for snake and scorpion bites and perhaps dragon bites as well. The name may also be derived from the Greek word 'basilikon' meaning royal or regal, for in Greek, basil is called the 'king of herbs'.

With or without cursing, the seeds will germinate in about two weeks once the ground is warm. The flowering tops of the plants should be pinched back often to encourage more and fuller leaf growth. The plant can be cut back for harvest down to the second pair of leaves in mid-summer and again in the fall. Leaves can be picked fresh as they are needed for cooking all summer long.

Basil leaves can be preserved by drying, freezing or packing them in salt. If frozen they will turn an ugly brown color when defrosted, but nonetheless retain their flavor and aroma very well. I find freezing the best and easiest way to preserve basil.

Some common varieties of basil grown, other than the one described are: Ocimum minimum, bush or dwarf basil; Ocimum basilicum purpurascens, purple or dark opal basil; Ocimum citriodorum, lemon basil; and Ocimum sanctum, sacred basil.

BAY LAUREL

Classification: Perennial, tender tree
Height: 2 to 40 feet
Conditions preferred: Full sun, shelter
Part of plant used and storage: Leaves, fresh and dried
Laurus nobilis
Lauraceae
Common names: Sweet bay, True laurel, Laurel

There is a legend that the Greek god Apollo fell in love with the nymph Daphne. He pursued and she ran. When she called to the gods for help, they took pity on her and changed her into a laurel tree. It is said that Apollo wore wreaths made of her sweet laurel leaves to show that he still loved her. Groves of laurel trees still surround the temple of Apollo in Greece.

The Romans wore bay leaves as protection against thunder and lightning. Rumor has it that the Emperor Tiberius (42 B.C. to 37 A.D.) would place a wreath of laurel on his head and hide under a bed during electrical storms. Bay laurel was considered a symbol of glory and the Romans decorated statues and crowned victors with wreaths made of laurel, as did the Greeks.

The derivation of the name of this tree is most

interesting, since it seems to be related to many grandiose concepts. In Latin, lauris means 'to praise' and noblis is 'famous or renowned'. The common name, laurel, comes from the Roman word landare, 'to praise', while bay comes from the Anglo-Saxon 'to crown'. The term 'poet laureate' in England symbolized the grand tradition associated with the name. And the word 'baccalaureate' means the successful completion of one's studies.

Bay laurel is the true laurel of antiquity and is native to the Mediterranean area and Asia Minor. In tropical climates, bay laurel is a tree, growing as tall as from twenty to forty feet in height. The same tree bears both male and female flowers. These small yellow flowers are followed by dark purple berries which are poisonous if eaten.

In temperate climates, bay laurel is a slow growing shrub that will reach two to three feet in height. It does need protection in the winter and is usually grown in pots that can be brought indoors. A mature plant can sometimes be left outside for the winter if it is well protected.

For home use, individual leaves can be picked from the plant when needed. Pick leaves from around the sides of the plant rather than from the top. For commercial use, the leaves are pressed to keep them flat when dried.

An exception to the rule, bay leaves are much more pungent when they are fresh. As they dry they become milder and more aromatic in flavor. Bay leaves commonly grown in California (called California bay or Oregon myrtle) are different from true laurel leaves. Although used in the same way, they are much stronger in flavor.

BORAGE

Classification: Annual
Height: 18 to 30 inches
Conditions preferred: Sun or partial shade
Parts of plant used and storage: Leaves, fresh; Flowers, fresh and candied
Borago officinalis
Boraginaceae
Common names: Bee bread, Starflower, Tale-wort, Cool-tankard

The Greeks called borage 'euphrosinum' and used it to flavor wine, which when imbibed, was supposed to make you joyful and merry. Enough wine by itself would probably have worked as well. Native to North Africa, this plant was carried throughout Europe by the crusaders.

In Latin the word 'borra' means hair, a name given to the plant because of the fuzzy or hairy coating on its large gray-green leaves. Borage is an annual plant with a cucumber-like aroma. Its leaves do have a mild and slightly bitter cucumber flavor and can be eaten as a salad green when they are very young and still tender. They have been used to flavor teas, as a medicinal and as a potherb.

Borage leaves contain a lot of moisture and do not dry well. They are best used only when fresh. The plant bears beautiful pink and blue star shaped flowers which can be candied or floated in wine bowls.

BURNET

Classification: Perennial
Height: 2 feet
Conditions preferred: Full sun
Part of plant used and storage: Leaves, fresh
Poterium sanguisorba
Rosaceae
Common name: Garden burnet

Native to Europe, this perennial herb is a member of the rose family. Its Latin name comes from the Greek word meaning 'drinking cup', as burnet was often used to flavor wines. The leaves have a cucumber-like taste, similar to borage, but are a little more bitter. They have been used as a medicinal, a salad green and to make tea.

Called 'pimpernella' in old French and Italian cookbooks, it was and still is used only when fresh, for when cooked the leaves turn very bitter. I find this herb much too bitter for my taste even when raw. Burnet does not dry well.

Burnet is called 'chabairji' in Hungarian, meaning 'chaba's slave'. It was said that after a great battle, the Hungarian King Chaba (Csaba) cured the wounds of fifteen hundred of his soldiers with the juice of the plant. Burnet has been used by the Chinese for several hundred centuries for this purpose as well.

CAPSICUM PEPPERS

Classification: Annual
Height: 1 to 4 feet
Conditions preferred: Sun
Part of plant used and storage: Fruit, fresh and dried
Capsicum annuum
Solanaceae
Common names: Red pepper, Green pepper, Bell pepper, Sweet pepper, Cherry pepper, Red cherry pepper, Pimento, Cayenne, Chili pepper, Paprika

As you can see from some of the common names listed, the classification of this plant can be quite confusing. The main type of peppers cultivated in the Americas today is of the Capsicum annuum variety. There are five main groupings of capsicum peppers with well over one hundred species grown.

Capsicum frutescens, commonly called 'tabasco pepper' is a very pungent, late maturing pepper mainly used in the commercial production of hot sauces. Both the annuum and frutescens varieties are indiginous to Mexico, the West Indies and Central America. They were used by the Indians there for centuries as a condiment.

BURNET

HOT RED PEPPERS

ASSORTED CAPSICUM PEPPERS

CARDAMOM

CELERY

APPLE PIE FARM, MALVERN, PENNSYLVANIA

Chanca, a physician to the fleet of Columbus, mentions their use by the native Indians in a letter he wrote to his friend Hernandez, court physician to King Philip of Spain. The peppers were carried to Europe by the Spaniards by 1650 and from there made their way to Asia and Africa. The varieties of capsicum grown in those continents were changed by the differences in soil and climate from their native environment.

Capsicum annuum is a herbaceous plant, usually one to three feet high, with highly diversified fruits. In colder climates, these fruits are eaten as a vegetable. The green fruits turn red, orange or yellow as they mature. They vary a great deal in size, shape and pungency. Paprika powder, which is made from a member of this species, will be described separately.

Ground cayenne pepper is really an umbrella term which means ground chili pepper and can be either C. annuum or C. frutescens. India is the world's largest exporter of chili peppers, the best being grown in nearby Nepal.

All capsicum are from the nightshade or potato family. The pungency of the pepper is due to a crystalline substance, capsaicin, found somewhat in the skin and seeds of the peppers, but mostly in their inner spongy placental area, to which the seeds are attached. When eaten, this capciasin tends to raise the body temperature, thereby inducing perspiration, which causes the outer air to seem cooler to the skin. This is why peppers are used to such a large degree in the cuisines found in many tropical climates.

Of the types of fresh hot peppers readily available in my part of the country for cooking, yellow chilies are considered hot, short round green jalapenos hotter and serranos the hottest. Supposedly, the smaller the pepper, the hotter it is, but the only true way to tell is by tasting them, if you are brave enough.

Paprika
Capsicum annuum var. Longum
Solanacae

Paprika is the dried stemless pod of a mature red sweet pepper which has been ground. Even though we associate paprika as being native to Hungary and Hungarian cuisine, it was most likely brought there by the Spaniards. The Hungarians were the first, however, to use paprika alone in pure powder form, for in other countries it was used as part of a spice mixture. Popular at first with only the peasant class, it was soon used by the gentry as well. Paprika, along with brandy gained a reputation of being a remedy for just about anything.

All peppers, including those used for paprika, have a very high content of vitamins C and A. As a matter of fact, peppers are a richer source of vitamin C than most citrus fruits. In 1937, a Nobel prize was awarded to a Hungarian, Dr. Szent Gyorgyi, for isolating the vitamin C content of the paprika pepper.

The variety of C. annuum used to make paprika powder requires a warm climate with lots of sunshine and plenty of rain to grow well. These perfect conditions exist in the village of Szeged in Hungary and its surrounding areas. Hungary produces over 10,000 tons of paprika each year. The quality is controlled by the Minister of Agriculture and true Hungarian paprika is considered to be the finest product available.

In Hungary, the planting and harvesting of paprika peppers has grown into a ritual. On St. Gregory's Day, at the beginning of March, the seeds are set in water. This water is changed daily for one week. The seeds are removed, dried and kept warm for a few days. They are then sown in hothouses prior to being planted outside. On September eighth, the Feast of the Nativity of the Holy Virgin, the peppers are harvested. They are strung into garlands and then hung under the eaves of houses to cure for about twenty-five days before they are dried and ground.

Until 1859, there was no method to control the strength of paprika powder. The Palffy brothers (in Szeged) found that by removing the seeds and veins of the peppers before grinding, a new mild or 'noble sweet rose' powder could be made. By controlling the amount of capciasin they added back into the powder, a variety of powders of varying strengths were possible.

In the United States, only a very mild variety of paprika powder is used to any large extent. However, many strengths of paprika powder are made in Hungary, such as: Exquisite delicate, which has a mild aroma and a deep color; Delicate, a fine grind with two versions, both hot and tame; Noble sweet, more pungent than the other two, but still mild; Semi-sweet, hotter; Rose, refined but firey; Hot, the name describes the powder.

Several years ago, a new subspecies of capsicum, C. annuum var. Longum Szegedense was developed. The entire pepper including the seeds and the pulp is ground to make paprika powder, for this pepper is sweet throughout.

CARAWAY

Classification: Biennial
Height: 2 feet
Conditions preferred: Full sun
Part of plant used and storage: Fruit (seeds), dried
Roots, fresh
Carum carvi
Umbelliferae

Caraway is one of the oldest known plants, inasmuch as its seeds have been found in the debris of Swiss lake dwellings that are over 5000 years old. Both caraway seeds and roots have been used for food and medicine since earliest times. The seeds are rich in protein and were used by the Romans to relieve indigestion. The roots were mixed with milk and made into a bread called 'chara' (by

Julius Caesar) that was eaten by the soldiers of Valerius.

Since caraway does not transplant well because of its deep tap root system, plant it in a nice sunny spot where it will remain, as it is a biennial plant. It will grow to a height of anywhere between eight to fifteen inches during its first year and produce green feathery carrot-like leaves. This plant will die back during the winter but will grow to two feet in height the following summer. Umbrella-like clusters of flowers resembling Queen Anne's lace then develop. The seeds can be picked by mid-summer.

Caraway seeds have to be harvested before they fall to the ground or they will be lost because the seed heads will burst when they are ripe. Once this happens, the caraway plant will resow itself, but you will have to wait two more years for seeds that can be used for cooking. Cut the stalks (with seed heads attached) off at the bottom, hang and allow them to dry for about ten days. Then thresh to remove the seeds from the seed heads. Be careful when sorting over the seeds, as many times tiny bugs hide in the seed heads.

After the seeds are harvested, you can dig up the plant and use the edible roots. Cook them as you would carrots. They resemble parsnips in flavor and are sometimes served in Europe as a vegetable. If you decide that you do not want to harvest the caraway seeds, then pinch off the flowers as they form and the plant will live for another year.

CARDAMOM

Classification: Perennial
Height: 6 to 10 feet
Conditions preferred: Tropics, rain
Part of plant used and storage: Seed, dried
Elettaria cardamomum
Zingiberaceae
Common names: Malabar cardamom, Ceylon cardamom

Cardamom is a very old and very aromatic spice. Both ancient Greeks and Romans imported it in great quantity from India and used it for a seasoning and a medicament. It was thought to aid digestion and help cure urinary problems. Records show that cardamom was grown in the garden of the King of Babylon in 721 B.C.

This perennial plant is a member of the ginger family and grows from a thick underground rhizome. It can be propagated either by seed or from a section of the rhizome itself. Native to India and Ceylon, it grows and flourishes in warm dark rain forests. The plant bears fruit in its fourth year and will continue to do so for ten to fifteen years. The fruits or capsules are harvested while they are still green and only about three-quarters ripe.

Each small pithy cardamom capsule contains fifteen or twenty dark brown aromatic seeds. The outer capsule cover has no flavor and ranges in color from green to white, depending on the variety grown. But it is the drying method used that often determines the final color. 'Greens' are dried artificially in kilns or rooms with forced hot air and therefore retain some of their natural green color. Lighter colored capsules have usually been dried in the sun. Sometimes the cardamom is treated with sulphur to bleach the capsules to a pure white color.

There is a variety of cardamom grown in India that has very large brown capsules. It is used in Indian cooking and is not readily available in the United States.

Cardamom is used to a large degree for baking in many European countries in the same way that we use cinnamon here in the United States. Arab countries use it as a flavoring for their coffee, called 'gahwa'. Malabar cardamom is considered to be the best now available for cooking purposes.

CATNIP

Classification: Perennial
Height: 18 inches to 3 feet
Conditions preferred: Full sun
Part of plant used and storage: Shoots (before flowering), fresh and dried
Nepeta cataria
Labiatae
Common name: Catmint

This perennial plant has an aroma that cats adore, as it makes them very playful. Native to Europe, the name 'nepeta' was given to this herb by the Tuscans who found catnip growing wild in the village of Nept.

Catnip was used as a culinary herb during the fifteenth century. The leaves were rubbed on meats and eaten as a salad green. Eating catnip was supposed to give one courage. Today catnip is used only as a medicinal tea and, of course, for cats.

CELERY

Classification: Biennial
Height: 2 to 3 feet
Conditions preferred: Temperate climate, shelter
Part of plant used and storage: Seeds, dried; Leaves, fresh and dried; Stalks, fresh
Apium graveolens L. var. dulce
Umbelliferae

Celery favors cool weather and does well in a temperate climate. It needs a long growing season, lots of water and a rich soil. Both the leaves and the seeds of the celery plant are used for flavoring, while the stalk is eaten as a vegetable. Celery is a biennial plant belonging to the parsley family. In its first year, it will grow leaves and thick roots. It is usually harvested at the end of this first year, while still immature. If left for a second year, the plant should grow to two or three feet in height and produce umbels of white flowers which develop into tiny seeds (really the fruit of the plant). I have not had much luck with this plant coming back a second year in my garden. Celery leaves are very rich in vitamins C and A. The tiny light brown seeds have a slightly bitter taste.

Celery should be banked with soil while it grows so that the stalks will remain white and tender, the same as asparagus. Or it can be wrapped with brown paper bags (tied on with string) leaving only the very top leaves exposed for about two weeks before harvesting. Commercially, the plant can be picked while green and packed into boxes with its roots covered with soil. It is then stored in a cool dark place until the stalks lighten in color.

Both celery stalks and leaves were used by the Egyptian, Greek and Roman civilizations. A garland containing wild celery was found in an Egyptian tomb dating back to about 1000 B.C. (20th dynasty). The ancients used it more for its medicinal qualities than as a food.

In the past, a wild variety of celery called 'smallage' was the only type grown. This smallage would seem quite bitter to our taste today. The mild variety of celery that we now know and eat was developed by gardeners in Italy during the seventeenth century.

Celeraic, commonly called celery root or celery knob (A. graveolens var. rapaceum) is very popular in Europe. It is grown for its large and ugly but very edible root crown. The leaf stalks are very pungent and usually not eaten. Celeraic is used for soups and salads and as a vegetable.

CHAMOMILE

Classification: Annual
Height: 18 inches to 3 feet
Conditions preferred: Full sun
Part of plant used and storage: Flowers, dried
Matricaria recutita
Compositae
Common name: German chamomile, Camomile

While there are both annual and perennial varieties of chamomile, we are only concerned with the annual variety for culinary purposes. The flowers of the annual or German chamomile are dried to make a medicinal tea. Roman or English chamomile (Anthemis noblis) is a perennial and is often grown as a substitute for grass because it makes an excellent ground cover.

Chamomile has been used from the time of the Egyptians as a medicinal and a dye. It's name comes from the Greek 'chamimelon' meaning ground or earth apple, because of the apple-like scent of its leaves. In Spanish the plant is called 'Manzilla' which means little apple. There is a Spanish sherry made called Manzilla, that is flavored with chamomile and produces a fortified wine with an apple-like scent.

GERMAN CHAMOMILE

CHERVIL

CHIVES

Chamomile has been called the 'plant's physician', for it is said that any plant which grows nearby will flourish. During the Middle Ages, chamomile was a popular strewing herb because of its scent.

CHERVIL

Classification: Annual
Height: 4 inches to 1 foot
Conditions preferred: Shade, shelter
Part of plant used and storage: Leaves, fresh and dried
Anthriscus cerefolium
Umbelliferae
Common names: Sweet chervil, Gourmet's parsley, Salad chervil

Chervil, a member of the parsley family, will develop a tap root system and does not like to be disturbed. Plant it where you want it to grow, as it tends to bolt (go to seed) if it is moved. A low-growing annual, chervil does not need a lot of sunshine and does well when planted in the shade of taller plants. Chervil does not thrive in the heat of summer and is best grown as a spring or fall crop.

Chervil seeds germinate quickly and can be sown every few weeks. It takes only six to eight weeks for the production of edible leaves. A difficult plant to grow, I never seem to have enough left over for harvesting, no matter how much chervil I plant. Like parsley, chervil leaves do not dry especially well. This is one herb I prefer to use fresh only. The seeds remain viable for a few years, so if you have any left, save them for next year. The refrigerator is the safest place for storage.

Cut the leaves from around the outside of the plant for daily use. Flowers should be pinched off as they form to keep up the plant's production of leaves. As I said, chervil is not an easy herb to grow, but its delicate flavor makes it worth the effort. Both the stems and the leaves have a mild anise-like flavor and aroma. The taste is similar to parsley, but sweeter.

When combined with other herbs, chervil tends to enhance or bring out their flavors. Heat tends to dissipate its taste and aroma, so add at the last moment when cooking. It is traditionally used as part of a 'fines herbes' combination in French cuisine.

Chervil was used by the early Greeks and Romans for both culinary and medicinal purposes. Its roots were boiled and eaten in Europe during the time of the plagues because they were thought to be a preventative. Because it was believed to have blood-cleansing properties, chervil was traditionally eaten during Lent.

CHIVES

Classification: Perennial
Height: 2 feet
Conditions preferred: Sun or semi-shade
Part of plant used and storage: Leaves, fresh and frozen
Allium schoenoprasum
Liliaceae

Chives are a member of the onion family and grow in thick grass-like clumps that reach two feet in height. The plant grows from tiny bulblets clustered on very small rhizomes and is a perennial. Chives are frost resistant and remain dormant in the winter but will reappear very early every spring.

After the second year, beautiful purple flowers appear on tall flower stalks, which if allowed to remain, will produce tiny black seeds. Some gardeners say that chives will have a better flavor if the plant is not allowed to flower. This may be true, but the flowers are so pretty that I let them bloom and still find the leaves very edible. Cut off the tall flower stalks either before or after flowering, as they are tough to eat and can easily be mistaken for the softer leaves.

Grow chives in a nice sunny spot. Every three to four years, in the early spring or fall, the clumps should be gently dug out and separated into bunches of four or five bulblets each. Chives tend to exhaust the soil, so move them to a different place in the garden or enrich the soil if you replace them in the same spot.

Chives can be snipped any time they are needed for daily use. You should cut the outer leaves off first. The plant can be harvested three or four times during the growing season, just be careful not to cut the leaves back to less than two inches above ground level.

Do not dry chives as they will lose their flavor. My preference in preserving them is freezing. Rinse and dry the leaves, then chop and pack them into a freezer container. Frozen chives keep beautifully. They can be used while still frozen, you do not have to wait for them to defrost.

Chives, although native to Northern Europe and Asia, were not used in Europe until the sixteenth century. It is said the Dutch settlers in the United States used to put their cows out to graze in fields rich with chives, producing milk with a characteristic onion-like flavor. It was probably, in reality, wild onions on which the cows were feeding, it just sounds more romantic to say chives.

Allium tuberosum, or garlic chives, is a variety of chives native to regions of China and Mongolia. The plant has a long history of use in China and was cultivated there for both culinary and medicinal purposes since 3000 B.C. Garlic chives have large flat green leaves when compared to the thin hollow leaves of regular chives. They grow from underground rhizomes or tubers and will bear white flowers, usually during the month of September. This variety has a definite garlic odor and flavor and tastes like a combination of garlic and chives.

CINNAMON

Classification: Perennial, tree
Height: to 30 feet
Conditions preferred: Tropics, rain
Part of plant used and storage: Bark, dried
Cinnamomum zeylanicum
Lauraceae
Common names: Ceylon cinnamon

A great deal of confusion exists between what is called 'true' cinnamon and cassia, but since this problem began about 4000 years ago, it is certainly nothing new. Cinnamon and cassia both come from the bark of two different but similar trees of the laurel family. They have, for centuries, been used interchangeably and can both be numbered among the oldest known vegetable products to be used by man as a flavoring.

Called 'kwei' in early Chinese herbals, the spice referred to was probably cassia. Cinnamon was used in Egypt as an ingredient in perfume and as one of the annointing oils mentioned in the Old Testament by Moses. Nero was said to have burned a three year supply of the sticks on the funeral pyre of his wife.

I will describe cinnamon and cassia separately so that perhaps you can become aware of what you are really buying, for there is a subtle difference in flavor between the two. In the United States, most of what is sold as cinnamon is really cassia.

True cinnamon is the dried inner bark of an evergreen tree of the laurel family which can grow from eighteen to thirty feet in height. Using special knives, the smooth tan colored bark is peeled from the young shoots of the tree in May and October. The bark is left in bunches for a day or two to ferment. The corky outer layer of the bark is then scraped off and the cleaned inner portion is left for a few more days to dry. As these pieces of bark dry, they curl into quill-like shapes.

True cinnamon quills are lighter in color and more flexible than cassia quills. Cinnamon is now cultivated in the rain forests of many tropical countries such as Ceylon, India and Jamaica, with the best quality coming from Ceylon.

CASSIA

Classification: Perennial, tree
Height: to 40 feet
Conditions preferred: Tropics
Part of plant used and storage: Bark, dried
Cinnamomum cassia
Lauraceae
Common names: Chinese cassia, False cinnamon, Chinese cinnamon, Cassia bark tree, Bastard cinnamon

The cassia tree is taller than the cinnamon tree and has a thicker bark with a red-brown color and has smaller leaves. Cassia bark is peeled from the young shoots of the tree the same as cinnamon, but the outer part of this bark is not removed by fermentation. Both the inner and outer bark are dried together to form the quills. Therefore cassia quills are thicker and darker in color than true cinnamon. Cassia has a more intense aroma and a less delicate flavor than cinnamon.

Cassia is native to China, the Eastern Himalayas and South Vietnam and is now mainly cultivated in China, Burma and Indonesia. Some of the best quality cassia produced today comes from Saigon (now called Ho Chi Mihn City).

CLOVES

Classification: Perennial, tree
Height: 30 to 40 feet
Conditions preferred: Tropics, rain
Part of plant used and storage: Unopened flower buds, dried
Syzygium aromaticum
Myrtaceae

Cloves are the dried, unopened flower buds of a tropical evergreen tree of the myrtle family. The tree is native to the Moluccas, which are a group of volcanic islands in Eastern Indonesia. Clove trees will reach a height of thirty to forty feet and bear fruit from the time they are six until they are one hundred years old or more.

Records found of the Han dynasty, in the third century B.C., show that cloves were used in China at that time. Called 'chicken-tongue spice', courtiers were required to keep them in their mouths to sweeten their breath when addressing the Emperor.

Cloves were used extensively throughout Europe by the fourth century. Arab traders carried them by overland routes until sea routes were opened in the sixteenth century. First the Portuguese and then the Dutch monopolized all of the clove trade from the Molucca Islands for many years. Their tight control was broken when a few seeds were taken out secretly and planted in Zanzibar and other islands.

The name clove comes from the French word 'clou' meaning nail. The dried flower buds with a bit of the stem attached do look like dark brown nails. The buds contain a high percentage of volatile oils and a good quality clove will exude a little bit of this oil when pressed hard with the fingernail. Oil of cloves is used commercially to a great extent and is one of the main ingredients used in the manufacture of artificial vanilla flavoring.

For centuries, cloves have been used as a remedy for toothaches and as their taste has a way of reminding me of trips to the dentist when I was young, I don't use them very often. Whole cloves are still used to make pommander balls as seen in many stores, especially during the Christmas season.

CORIANDER (CILITRANO)

COSTMARY

CURRY LEAF

CORIANDER

Classification: Annual
Height: 3 feet
Conditions preferred: Full sun or partial shade
Part of plant used and storage: Fruit (seed), dried; Leaves, fresh and frozen
Coriandrum sativum
Umbelliferae
Common names: Leaves called Cilitrano, Chinese parsley, Indian parsley

Both the leaves and the seeds from this plant are used for culinary purposes. The name coriander comes from the Greek word 'koris' meaning bug or bedbug and was given to this plant because of its foul odor. The leaves do have a very unpleasant smell. The seeds, however, lose this odor when dried and have a pleasant and mild orange-like flavor.

The use of this herb as both a stimulant and a flavoring date back to antiquity. Seeds have been found in Egyptian tombs of the twenty-first dynasty (1085-945 B.C.) as well as in shops found among the ruins of the ancient city of Pompeii. In the Old Testament, Moses compared the color of manna to that of coriander seed. Its leaves may have been used as the bitter herb associated with the holiday of Passover. Coriander has been used in China as a seasoning since the fifth century B.C.

Coriander or cilitrano leaves are used as a staple in Chinese as well as Mexican, Spanish and Indian cuisines, much the way that we use parsley for many dishes in this country. Coriander was brought to Mexico by the Spanish conquistadors. The leaves are very pungent in flavor, so use them with caution if you are not familiar with the taste. It is not one of my favorites, but a Chinese friend has told me that as I get older I will learn to better appreciate cilitrano. I'm still waiting for this to happen, although I do find the flavor of the seeds quite pleasant.

Grow the plant where it will remain as it has a deep tap root system and does not transplant well. It will grow to about eighteen inches in height and likes a lot of sun. The seeds remain viable for a few years and can be stored in the refrigerator for future planting.

Coriander leaves do not dry well as they tend to lose their flavor quite easily. For preserving, I would recommend freezing the leaves of this herb, although it really is best when fresh. I would also be very cautious about growing coriander indoors because of its unpleasant smell.

COSTMARY

Classification: Perennial
Height: 2 to 4 feet
Conditions preferred: Sun or partial shade
Part of plant used and storage: Leaves, fresh and dried

Chrysanthemum balsamita
Compositae
Common names: Bible leaf, Alcost, Alecost

The name costmary comes from the Greek word 'costus' meaning spicy plant and the name Mary, after the Virgin Mary, for this plant is dedicated to her in many parts of Europe. It has a strong balsam-like odor with lemony overtones. Costmary was used to sweeten water for washing and was stored in cupboards along with clothing.

The leaves were used in salads, soups, teas and stuffings. This perennial herb is no longer used for culinary purposes today and has never been very important medicinally. Some of the common names given to costmary do, however, show many of its original uses. Our early colonists used to dry and press the long leaves for use as bookmarks for their bibles. Costmary was employed long before hops as a flavoring for beer and ale, therefore the name alecost.

CUMIN

Classification: Annual
Height: 2 to 6 feet
Conditions preferred: Sun, shelter
Part of plant used and storage: Fruit (seeds), dried
Cuminum cyminum
Umbelliferae
Common names: Green cumin, Cumino

Originally grown in Upper Egypt and the Mediterranean region, this plant dates well back into antiquity, for seeds have been found in the Egyptian pyramids. Cumin was used as a medicine, a food preservative and a seasoning. The Romans used cumin as a substitute for pepper on their food. During biblical times many aromatic seeds, including cumin, were used in place of money for the payment of tithe or taxes.

The folklore surrounding this herb is most intriguing. It was supposed to keep poultry from straying away from home as well as to keep lovers from being fickle. Cumin seed was carried by both bride and groom (along with dill seed and some salt) in their pockets at wedding ceremonies in Germany during the middle ages. Very popular in medieval cookery, it was used to season fowl, breads, cakes, cheeses and relishes.

Cumin seeds are the dried yellow-brown fruit of an annual plant which belongs to the parsley family. In the north, cumin can be started indoors. It needs a long warm summer and lots of sunshine to grow to full maturity. The seeds do not form until late summer and grow inside of the plant's pretty white flowers. The stems are not very strong and sometimes need to be staked to keep them from flopping over. The seeds are similar to those of caraway in appearance, except that they are just a little bit longer.

Cumin seeds can be bought either whole or ground. When buying this spice, I prefer to purchase the seeds whole as they will retain their flavor longer. Before using the seeds, toast them to bring out their full flavor and aroma by heating for about ten minutes in a moderately warm oven (or about two minutes in a microwave). Then grind, if desired. Cumin is a common addition to commercial chili powder.

There is also a black cumin that is used for cooking in India and many countries of the Middle-East. It is, however, not true cumin seed and comes from a different family (Nigella sativa of the Ranunculaceae family). These aromatic dark seeds are very small and have a peppery flavor.

CURRY LEAF

Classification: Perennial
Height: 2 feet or more
Conditions preferred: Sun
Part of plant used and storage: Leaves, fresh and dried
Murraya koenigii
Rutaceae

The name of this plant tends to cause some confusion, but the curry leaf plant is not and cannot be considered a substitute for curry powder. However, its leaves do have a curry-like scent. The leaves are used, along with other herbs and spices, to flavor some curry pastes and will add a touch of piquancy to cooked curries.

Native to India and Ceylon, the curry leaf plant is quite pretty, with slender silvery gray-green leaves. It will develop tall spikes with yellow flowers in mid-summer. This herb prefers a lot of sun and a sandy soil, but will grow well almost anywhere. The leaves can be dried.

DILL

Classification: Annual
Height: 3 to 4 feet
Conditions preferred: Full sun
Parts of plant used and storage: Fruit (seeds), dried; Leaves, fresh and frozen
Anethum graveolens
Umbelliferae
Common names: Dill weed

The scraggly looking appearance of this plant is the cause for it to be called a weed. Dill is an annual plant which grows to three or four feet in height and should be staked or grown next to a wall. Plant it where it is to remain, as it is a member of the parsley family with a deep tap root which does not like to be disturbed. I never have too much luck with dill in my garden, as it is always true to the weed part of its name and produces mostly stems with very little leaves. I seldom have enough left to harvest any appreciable amount.

If your plants produce enough for harvest, then wash, dry and freeze the feathery-like leaves. They do not dry well at all, but will freeze beautifully. Dill seeds will keep their flavor for several years if stored in an air-tight container. They have been used as a pickling spice in many countries for centuries. The leaves impart a more delicate flavor to food than does the seed and is used much more frequently for cooking purposes.

One word of caution about growing dill—several gardening books recommend that you do not plant dill near fennel or the two plants will cross-pollinate. If you would like to grow dill indoors, try a low growing variety of seed such as Dill Bouquet. Most of the dill seed we use today comes from India.

Dill is native to the Mediterranean region and Southwest Asia. It has a long and ancient history, being mentioned some five thousand years ago in Egyptian writings. Its Latin name, anethum, comes from the Greek 'ono', meaning upward and 'theo', meaning I run, probably given because the plant grows very quickly. Roman gladiators ate something called 'aneth' which was supposed to give them strength for fighting.

The English name, dill, comes from the Norse 'dilla', meaning to lull. A decoction was made from dill seeds and fed to babies to lull them to sleep. An interesting and contradictory story which I came across in several books said our American ancestors called dill seeds 'meeting seeds' and nibbled them in church to keep awake during the long sermons. Knowing the soothing effect of the seeds, I have a feeling they were really eaten to induce a quiet cat nap or two during the sermons.

FENNEL

Classification: Perennial (grown as annual)
Height: to 5 feet
Conditions preferred: Sun
Parts of plant used and storage: Fruit (seeds), dried; Leaves, fresh and dried; Base of stalk, fresh
Umbelliferae
Foeniculum vulgare
Common name: Common fennel
Foeniculum dulce
Common name: Sweet fennel
Foeniculum azoricum
Common name: Florence fennel, Finocchio

Native to the Mediterranean area, fennel dates back to ancient times, having been used by the Chinese, Indian and Egyptian cultures. Fennel is mentioned in the scrolls of papyrii found in some Egyptian tombs and was grown in the gardens of Charlemagne. Used as both a medicine and a food, it was thought to restore failing eyesight and make fat people thin.

Common fennel is cultivated for its leaves and seeds while Florence fennel is grown for its swollen base stalks which can be eaten as a vegetable. Sweet fennel, while often confused with Florence fennel, is somewhat different and is mainly grown for the essential oil in its fruit. All varieties of fennel are members of the parsley family and have a typical tap root system that does not like to be disturbed. Fennel is a perennial plant but is often grown commercially as an annual. Common fennel resembles dill but is more aromatic with a slight anise or licorice flavor.

Some references say that fennel seeds were the true 'meeting seeds' of our Puritan forefathers, rather than dill seed. They were nibbled during long church sermons to stave off hunger pangs.

The name fennel comes from the Latin word 'foeniculum' meaning hay. When dried, fennel does smell like a variety of fragrant hay and was used as a strewing herb in medieval times. Florence fennel has an anise-like flavor and can be used much as we use celery stalks. To keep the growing fennel white, pack dirt around the stems when they are just a few inches high. Otherwise, they will turn green and tough as they grow.

FENUGREEK

Classification: Annual
Height: 2 feet
Conditions preferred: Heat, rain
Parts of plant used and storage: Seed, dried; Leaves, fresh and dried
Trigonella foenum-graecum
Leguminosae
Common names: Foenugreek, Bird's foot, Greek hay seed

Fenugreek is an annual plant which belongs to the legume or pea family. It likes a lot of sunshine and will grow to about eighteen inches high. Since it is a legume, it will restore nitrogen to the soil and because of this, is often used as a cover crop in citrus groves.

Since ancient times, fenugreek has been used as a seasoning, a medicine, a dye and even as fodder for animals. The fenugreek plant produces string bean-like pods which each hold from ten to twenty hard yellow-brown seeds. In India the seeds are roasted and used as a substitute for coffee. Commercially, oil extracted from fenugreek seeds is used as a primary ingredient in the manufacturing of imitation maple flavoring.

The leaves are dried and used in Indian cooking. Called 'methi' they are very aromatic and have a bitter flavor reminiscent of bay leaves. The dried and ground seeds are a frequent ingredient in curry mixtures.

Ancient Egyptian papyrii list fenugreek as one of the ingredients of the 'kelpi', or holy incense, used for both embalming and fumigation. The Romans obtained this plant from the Greeks and named it 'foenum-graecum', which means 'Greek hay', probably because of its use as animal feed. Trigonella is the Latin word for 'little triangle' and refers to the shape of the small yellow-white flowers produced by the plant.

GARLIC

Classification: Perennial (bulbous)
Height: 2 feet
Conditions preferred: Sun
Part of plant used and storage: Bulb, fresh and dried
Allium sativum
Liliaceae

Garlic, along with onions, are among the oldest known of all cultivated plants. Records show that garlic had been used as food and medicine by the Sumerians over 5000 years ago. Garlic was part of the daily ration given to the slaves while they were working on the great pyramid of Cheops in Egypt. Its 'spirit' was invoked by the priests when communicating with their gods.

There has always been much folklore associated with this plant and many an adult, child or even cow has had garlic hung around his (or its) neck to avert evil spirits or to prevent colds. Modern medical research has shown that garlic contains essential oils that have antiseptic and disinfectant properties. This is not to say that I would recommend wearing a garlic necklace.

The base of this perennial plant consists of a composite cluster of tiny bulblets or cloves that are held together by a thin paper-like skin. Individual bulblets should be planted about two inches deep in the soil. As they mature they will multiply into a cluster of eight to twenty small bulblets.

There are several varieties of garlic which can range in size from tiny to giant. The flavor can vary from sweet to nutty and the strength from mild to strong. European varieties tend to be milder than those grown in the United States. Even the color of the skin that holds the cloves together can vary from white to purple, again depending on the variety.

Snip off the flower stalks as they form so that the plant's energy will be diverted to the bulbs. When the leaves die down, dig up the bulbs of garlic and store them in a cool dry place.

The name of this plant comes from the Anglo-Saxon 'gar' meaning spear and 'leac' meaning potherb or plant. The name probably refers to the spear-like shape of the stems.

GINGER

Classification: Perennial
Height: 2 to 3 feet
Conditions preferred: Tropics, rain
Part of plant used and storage: Rhizome, fresh and dried
Zingiber officinale
Zingiberaceae
Common names: Common ginger, True ginger, Canton ginger, Ginger root

DILL

FENNEL

ORIENTAL GARLIC

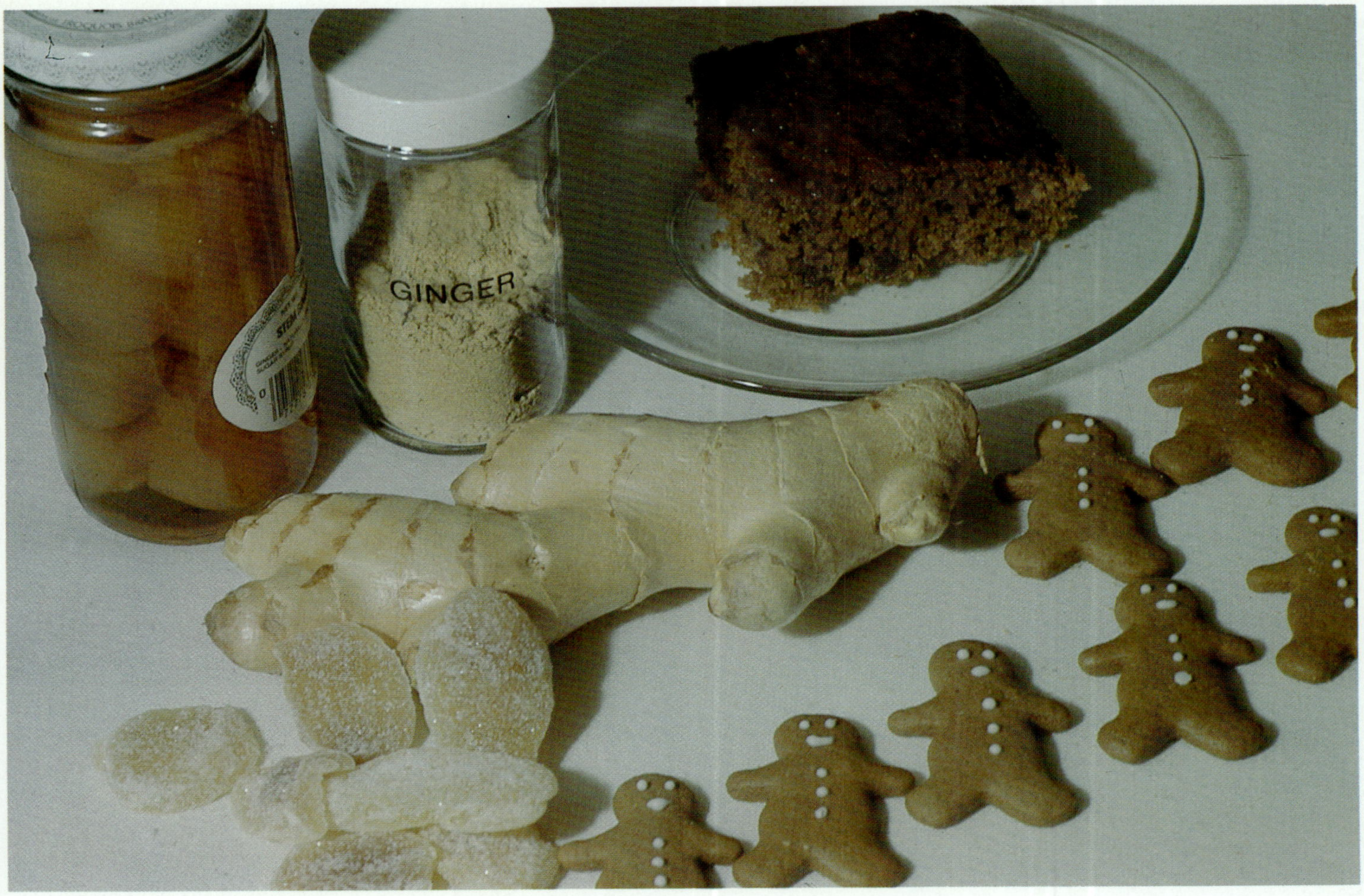

GINGER, from top left: preserved, powdered, oatmeal ginger cake, gingerbread men, candied, ginger root.

HORSERADISH, from top left: horseradish root, beets, grated horseradish with beets, grated horseradish.

Ginger was grown by the ancient Chinese and Hindu peoples for use as a spice as well as a medicinal. Marco Polo claimed to have discovered it in China but records indicate that builders of the Egyptian pyramids ate sweet unleavened ginger cakes. Arab traders brought ginger to the Greeks and Romans and a Greek baker in Rhodes in 2400 B.C. is credited with making the world's first gingerbread.

Ginger is a tuberous underground rhizome which flourishes in tropical rain forests. Although native to Southeast Asia, today the best quality ginger comes from Jamaica. The Latin name zingiber comes from the Sanskrit 'singabera' which means shaped like a horn, referring to the antler-like formation of the rhizome.

Pieces of the rhizome are usually planted in early summer. They will die back in the winter and should be dug up nine months to one year after planting. The young underground sprouts are the most flavorful, for if left in the ground too long, the root will become fiberous. The perennial underground stems or 'hands' as they are called, will exhaust the soil and should be grown in rotation. Each ginger root will yield about eight tubers and one acre of land will produce about four thousand pounds of ginger annually.

Fresh ginger root can be kept in a plastic bag and stored in the refrigerator for a few weeks. Or you can peel the root and keep it in a jar filled with Sherry for a longer period of time. The root can be frozen, but it will become mushy when thawed. Fresh ginger root is used to make ginger ale and ginger beer.

Crystallized ginger is a candy-like product which is made from fresh root that has been cooked in a syrup. Crystallized ginger root is usually used as a condiment, not as a spice.

HOREHOUND

Classification: Perennial
Height: 18 to 32 inches
Conditions preferred: Sun
Part of plant used and storage: Leaves, fresh and dried
Marrubium vulgare
Labiatae
Common names: White horehound, Common horehound

Horehound is one of the oldest known medicinal plants. This perennial herb was used as a cough remedy by the early Egyptians. The Latin name comes from the Hebrew 'marrot', meaning bitter juice, because of its exceedingly bitter taste. Horehound was used as an antidote for poisoning by the Greeks and Romans.

The leaves have long been used as a flavoring for tea and ale and are still a popular ingredient in many cough preparations. There are many recipes for horehound candy found in old cookbooks. Usually the leaves are boiled until the juices are just about evaporated, then the residue is mixed with sugar.

HORSERADISH

Classification: Perennial (grown as annual)
Height: 3 to 4 feet
Conditions preferred: Semi-shade, cool temperatures
Part of plant used and storage: Roots, fresh
Armoracia rusticana
Cruciferae
Common name: Red cole

The horseradish plant originated in Eastern Europe some one thousand years ago. Called 'wild radish' by the ancients, it was used as a medicinal. This plant has been used as a food only since the sixteenth century. Horseradish is the thick fleshy root of a perennial plant belonging to the mustard family. Its essential oils are similar to those found in mustard seeds, hence its pungent aroma (once cut) and flavor. A valuable source of Vitamin C, horseradish is most often eaten raw, for it loses much of its pungency when cooked.

Raw horseradish root is usually peeled, grated and covered with vinegar. If refrigerated and stored this way, it will keep for about three months. You can buy grated horseradish root plain, or in combination with grated beets. Store the whole root in a dark place, as light will turn the white color to green. Horseradish is said to improve the digestion when eaten with rich and fatty foods.

This plant grows very well in a temperate climate. Sow in the spring by planting a piece of the root in a somewhat shady area. If you want to grow a really large root, dig the dirt out from around the plant when the leaves are eight to ten inches long. Then rub or cut off any of the side shoots formed along the main root. Re-cover the main root with soil. The side shoots that have been removed can also be planted, if you like a whole lot of horseradish. Repeat the process again in about six weeks and harvest the root in the late fall.

I do not bother doing all of this and just leave my plant alone, as I do not use all that much horseradish. Harvest late in the fall by digging out the root. If any of this root is left in the ground, the plant has a good chance of re-appearing again the next year. The leaves will grow quite large, so allow enough room when planting.

HYSSOP

Classification: Perennial
Height: 18 inches to 2 feet
Conditions preferred: Sun or partial shade
Part of plant used and storage: Leaves, fresh and dried
Hyssopus officinalis
Labiatae

This evergreen perennial is native to the Mediterranean area. The name hyssop comes from the Hebrew word 'esob' meaning holy plant because the Bible mentions hyssop as one of the ritual or sacrificial herbs used to cleanse holy places. There is a good chance that the plant used then was not really the hyssop we know today, but rather a variety of marjoram.

The flavor of hyssop is unpleasant to the modern palate and it is no longer used as a culinary herb. The leaves were used in salads and soups and to make tea. Hyssop is still used as a flavoring for liqueurs, such as Chartreuse.

JUNIPER BERRIES

Classification: Perennial, tree (coniferous)
Height: 4 to 35 feet
Conditions preferred: Sun
Part of plant used and storage: Berries, dried
Juniperus communis
Cupressaceae

Juniper can be either a bushy evergreen shrub or a small branched tree depending upon its environment. A member of the cyprus family, juniper is dioecious, meaning that male and female trees grow separately. Both are necessary for the production of flowers, but only the female tree yields the fruit or berry.

Juniper berries take from two to three years to ripen and their color turns gradually from green to blue-black. Each berry contains three seeds and has a fragrant slightly resinous smell and flavor. Throughout the year, the trees have berries at various differing stages of ripeness, all at the same time.

Native to many of the northern countries (such as Norway) juniper has been used both as a flavoring agent and a medicinal since biblical times. Early folklore mentions that juniper was believed to be a symbol of protection against both evil spirits and wild animals. In the middle ages, branches were burned as a fumigant to keep the air fresh. Today, in parts of Scotland, branches are still added to the fire to impart their flavor to smoked salmon.

While they are left whole in some marinades, juniper berries are for the most part crushed before using in order to bring out their full flavor and aroma. Juniper berries are a prime flavoring agent in the production of gin.

LAVENDER

Classification: Perennial
Height: 2 to 3 feet
Conditions preferred: Sun
Parts of plant used and storage: Leaves, fresh and dried; Flowers, candied
Lavandula augustifolia
Labiatae

There are numerous varieties of lavender that grow in different shapes and sizes. All are perennials and all have flowers which appear on spikes. The name lavender comes from the Latin 'lavare', meaning to wash, because this herb was used by the early Romans to scent their bath water. The entire plant has a wonderfully clean smelling aroma. Lavender was not used medicinally until Tudor times.

In early European cooking, lavender leaves were used to flavor meats. The flowers were candied as a sweet and still are to this day, being used as a garnish for desserts and confectionary. The plant is now used commercially for perfumes, soaps and to make spirits of ammonia.

LEEKS

Classification: Biennial (grown as an annual)
Height: 2 to 3 feet
Conditions preferred: Sun, cool temperatures
Part of plant used and storage: Leaf stalk and base, fresh
Allium ampeloprasum v. porrum
Liliaceae

Leeks are a biennial member of the onion family usually grown as an annual. The plant has been used both as a food and a medicament since ancient times. Considered a symbol of honorable service, Welsh soldiers wore them in their caps while fighting the Saxons in 640 A.D.

In Europe, leeks are called 'poor man's asparagus' and are frequently eaten as a vegetable. For the most part here in the United States, we use the white part of the stems and discard the upper green portion. This is a terrible waste, as there is a lot of flavor in these greens. I like to save and use them for stocks and soups.

As the plant grows, soil is piled up around the base to blanch or whiten the bottom part of the stalks. Leeks grow in concentric, very tightly packed layers. Care should be taken to wash the leaves well before cooking, especially at the root end of the plant.

To wash a leek properly, cut off the hairy root portion, leaving just enough of the base to keep the leaves attached to each other. Then split the leek in half, lengthwise. While holding each half under running water, force the leaves apart with your fingers to wash away any dirt that is trapped between the layers.

Leeks are quite hardy and will grow well in a temperate climate. They can even withstand the frost if left outside over the winter months.

LEMON BALM

Classification: Perennial
Height: 2 to 3 feet
Conditions preferred: Sun or partial shade
Part of plant used and storage: Leaves, fresh and dried

LAVENDER

LEEKS

LEMON BALM

Melissa officinalis
Labiatae
Common names: Balm, Sweet balm, Common balm, Bee balm

Native to the Mediterranean area and Southern Europe, lemon balm has been cultivated for about two thousand years and was used by the early Greeks and Romans as both a seasoning and a medicinal. Because of its delicate lemon-mint smell, lemon balm was one of the strewing herbs used in medieval times to freshen the always dank indoor air.

Bees have long been attracted to this herb because of its pleasant aroma. In the past, beekeepers used to rub balm leaves on their hives, for they thought it would keep their bees from straying. The name 'melissa' is the Greek word for bee and 'balm' is an abbreviation for balsam, meaning aroma.

Through the early nineteenth century, people carried leaves of lemon balm in their clothing. It was thought that by doing so, the person would be more lovable and attractive. Before the days of modern dry cleaning, this was probably a very good idea. Hopefully, they attracted only other people, not bees.

This perennial plant does well in full sun or partial shade. It spreads easily and will grow up to three feet in height. The plant can be lifted and divided after the second year. Pinch back the top leaves to encourage side growth as you would basil. Lemon balm leaves can be dried, but are better when used fresh. They can be used as a substitute for lemon peel in cooking.

LEMON GRASS

Classification: Perennial
Height: 2 to 6 feet
Conditions preferred: Tropics
Part of plant used and storage: Leaves, fresh and dried
Cymbopogon citratus
Graminae
Common names: West Indian lemon grass, Flower grass

Lemon grass is a perennial member of the grass family that has very long leaves. Any of several varieties of grass go by the name of lemon grass. All of them grow in large clumps and have similar properties.

Lemon grass is native to tropical Southeast Asia. It will, however, grow in temperate climates if wintered indoors. Lemon grass was used by the Egyptians, Greeks and Romans as a cosmetic and a medicament. It is now widely used as a seasoning for Indonesian cooking. It flavors soups, sauces, fish dishes, curries, teas and wines. Lemon grass is used commercially for its lemon scented oil.

LEMON VERBENA

Classification: Perennial (tender)
Height: 2 to 20 feet
Conditions preferred: Sun, shelter
Part of plant used and storage: Leaves, fresh and dried
Aloysia triphylla
Verbenaceae

Lemon verbena is native to Central and South America and was taken to Europe and the United States at the end of the eighteenth century by the Spanish explorers. The name aloysia comes from Louisa, as the plant was named for Marie Louisa, wife of King Charles IV of Spain.

The plant is considered a semi-shrub in tropical climates and can grow up to ten feet in height there. It can grow as tall as six feet even in a temperate climate if planted in a hot and sunny sheltered spot in the garden. The stems are very woody and should be cut back at the end of each growing season.

If you decide to bring this plant indoors for the winter, it will often lose its leaves. New growth usually appears around February, so have patience. If left outdoors in a temperate climate and if very well protected, verbena has a chance of surviving the winter. But to be safe, it is probably better to bring the plant inside. Verbena grows best in a greenhouse where the temperature never goes below fifty degrees.

Lemon verbena is very aromatic, for its leaves have the strongest lemon scent of all the lemon flavored herbs. Use it sparingly as a substitute for lemon or lemon rind. The leaves are at their peak of flavor just before the flowers begin to bloom. They can be picked and dried for winter use.

LOVAGE

Classification: Perennial
Height: to 6 feet
Conditions preferred: Sun or partial shade
Parts of plant used and storage: Leaves and stems, fresh; Seeds, dried
Levisticum officinale
Umbelliferae

Lovage is a large perennial plant native to West Asia. It grows six or more feet in height and develops a long tap root system which does not like to be disturbed. The Greeks and Romans used every part of this plant to make medicinals and as a deodorant.

The stems and leaf stalks of the lovage plant have a spicy celery-like flavor. They can be blanched and eaten as a vegetable (like celery) or used as a flavoring for soups, meats and sauces. Much like angelica, lovage stems can be candied and the seeds dried and used to flavor confectionary.

LEMON VERBENA

LOVAGE

MARIGOLDS

Tea made from this plant has a meaty or yeasty flavor. In fact, it will taste more like a broth than a tea. Because of this property, lovage is used commercially as an ingredient in some dried seasoning mixes. Lovage root was once ground and used as a substitute for pepper.

MARIGOLD

Classification: Annual
Height: 8 to 24 inches
Conditions preferred: Sun
Part of plant used and storage: Flower petals, fresh and dried
Calendula officinalis
Compositae
Common name: Pot marigold

Marigold petals, because of their deep yellow or orange color, have been used throughout history as a substitute for (or an adulterant of) the more expensive saffron powder. The flower petals can be used as a coloring for butter, rice dishes, baked goods and cheeses. The finished dish will have the same color but none of the taste that saffron imparts. The ground petals are often added to chicken feed to give the chicken skin a deep yellow color.

Marigolds are native to Southern Europe. Both the leaves and petals of this annual have been used as a medicinal throughout history. The flowers are often seen decorating temples in India.

The Latin name can be interpreted to have two different yet similar meanings. Calendula may come from the word 'calende' or 'calendae' meaning through the months because of the long blooming period of this flower. Another interpretation is that the name stems from 'kalendis' meaning first day of the month, for marigolds were thought to always flower on the first day of the month.

MARJORAM

Classification: Perennial (tender)
Height: to 2 feet
Conditions preferred: Full sun, shelter
Part of plant used and storage: Leaves, fresh and dried
Origanum marjorana or Marjorana hortensis
Labiatae
Common names: Sweet marjoram, Annual marjoram

The name origanum comes from the Greek words 'horos' meaning hill and 'ganos' meaning adornment. It has been liberally translated to mean 'joy of the mountain'. Known since ancient times as a symbol of happiness, marjoram was used to make love potions. In ancient Greece and Rome, young married couples were crowned with wreaths made from the stems. It was also planted on graves to ensure the departed of a happy afterlife.

Marjoram is a member of the mint family and is native to the Mediterranean area. It grows as a perennial in warm climates and is supposed to be an annual in cooler areas, although this is not always the case. It may surprise you by reappearing year after year.

There is a great deal of confusion, even among botanists, between marjoram and oregano. Many plants grown and sold in nurseries as marjoram are really varieties of oregano. True marjoram can sometimes be difficult to obtain. Marjoram has a small green leaf and usually, knot-like white flowers. Some varieties, however, can have pink or purple flowers as does oregano, which only helps to add to the confusion. There is a difference in the flavor of the leaves with marjoram being milder and to me, more aromatic than oregano.

Varieties most often cultivated for culinary purposes are sweet or knotted marjoram and pot marjoram (O. onites). Pot marjoram has a larger dark green leaf which is stronger in flavor than sweet marjoram. I use both, but prefer the more delicate flavor of the knotted marjoram.

MINT

Classification: Perennial
Height: 1 to 3 feet
Conditions preferred: Partial shade
Part of plant used and storage: Leaves, fresh and dried
Labiatae
Mentha spicata
Common names: Spearmint, Garden mint
Mentha piperata
Common name: Peppermint

Of the hundreds of species of mint grown, spearmint and peppermint are the two types most often used for culinary purposes. Spearmint is the oldest member of the mint family and was used by the Assyrians during rituals to their fire god. Mint has been used as a food flavoring for a very long time. The invention of mint sauce can be traced back and credited to early Roman cooks.

There is no record of peppermint until 1696, when it was described by John Rey, an English botanist. Peppermint is a hybrid and is really a cross between watermint and spearmint. Peppermint is the variety, however, always associated with the ever popular Mint Julip.

It is said that a beautiful nymph named Minthe was loved by Pluto, the lord of the underworld. His jealous wife, Proserpine, changed her into the herb known as mint. Because of its fresh and clean aroma, mint was used to perfume bath water and as a strewing herb.

All mints tend to hybridize easily and will do so even in your own garden if many varieties are planted near each other. Mint will spread unmercifully if left unchecked, because its underground runners take over your entire garden, if they could. The only way to keep mint under control is to grow it in a separate area from your other herbs, or to surround it with a brick or metal edging that has been buried deeply in the ground. The clumps can and should be dug up and divided every few years. Mint likes lots of moisture and grows best in a semi-shady spot.

Some of the more common types of mint other than the two mentioned are; apple mint, lemon mint, pineapple mint, pennyroyal, Corsican mint, curly mint, watermint and bergamot. These are but a few of the many varieties available for mint lovers to grow at home. Most of them have a commercial use in the manufacturing of the large number of products that have a mint smell or taste.

MUGWORT

Classification: Perennial
Height: to 6 feet
Conditions preferred: Weed, will grow anywhere
Parts of plant used and storage: Buds and leaves, fresh and dried
Artemisa vulgaris
Compositae
Common name: St. John's plant

This perennial plant grows like a weed in many parts of the world. Commonly called St. John's plant, mugwort was believed to possess magical properties. Travellers placed sprigs of this herb in their shoes before embarking on a journey. They thought that by doing so they would feel no fatigue and have a safe journey as well.

In Germany, mugwort is called 'beifuss' and its leaves were often cooked with fatty meats to make them more digestible. Before the advent of hops, the leaves were used to flavor beer and ale. Sometimes even the dried flower buds were used as a seasoning. Mugwort is not used very much for cooking today.

MUSTARD

Classification: Annual
Height: White and Brown, to 4 feet; Black, to 6 feet
Conditions preferred: Sun
Part of plant used and storage: Seeds, dried
Cruciferae
Brassica hirta b. alba
Common name: White mustard
Brassica nigra
Common name: Black mustard
Brassica juncea
Common names: Indian mustard, Brown mustard, Leaf mustard, Mustard greens

There are three types of mustard seeds that can be used for culinary purposes. The seed of the white mustard plant is actually yellowish in color and larger in size than the other two, with a pungent flavor and little or no aroma. Black seeds are dark brown in color with a pungent taste and a very strong odor. Since the black mustard plant has not adapted well to our modern harvesting methods, it has mostly been replaced with the brown or Indian variety. Brown mustard seeds are less pungent than black, but the two are very similar in appearance. Mustard powders or pastes bought commercially contain a combination of at least two of the three types of seeds.

The name mustard is thought to be from the Latin word 'mustum' or 'must'. Must is the name given to juice that is pressed from grapes. The Romans made a paste of this juice which they mixed with ground mustard seeds. They called this mixture 'mustem ardens', a hot or burning must, and used it as a condiment on their food.

All mustard seeds contain sugar compounds or glycosides and an enzyme that in the presence of water will react to produce a sulphur compound. This is why foods that have mustard in their preparation will discolor silverware. Sulphur turns silver black.

Mrs. Clements of Durham, England, has been credited with the invention of mustard powder in 1720. The dry powder is a mixture of white and black or brown seeds. It can be stored for a long period of time and has no odor until activated. To activate the powder, mix it with a cold liquid (water or wine) and allow it to stand for five to ten minutes. Once liquified, the mustard cannot be stored for long or it will lose its strength. Adding an acid such as vinegar or lemon juice will stop the enzyme action and help it to keep longer. 'DSP' on the label of dried mustard powder means 'double super fine' and is indicative of a high quality mustard powder.

The yellow or 'ball-park' mustard commonly sold in jars is a mixture of ground seeds, salt, vinegar or wine and spices. Its bright yellow color comes from the addition of turmeric. Some of the finest quality mustard seeds as well as prepared mustards come from the Dijon region of France. Dijon-type mustards are now produced in the United States and are also of a very good quality.

NASTURTIUM

Classification: Annual
Height: 8 to 15 inches
Conditions preferred: Sun
Parts of plant used and storage: Leaves and flowers, fresh; Seeds, pickled
Tropaeolum tropaeolum
Tropaeolaceae
Common names: Indian cress, Garden nasturtium, Tall nasturtium

There are several edible varieties of nasturtium that have extremely pretty blossoms of varying colors. This plant is native to South America and can be found growing wild there. Nasturtium seeds were taken from Peru to Europe in the sixteenth century by the Spanish explorers.

Its name comes from the Latin word meaning

GOLDEN AND POT MARJORAM

PEPPERMINT

SPEARMINT

BLACK MUSTARD

'to twist the nose' because of the plant's spicy or peppery flavor. Nasturtium is a sun loving annual and is a member of the watercress family. The seed pods can be pickled and used much like capers. Because of their sharp and peppery flavor, the leaves, and even the flowers, are used fresh in salads.

NUTMEG and MACE

Classification: Perennial, tree
Height: 40 to 70 feet
Conditions preferred: Tropics, rain
Part of plant used and storage: Seed, dried; Aril, dried
Myristica fragrans
Myristicaceae

Nutmeg and mace are a unique duo in nature as they are the only two separate and distinct spices which grow on the same plant. They both come from the same one-seeded, oval shaped, apricot-like fruit of a tropical evergreen tree. Nutmeg trees are native to the Molucca Islands and although exclusive to these islands for many years, are now grown in other parts of the tropics.

There is no historical record which shows either nutmeg or mace being used before the sixth century. Around that time they were brought to Constantinople by Arab traders. Both spices reached Europe by the twelfth century and were widely used as a flavoring and a medicament. The trade in these spices was controlled and monopolized for centuries, first by the Portuguese and then the Dutch.

Male and female trees grow separately, but only the fertilized female trees bear fruit. The trees will produce blossoms all year long and continue to bear fruit for about eighty years. When the fruit of the tree ripens, it splits in half. Inside can be found a wrinkled brown nut covered by a scarlet net-like membrane or aril, as it is called. This aril is mace, while the kernel found inside the brown shell is nutmeg.

The aril is separated from the nut before it is dried. This scarlet aril, called a blade when it is whole, is flattened and sun dried for ten days to two weeks. Drying turns the red aril to a yellow-brown color and once dried it takes on a typical mace aroma. The seeds (nuts) are dried for up to two months, or until the kernels rattle around in their shells. The shells are then broken and the nutmeg removed.

Nutmeg, once grated, loses its strength quickly. This is probably why nutmeg graters have been so popular throughout history. Gentlemen often carried their own personal graters with them when travelling or dining out. If you buy nutmeg whole and grate it as it is needed, the taste will be far superior to that which has been grated ahead of time.

Mace is a much more pungent spice than is nutmeg. Substituting one for the other in cooking will not always work, for each has its own unique

NASTURTIUM

ONIONS

MUSTARD, at top prepared mustards; in foreground from left: white seed, powdered, and black seed.

and different flavor even thought they come from the same fruit.

ONIONS

Classification: Biennial (bulb)
Height: 2 to 6 feet
Conditions preferred: Full sun
Part of plant used and storage: Bulb, fresh
Allium cepa
Liliaceae
Names of common varieties: Scallions, Ciboule, Spring onions, Green onions

Onions, along with garlic, are among the oldest of all cultivated plants. We have proof that they were grown in Egypt, China and India long before man began to formally record his history. Onions were used both as a medicine and a food because of their natural antiseptic qualities and their high vitamin C content.

The onion is a member of the lily family and is considered an herbaceous biennial plant. An onion consists of a single large bulb made up of concentric layers of flesh. The underground bulb sends up a tall leafless stalk. What we usually eat is really the swollen ball at the base of the leaf stalk. The word 'cepa' in Latin means head, probably given to this plant because of its shape.

The amount of sunlight present determines just how long it takes an onion to grow. In the tropics, the plant can and does complete a full life cycle in just one year, while it takes two years in a temperate climate. The flavor of onions will vary, depending on the climate in which they are grown. Onions are sweet and juicy when cultivated in a warm climate. Elsewhere they tend to be quite strong—enough to make your eyes water when you cut them.

In the tropics, onions are usually started from seed, while in temperate climates, sets (tiny bulblets which are retarded and stored under refrigeration) are used. All members of the onion family like a rich soil and lots of sunshine and moisture. They should be harvested in the fall when the stalks turn brown.

There are several varieties of edible onions. Allium cepa vivaparum, or Egyptian onions are one of the more interesting types. The tiny bulbs develop on top of the stem and the whole plant appears to be growing upside down.

Scallions or spring onions are small elongated bulblets that grow in clumps. We eat their sweet tender green stems as well as the white bulblets. Scallions have an extremely high vitamin C content, containing about fifteen times the amount found in onions. Even though their flavor is different from chives, they can be substituted for each other in many recipes.

Mentioned in Chinese literature over two thousand years ago, Welsh onions (A. fistulosum) is a perennial plant grown for its large green chive-like leaves. The plant grows well in colder climates and can be harvested in just three to four weeks.

OREGANO

Classification: Perennial
Height: 2 to 3 feet
Conditions preferred: Full sun
Part of plant used and storage: Leaves, fresh and dried
Origanum vulgare
Labiatae

Common names: Wild marjoram, Pot marjoram, Origano, Organy

Oregano and marjoram are often and easily confused with each other. Some botanists claim oregano is just a strain of wild marjoram while others think it is a different species. There is some truth to this, for most of what we think of as marjoram is, in reality, varieties of oregano. Be that as it may, I will leave the technical arguments to the botanists and say that I think of marjoram and oregano as two separate herbs for culinary purposes.

Oregano has fairly large leaves and bears tiny pink or purple flowers. If left unchecked, it can grow to almost bush-like proportions and has done so in my garden. Even though I keep just one plant, I always end up with far more oregano than I can ever hope to use each year. Divide and replant (or give away) every few years.

The pungency of this herb will vary, depending on the particular variety as well as where the plant has been grown. Oregano from Mexico is different from the strain that comes from Europe. Here in the United States, we usually use the European variety.

Legend has it that a servant to Cinyras, King of Cyprus, dropped and spilled a large vessel of perfume he was carrying. Afraid of being punished for this deed, he fainted and was metamorphosized into oregano. This herb was used by the ancients as both a condiment and a medicinal.

Oregano was not used to any great extent in the United States as a culinary herb much before the 1940's. The GI's returning from the war probably created a demand for this herb because of their fond memories of the wonderful dishes they had eaten in Europe, most especially the pizza in Italy.

PAPRIKA, see Capsicum peppers, page 27.

PARSLEY

Classification: Biennial (grown as annual)
Height: 1 to 3 feet
Conditions preferred: Sun or partial shade
Parts of plant used and storage: Leaves, fresh and dried; Roots, fresh
Petroselinum crispum var. carum
Umbelliferae

Parsley is, no doubt, the most widely used herb in this country, as both a flavoring and a garnish.

Parsley sprigs appear like magic on most platters served in restaurants as if they had grown there. Both the curly and flat leafed (or Italian) varieties are readily available year-round. Many cooks claim that the flat leafed variety has more flavor than does the curly. It is a little stronger, but there is not a great deal of difference between the two, so use whichever pleases you.

Parsley is a biennial plant, but it is usually grown as an annual. It prefers a fairly rich soil and partial shade. If you wish to grow this plant as a biennial, do not cut the leaves below four inches from the ground when harvesting the first year. After the second year's growth, wait to cut the plant back until the first frost. You can even get parsley to return for a third year if you cut back the stems and do not allow this herb to flower during its second year.

Parsley seeds are extremely slow to germinate and it will take several weeks before any growth appears. Soaking the seeds in warm water for twenty-four hours before planting should help some. There was a medieval superstition to explain this slow germination time. It was said that the parsley seed had to travel down to the devil and back seven times before it could begin to grow. Another strange but interesting tale assures a good harvest only if the seeds are sown on Good Friday by a pregnant woman.

The plant's Latin name comes from the Greek 'petros' meaning rock, probably given because parsley was often found growing among the rocks. The Greeks did not eat parsley but used it to crown the victors of athletic games and as fodder for their horses. Considered a symbol of death, they placed parsley springs and wreaths on their tombs. The Romans were probably the first to eat this herb in about the third century.

Fresh parsley is high in vitamins A and C and contains lots of iron and minerals. Parsley has been used as a natural breath freshener for centuries. The leaves have little flavor or aroma when dried. They can be frozen but are really best when used fresh. Parsley roots are excellent as a flavoring for soups.

OREGANO

PARSLEY

PEPPER

Classification: Perennial (climbing vine)
Height: to 30 feet
Conditions preferred: Tropics, rain
Part of plant used and storage: Berry, dried
Piper nigrum
Piperaceae
Common names: Black pepper, White pepper, Pepper plant

PARSLEY, from top left: flat, curly, cilitrano, root.

Pepper is considered to be the world's most important spice. Throughout history, pepper has been given the same value as hard currency and it has been used from time to time as payment for taxes, dowries, rents, tithes, and so on. Spice merchants during the middle ages were called 'Pepperers' in English, 'Poiviers' in French and

'Pfeffersacke' in German. History records that the Guild of Pepperers became incorporated into the Guild of Grocers who, in turn, lost their spice trade to the Guild of Apothecaries.

Pepper is the small round berry of a woody vine native to the Malabar coast of India. It is now cultivated in many tropical climates. The vines can climb as high as thirty feet and are grown against wooden supports or trees. The flavor and strength of pepper will vary depending on the area in which it is grown. Pepper is, in fact, graded and identified geographically (for example, Malabar, Tellicherry, Sarawaka, etc.).

Both black and white pepper come from the same berry, the difference being in when it is picked and how it is then treated. Black pepper is picked while still green, before the berries ripen. They are piled into heaps and allowed to sit and ferment for a few days before they are dried. The peppercorns will shrivel and turn black or brown-black in color.

White pepper is picked once the berries have ripened, when they are green-yellow in color, just at the point of turning red. These berries are soaked in water for about eight days, then the soft outer pericarp or hulls are removed. When dried, they turn white.

There is a subtle difference between black and white pepper. Black peppercorns have a fuller aroma, while white pepper has a stronger flavor. For cooking, I like to use Richard Olney's pepper mixture, which consists of three parts black peppercorns to two parts white peppercorns to one part allspice berries. I keep this mixture in my peppermill and find that the combination of flavors and aromas is excellent.

An item now readily found in stores (and recipes) is the 'so-called' green peppercorn. It is exactly what its name implies, unripe fresh pepper berries. Green peppercorns are available either in a salt brine or vinegar solution or as a freeze-dried product. I prefer to use them in their freeze-dried state because there is no problem of shelf life once the container is opened. Green peppercorns have a pungent spicy flavor and are used a great deal in the 'Nouvelle Cuisine' wave of French cooking. So-called red peppercorns now sold are not true pepper berries and should be avoided. They can be poisonous when used in quantity.

POPPY SEEDS

Classification: Annual
Height: 3 to 4 feet
Conditions preferred: Sun
Part of plant used and storage: Seed, dried
Papaver somniferum
Papaveraceae
Common name: Opium poppy

The opium poppy, which has been cultivated for thousands of years for use as both a food and a medicine, provides us with poppy seeds. Cooking oil extracted from the seeds was used by the Egyptians as early as 1500 B.C. The ancients often ate poppy seeds mixed with wine and honey.

Opium comes from the shell of the plant's seed capsule. Incisions are made in the outside of the capsule so that the sap or juice will ooze out. This sap dries on contact with the air and solidifies into tiny white droplets or 'tears'. Opium and morphine are produced from this dried sap.

The women of Crete cultivated poppies for their opium content as early as 1400 B.C. and a statue of the Greek god of sleep, Hypnos, has a wreath of poppies around its head. The name 'somniferum' means sleep-bearing, given to the plant because of its narcotic qualities.

Poppy seeds are not formed until after the plant loses its opium bearing potential. The slate-blue seeds contain no narcotic qualities and have a pleasant, crunchy nut-like flavor. They are rich in oil (30%) and extremely tiny in size. About 400,000 seeds weigh just one pound. Today, their main culinary use is in baked goods. The seeds are extremely hard to grind and can be bought ground as well as whole. Store ground poppy seeds in the freezer to keep them fresh longest.

The flowers of the poppy plant are usually red, but they can also be white, pink or purple in color. An annual plant, poppies are native to Southwest Asia. Today, poppies are grown commercially in the Netherlands, Poland and Iran.

ROCKETTE

Classification: Perennial
Height: 12 to 30 inches
Conditions preferred: Sun
Part of plant used and storage: Leaves, fresh
Eruca vesicaria
Cruciferae
Common names: Rugula, Arugula, Roquette, Rocket salad

This annual plant is native to the Mediterranean area and West Asia and was used by the Romans as a medicinal. Rockette is a wonderful salad green and until recently used mostly in the south of France and Italy. It is now just beginning to become popular in the United States.

The leaves have a very pungent, almost nut-like bitter flavor and should be eaten only when they are young and tender. Pick the leaves often and do not allow the plant to flower. In the past the only way to obtain this green was to grow it yourself, however, it can now be found fresh in many specialty stores when in season.

ROSE

Classification: Perennial (bush)
Height: to 8 feet
Conditions preferred: Sun
Parts of plant used and storage: Petals and hips, fresh, dried and candied
Rosaceae
Rosa centifolia

Common name: Cabbage rose
Rosa damascena
Common name: Damask rose
Rose eglanteria
Common names: Sweet briar rose, Eglantine
Rose gallica
Common names: Rose de Provins, French rose, Apothecary rose

There are hundreds of varieties of roses, but basically all are hybrids, descendants from one of three original kinds; the damask rose, the rose de provins and the China rose (Rosa chinesis). Most hybrids are not used for culinary purposes because they do not have enough aroma and flavor.

Roses were imported from Egypt and extremely large quantities were used by the early Romans for almost everything. The petals were strewn on the floors and in streets, stuffed into mattresses, made into cosmetics, used for bath water and as a medicinal. Oil of rose was first distilled by Avicenna, a Roman, during the tenth century.

Today, rose water and attar of rose are made mainly from the damask and cabbage varieties. Rose petals, usually from the rose de provins, can be candied or dried. This flower has long been considered a symbol of beauty, fidelity and happiness.

A special word about rose hips. They are small red-orange berries that remain on the rose bushes once the flowers have wilted and fallen. They are rich in vitamins C and A and can be used in fresh or dried form. The rose hips used today as a flavoring and to make tea usually come from the bushes of the sweet briar or wild dog rose (Rosa conviva). There is some evidence that rose hips were used as a food in Britian about 2000 B.C.

ROSEMARY

Classification: Perennial (tender)
Height: up to 6 feet
Conditions preferred: Sun
Part of plant used and storage: Leaves, fresh and dried
Rosmarinus officinalis
Labiate

The name rosemary comes from the Greek 'ros' which means dew and 'marinus', meaning of the sea or belonging to the sea. This plant is native to the Mediterranean area and grows wild there along the limestone coastline, bathed in the salty spray of the sea. In this natural habitat, rosemary is a woody evergreen shrub that will grow up to six feet in height. The leaves resemble pine needles and have a strong resinous smell and taste. Both creeping and upright varieties of this plant are cultivated.

Rosemary will never reach its full size or height in temperate regions. It should either be taken indoors for the winter or given lots of protection if left outside. The plant likes a lot of sun and a well drained limey soil. Harvest by cutting the side branches, not the woody stems. Rosemary can be dried, but it is better when fresh.

This herb was used as early as 300 B.C. as both a condiment and a medicament. Folklore abounds about rosemary in many countries, for it has long been considered a symbol of friendship and fidelity. Rosemary was carried at weddings, used at funerals and even rubbed in the scalp to make hair grow. Branches were hung in doorways so that those passing through would have to brush against it with their clothing. Its clean scent was valued long before dry cleaning existed.

Legend has it that when the Virgin Mary was enroute to Egypt while fleeing Herod's soldiers, she hung her blue cloak on a rosemary bush. The white flowers of the bush were said to have turned blue overnight. Hence its name, Rose of Mary.

RUE

Classification: Perennial
Height: 2 to 3 feet
Conditions preferred: Sun
Part of plant used and storage: Leaves, fresh
Ruta graveolens
Rutaceae
Common names: Herb o'grace, Common rue

Rue has been used since early Greek and Roman times as a seasoning and a medicament. Used to treat numerous ailments, rue was also considered to be an antidote for poison. The name comes from the Greek 'reuo' meaning to set free, inferring to set free from disease. In the past, the leaves have been used both as a salad green and for cooking.

Rue was once called herb o'grace, for in early church rituals, branches of rue were used to sprinkle holy water. The Greeks thought rue would grow better if the plants were stolen from a friend's garden. Stolen or not, rue has the most bitter taste of all the herbs. Use this herb with discretion as well as caution, for it can be quite irritating both internally and externally. I would stay away from it myself.

SAFFRON

Classification: Perennial (bulbous)
Height: 6 to 10 inches
Conditions preferred: Full sun
Part of plant used and storage: Flower stigmas, dried
Crocus sativus
Iridaceae
Common name: Saffron crocus

Pepper may be the most important spice in the world, but saffron is considered to be the most expensive. Saffron is the dried stigma of the flower produced by the saffron crocus. In the fall, each

FROM TOP LEFT: BLACK PEPPERCORNS, WHITE PEPPERCORNS, ALLSPICE BERRIES, GREEN PEPPERCORNS

POPPY SEED HEAD

PEPPERCORNS

ROCKETTE

ROSEMARY

RUE

COMMON SAGE

DWARF SAGE

SUMMER SAVORY

WINTER SAVORY

six-petaled violet flower blooms and will produce three stigmas. These bright orange stigmas must be picked by hand once the flower opens. There are varying estimates as to how many stigmas it takes to make a pound of saffron with the average guess being about 70,000 flowers or 210,000 stigmas or threads.

This particular species of the iris family can be started from seed or by planting the tiny bulbs or corms. When started from seed, the crocus will take three years to produce a corm. A perennial, the plant will bloom and produce flowers for twelve to fifteen years. Commercially, the corms are lifted, divided and replanted every few years.

The bright orange stigmas will turn red-brown in color when they are dried. They can be bought either in thread form or as a powder. Since saffron powder can be easily adulterated and has been for centuries, I would strongly recommend buying the threads. They can be pulverized or dissolved when needed. The best quality of saffron grown today is said to come from Spain.

Saffron has been used since ancient times as a condiment, dye, perfume and medicament. We find reference to saffron as early as 1552 B.C. in the medical papyrus of Thebes. King Solomon mentions saffron in his Song of Songs in the Old Testament.

Saffron produces an extraordinarily potent dye. A piece of silk cloth colored with saffron was found in the Egyptian dessert buried under the sands for over two thousand years. When dug out, the color of the cloth was still perfectly preserved. The name saffron comes from the Arabic word 'za'faran' meaning yellow.

This dye will color food, as well as fabric, a beautiful bright yellow. Use with caution, for while pleasant in small quantities, saffron will impart a bitter, musty-like flavor to your dish if used in excess.

SAGE

Classification: Perennial (shrub)
Height: 8 inches to 4 feet
Conditions preferred: Full sun
Part of plant used and storage: Leaves, fresh and dried
Salvia officinalis
Labiatae
Common names: Common sage, Garden sage

Sage, an evergreen shrub of the mint family, is native to the Mediterranean area. It has been cultivated for so long that hundreds of varieties have developed. Some of the most common types found are pineapple, dwarf, purple, golden, tri-colored and clary sage. The plant can grow anywhere in size from eight inches to four feet, depending on the variety. The leaves can be green, purple, yellow, gray or a mixture of these hues.

The best type of sage to use for cooking purposes is the plain common or garden variety. Common sage grows to two feet in height and has grayish colored leaves. Sage bushes tend to get woody and should be renewed every four years or so. Trim the bush back well in the late fall or early spring. Sage leaves can be harvested twice a season, once in mid-summer and again in the fall. For preservation, the leaves are best when dried.

The Latin name 'salvia' means to save or to heal. Sage was used as a medicine by the Chinese as well as the Greeks. It was thought to be a symbol of immortality, for the ancients believed that anyone who ate sage would live a long life. Because of this, sage tea was a very popular beverage in China as recently as just a few hundred years ago. Shrewd Dutch merchants took advantage of this belief and were able to trade three pounds of Chinese tea for use in the West in return for only one pound of sage leaves for use in China.

Sage leaves can be quite pronounced in flavor, so use with caution. The French name for sage means 'wise', but interestingly, the Greek name translates to mean 'camel's tongue', because of the shape and texture of the leaves. Perhaps the Greeks were trying to tell us something. Admittedly, sage is not one of my favorite herbs.

SAVORY

Summer Savory
Classification: Annual
Height: 12 to 18 inches
Conditions preferred: Sun
Part of plant used and storage: Leaves, fresh and dried

Winter Savory
Classification: Perennial
Height: 6 to 12 inches
Conditions preferred: Sun
Part of plant used and storage: Leaves, fresh and dried
Labiatae
Satureja hortensis
Common names: Summer savory, Annual savory
Satureja montana
Common names: Winter savory, Mountain savory

Savory is a member of the mint family. Summer and winter savory can be used more or less interchangeably for cooking purposes although there is some difference in flavor. Both varieties have been used for over two thousand years. Both types can be dried for winter use. The Latin name 'satureja' means chosen plant of the satyrs, for this plant has long been regarded as having aphrodisiac qualities.

Summer savory is an annual with a very delicate flavor and is considered to be superior to the winter variety. It was used by the ancient Greeks and Romans as a potherb and a seasoning. Summer savory was often mixed with vinegar and served as a sauce during Roman feasts.

Winter savory is a dwarf evergreen perennial and has a less delicate, but nonetheless, good flavor. Most dried commercial savory is of the winter variety. Growth will slow as the plant ages. To keep a constant supply, in the fall spread out some of the branches and cover their bases well with soil. By spring, these branches should have grown roots. Cut them off for replanting.

Savory is called the 'bean herb' in Europe, because in many countries it is traditionally added to the pot when cooking beans.

There is an evergreen variety of savory (S. douglasii) which in earlier times grew wild and was native to the West Coast of the United States. Found on many hillsides, it was named 'yerba buena' by the Spanish. Yerba Buena is the original name of San Francisco.

SCENTED GERANIUMS

Classification: Perennial (tender)
Height: up to 4 feet
Conditions preferred: Sun, shelter
Part of plant used and storage: Leaves, fresh and dried
Pelargonium graveolens
Geraniaceae
Common names: Rose geranium, Sweet scented geranium

Scented geraniums or pelargoniums were very popular during Victorian times. Of the over two hundred and eighty varieties known, the rose geranium was and still is the favorite. Pelargoniums are unusual because it is the leaves and not the flowers which contain the aroma that is characteristic to the variety. Usually the larger the leaf, the more pronounced the aroma.

The leaves of this plant are used for cooking, usually when fresh. Many old recipes for custards and cakes call for the fresh leaves to be placed in the pan before baking to impart a subtle flavor and aroma to the finished product. Today pelargoniums are mainly used as a source of commercial geranium oil.

Scented geraniums do not survive the frost. In a temperate climate they should be brought indoors during the winter. They prefer lots of sunshine and need some protection from the wind.

SESAME SEEDS

Classification: Annual
Height: 2 to 3 feet
Conditions preferred: Sun
Part of plant used and storage: Seeds, dried
Sesamum indicum [*s. orientale*]
Pedaliaceae
Common name: Benne seeds

The ancient Assyrians believed that the gods drank sesame seed wine while they contemplated the creation of the earth. Sesame is among the oldest of man's cultivated spices, having been mentioned by its Egyptian name 'sesamt' in the Ebbers papyrus written in 1500 B.C. Originally grown in the Nile valley, India and Africa, this plant was used as a staple to produce a variety of products in many ancient lands.

Sesame seeds are the dried fruit of this tropical annual plant. The original cultivated variety had pods that shattered forcefully once ripe, with the seeds ejecting violently. The words 'open sesame' from the tale of Ali Baba refers to this fact. Newer varieties have been developed commercially with pods which do not shatter when ripe.

The sesame seeds we buy are usually hulled before they are packaged and are light in color. It takes between twenty and thirty plants to produce just one cup of these tiny seeds. When used for cooking, the seeds should always be toasted first to bring out their rich nut-like flavor.

Sesame seeds are the source of both sesame oil and sesame paste. They contain approximately fifty percent of a fixed oil which can be extracted and used for cooking. They will keep well if stored at room temperature for up to three months. For a longer period of time, keep the seeds refrigerated as they can easily turn rancid because of their high oil content. However, sesame oil has a longer shelf life and storage period than most other vegetable oils and is used a great deal in oriental cooking. A paste made from the seeds called 'tahina' is used in many Middle-Eastern dishes. Halvah, a popular and very sweet candy is also made from sesame.

Sesame seeds found their way to the United States from Africa by being brought here by the slaves. In the southern part of this country, sesame seeds are often called benne seeds. In Africa, the name for sesame is 'benne'.

SHALLOTS

Classification: Perennial (bulb)
Height: 16 inches
Conditions preferred: Sun
Part of plant used and storage: Bulb, fresh
Allium aggregatum
Liliaceae

Shallots are a perennial member of the onion family. It is believed that they originated in Ethiopia and were taken to Europe by the crusaders. Their original name, A. ascalonium, however, comes from the Palestinian town of Ascalon, where shallots were grown in large quantity.

Shallots can be planted from bulblets or sets in early spring or fall. Each bulblet will multiply into a clump. Harvest by digging out the clumps after the foliage dies down, as the plants do not flower. Shallots, like all members of the onion family, need rich soil and lots of sunshine to grow well. If you grow shallots every year, rotate your crop, as

ROSE SCENTED GERANIUM

FRENCH SORREL

GARDEN SORREL

this plant will tend to deplete the soil of valuable nutrients.

Depending on the particular variety, shallots can have either a red-brown or silver colored skin. Individual shallots can also vary in size from small to large. I find that the larger variety are sweeter in taste and easier to handle for cooking.

Shallots have a mild and delicate flavor which can be described as a cross between that of an onion and garlic. Used frequently in many cuisines, especially French, they are a great favorite in my kitchen. Once you become a shallot addict, nothing else will do.

SORREL

Classification: Perennial
Height: 18 inches to 3 feet
Conditions preferred: Sun
Part of plant used and storage: Leaves, fresh and frozen
Polygonaceae
Rumex scutatus
Common name: French sorrel
Rumex acetosa
Common names: Garden sorrel, Sour dock

Sorrel was cultivated by the fourteenth century in Europe and was used much in the same way that spinach is today. It was very popular and many recipes can be found in old cookery books that call for sorrel as an ingredient. The leaves have a very strong sour or acid flavor and are high in vitamin C. But they also contain large amounts of oxalic acid, so use with discretion. It is not a good idea to eat very large quantities of this plant on a regular daily basis.

Both the French and garden varieties of sorrel are perennial and either can be used for cooking. Beginning in the plant's second year, the tall flower stalks should be cut back before they begin to bloom. Sorrel leaves tend to get tough as the plant ages. Some gardeners suggest digging up the sorrel and starting a new patch every four years. But I find that sorrel, once started, grows like a weed and is difficult to get rid of.

Garden sorrel is the most common variety found growing in the United States. It has long flat leaves and a very strong acid flavor. French sorrel has much smaller arrow-shaped leaves and is milder in flavor. The name 'scutatus' comes from the Latin and means shield, so named because of the shape of the leaves.

The best way to preserve sorrel for winter use is to blanch and freeze the leaves. The bright green leaves will turn muddy brown in color and shrink down to almost nothing in size once they are immersed in boiling water. Refresh immediately in cold water and the leaves will retain their flavor. I pack the well drained leaves into ice cube trays and freeze them. Once they are frozen, I remove the sorrel cubes and wrap them individually for long term freezer storage. Frozen sorrel will keep very well for a year or two.

For cooking measurements, I find that each ice cube size block equals two tablespoons of blanched sorrel or about the equivalent of one-half cup of fresh sorrel leaves. Don't forget to label and date the packages.

SOUTHERNWOOD

Classification: Perennial
Height: 2 to 6 feet
Conditions preferred: Sun or partial shade
Part of plant used and storage: Leaves, fresh and dried
Artemisa abrotantum
Compositae
Common names: Lad's love, Maiden's ruin, Old man, Southern wormwood

Southernwood is a perennial plant native to Southern Europe. Its leaves have a strong lemon odor and a very bitter taste. It has a history of use as a medicinal and as a flavoring for alcoholic beverages. Southernwood was sometimes used in cakes.

The name for southernwood in French is 'garderobe' given because of the plants natural insect repellent qualities against moths and ants. Dried leaves were hung in closets to protect clothing from insects.

Southernwood has long been considered an herb of constancy that possesses aphrodesiac qualities. It was put into posies and love potions and used as a strewing herb in bedrooms. An ointment made from the leaves was rubbed by young men on their faces, hoping that this would promote the growth of a beard. This herb was given the name 'old man' because of its characteristic gray foliage, signifying age.

STAR ANISE

Classification: Perennial (tree)
Height: 8 feet or more
Conditions preferred: Tropics
Part of plant used and storage: Fruit, dried
Illicium verum Hook f.
Illiciaceae
Common names: Chinese anise, Aniseed star, Badiane

Star anise and anise seed both contain essential oils that are similar in chemical composition and therefore they have a very similar flavor. Interestingly enough, however, they differ from each other botanically with anise being a member of the carrot or parsley family and star anise related to the magnolia family.

Star anise grows on a small evergreen tree that bears tiny yellow flowers along with large magnolia-like leaves. When ripe, the fruit of the tree opens out to form a star. Collected while still green, the star shaped fruit is dried and turns reddish-brown in color.

SOUTHERNWOOD

TANSY

FRENCH TARRAGON

The tree begins to produce fruit by its sixth year and will continue for one hundred years or more. A mature tree is capable of producing fifty to sixty pounds of dried fruit every year. Star anise is one spice that will retain its flavor for many years. The taste is quite strong, so be careful when using it, as just a little bit of star anise will go a long way.

The Latin name for star anise is 'illicium' and means allurement or that which entices. It was so named because of the pleasant aroma of both the tree and its fruit. The trees are native to Southwest China and North Vietnam and have grown there since earliest times. Star anise was not used in the Western world until the sixteenth century. It is presently used in the manufacturing of many commercial preparations to give them an anise flavor.

SWEET CECILY

Classification: Perennial
Height: 3 feet
Conditions preferred: Shade
Parts of plant used and storage: Seeds, leaves and roots, fresh and dried
Myrrhis odorata
Umbelliferae

Sweet cecily is a very large and hardy perennial native to Europe. Its Latin name comes from the Greek word 'myrrh' meaning perfume, because of the pleasant anise-like smell of the plant. We do not know if this is the same myrrh referred to in the Bible or if the original was a different plant.

This herb has a long history of use as a medicinal and as a flavoring agent for liqueurs (Chartreuse). Sweet cecily leaves can be used in salads and desserts. When cooked with fruits, it will reduce their acidity, because the plant is considered to be a natural sugar saver.

The seeds can be eaten raw like a candy or dried to make tea. In medieval times the dried seeds were ground and used as a furniture polish. The large tap root of this plant is also edible, either raw or cooked. Sweet cecily is sometimes referred to as giant chervil.

SWEET FLAG

Classification: Perennial
Height: up to 6 feet
Conditions preferred: Sun or partial shade
Parts of plant used and storage: Leaves and roots, fresh and dried
Acorus calamus
Araceae
Common names: Calamus root, Flagroot, Myrtle

Sweet flag is native to India. It was used there as well as in China, Greece and Rome as a medicinal and for flavoring food. The plant has huge leaves, extremely small flowers and no fruit. The leaves were used as a moth and insect repellent and to flavor custards and creams.

The Latin name of this plant comes from the Greek 'kalamos' meaning reed or cane, because the reed-like foliage was used as thatching for roofs. Sweet flag is valued mainly for its root, which is a thickened rhizome with many attached fleshy rootlets. When the root is cut it has a pleasant lemon smell and is used in the manufacturing of beverages and for making cosmetics.

TANSY

Classification: Perennial
Height: 3 feet
Conditions preferred: Sun
Part of plant used and storage: Leaves, fresh and dried
Tanacetum vulgare
Compositae
Common names: Buttons, Common tansy, Golden buttons.

Tansy is no longer used today as a culinary herb. It can be poisonous if taken internally in large doses, acting as a strong irritant. 'Tansies' were the names given to cakes or puddings prepared and eaten after Lent at Easter time. They were thought to purify the digestive system and probably did somewhat because they act as a purgative.

Tansy is a perennial plant that has a camphor-like smell and a very bitter taste. The Latin name of this plant comes from the Greek 'anthansia' meaning immortality because of its everlasting qualities. Tansy will retain its bright green color even when dried. This herb also has a long history of use as an embalming agent. The leaves were also used as a preservative and rubbed on the flesh of fish or meat to prevent decay.

TARRAGON

Classification: Perennial (tender)
Height: 2 to 5 feet
Conditions preferred: Sun
Part of plant used and storage: Leaves, fresh, frozen and dried
Compositae
Artemesia dracunculus
Common names: French tarragon, Little dragon, Estragon
Artemesia dracunculoides
Common names: Russian tarragon, False tarragon

French and Russian tarragon are both shrub-like perennial plants of the sunflower family. Historically, tarragon was not used for medicinal purposes, therefore there is little in the way of legend or folklore handed down to us about this herb. Most tales about herbs are based on their healing or curative properties. Both varieties are native to Southern Russia and Western Asia.

The derivation of the name tarragon is a puzzle. The Latin name 'drancuculus' means little dragon. No one knows for sure why it was called this. Some references say it is because the roots of the plant coil in a serpentine fashion.

Of the two varieties, only French tarragon is good for cooking purposes. French tarragon cannot be started from seed, as the plant does not produce any (cuttings or root division are used for propagation). This is certainly one case where the easiest way to start tarragon is to buy a plant or two.

French tarragon is very aromatic and will grow to two or three feet in height. It spreads slowly by creeping underground rhizomes. The quality of the leaves will decline in time, so the plant should be dug up every four or five years, divided and replanted. It is advisable to move the plant or plants to a new location. Tarragon will need some protection during the winter in the North.

Tarragon leaves can be harvested two or three times during the summer and can be preserved by freezing or drying. I do dry some tarragon, but I prefer to freeze most of the leaves because I find that they retain much more of their original flavor and bouquet even though they will lose their color. Tarragon has always been one of my favorite herbs.

Russian tarragon can be grown from seed. The plant will reach up to five feet in height and looks similar to the French variety. The leaves have practically no flavor at all and should really not be used as a culinary herb. Beware of the seed packets of tarragon, as they are most certainly the Russian variety. This is one case where you should never start with seeds. Check the label carefully to make sure the plant you buy is French tarragon.

THYME

Classification: Perennial
Height: 8 to 18 inches
Conditions preferred: Sun
Part of plant used and storage: Leaves, fresh, frozen and dried
Thymus vulgaris
Labiatae
Common names: Garden thyme, Common thyme

There are well over one hundred species of thyme and even more counting hybrids, for this plant tends to hybridize quite easily. A member of the mint family, thyme is native to the Mediterranean area. This herb has been used as a fumigant and a medicinal for well over two thousand years. The Egyptians valued it as one of the ingredients necessary for their embalming processes, and other civilizations have burned the sweet smelling leaves during their sacrificial rites and as incense to appease their gods.

Thyme does not have much of a culinary history. There does exist, however, a description for a tea, dating from the Middle Ages, that was made with thyme and other herbs. The author claimed that this tea had the power to enable those who drank it to see nymphs and fairies. He could probably make a fortune with that recipe today.

Thyme flowers have always had a large attraction for bees. Some of the most famous honey in the world comes from Mount Hymettus in Greece, whose slopes are covered with wild thyme.

Of the several varieties of thyme grown, just three are used for cooking purposes. They are common thyme, lemon thyme and caraway thyme. Sprigs of caraway thyme (Thymus herba-barona) were used in medieval England to flavor the great barons of beef as they were roasted on spits over open fires.

Thyme should be replaced every three to four years as the plant does tend to get woody. Propagate new cuttings in the spring or fall. The leaves can be harvested twice during the summer. Cut just when the flowers begin to open, as they can be used right along with the leaves and then again in late summer.

For preservation, thyme can be dried or frozen. I like to dry the majority of thyme from my garden, but I do freeze a small container of sprigs each year. Whole sprigs can be used as part of a bouquet garni for making stocks and soups (they are removed once cooked). I do find a world of difference between home dried thyme and the kind bought commercially.

TURMURIC

Classification: Perennial (rhizome)
Height: to 20 inches
Conditions preferred: Tropics
Part of plant used and storage: Rhizome, dried
Curcuma domestica
Zingiberaceae

Turmuric is a member of the ginger family. This perennial plant grows from a thick round stem or rhizome with short branching finger-like appendages attached. It grows in the tropics, the same as ginger root.

To make turmuric powder, the rhizome is dug out of the ground, cleaned and boiled. It is then dried, either in the sun or by artificial heat and ground. The color of dried turmuric can vary from yellow to orange, depending on where it is grown and how it is dried.

Although long used as a condiment and a medicinal, this spice is known mainly for the exceptional quality of the dye it produces. Turmuric has the ability to color cloth as well as food and has been used throughout history for both purposes. The volatile oil found in the rootstalks has a sharp odor and contains a bright yellow pigment called 'circumin'. This circumin is the coloring agent.

As early as 600 B.C. we have mention of

CARAWAY THYME

COMMON THYME

FRENCH THYME

LEMON THYME

turmuric in an Assyrian herbal, listed because of its use as a dyeing agent. Turmuric was brought to Europe by Arab merchants. Often called 'Indian saffron', it was used a great deal during the Middle ages.

Turmuric will have a raw and musty flavor if it is not cooked properly. It needs to be simmered slowly in oil or butter for at least five to ten minutes (usually with other spices) in order to get rid of its initial raw taste. Use sparingly.

Powdered turmuric is light-sensitive and will lose its potency easily, so store it in a dark place or use a light-proof container. It is widely used as one of the ingredients in commercially produced curry powders. Turmuric also lends its bright yellow color to many prepared mustard products.

VANILLA

Classification: Perennial (climbing vine)
Height: to 80 feet
Conditions preferred: Tropics, rain, shade
Part of plant used and storage: Pod, dried
Vanilla planifolia var. fragrans
Orchidaceae

Vanilla beans are the dried fruit of a climbing perennial vine that belongs to the orchid family. It has long aerial roots which must fasten onto trees or posts for support. Each beautiful white orchid-like flower, once fertilized, develops into a long thin pod or bean. These beans are picked while they are still green in color. They have no taste or smell at this stage, but must undergo a long and slow fermenting and curing process for the characteristic vanilla flavor and odor to develop. It takes several months for the natural vanillin to be formed in the pods before the beans can be dried.

Early Aztec Indians used vanilla beans both as a medicine and to flavor their 'xoco-latl', a popular drink made from both vanilla and cocoa beans. Vanilla was taken to Spain by Cortez in the sixteenth century and its popularity soon spread to the rest of Europe. The name vanilla comes from the Spanish 'vainilla', meaning little scabbard, so called because of the shape of the pods.

Vanilla is native to Mexico. It is the only country in the world where the flowers of this vine are pollinated naturally (by the local Melipona bees). Although now grown in the Bourbon Islands, Indonesia and Tahiti, the flowers must be individually hand pollinated in these places in order for the vanilla bean to develop. Since the flowers are open only once and just for a few hours, this is a costly and laborious process.

To make vanilla extract, the beans are chopped and percolated in an alcohol and water solution. Pure vanilla extract is infinitely superior in flavor and aroma to imitation vanilla extracts. Check labels to be sure which you are buying. According to manufacturers, the best quality bean is now produced in the Bourbon Islands.

Dried vanilla beans will retain their flavor and aroma for a long period of time. Store them in a jar of sugar to make your own vanilla-flavored sugar for cooking or baking. The beans can also be stored in Cognac and will impart their flavor and aroma to the liqueur to create a home-made vanilla extract of sorts. Vanilla beans can be cooked in sauces and custards, then removed, dried and re-used a few times.

VANILLA

VIOLET

Classification: Perennial
Height: 6 to 12 inches
Conditions preferred: Sun or partial shade
Part of plant used and storage: Flowers, fresh or candied
Viola odorata
Violaceae
Common names: English violet, Sweet violet, Wood violet

VIOLETS

Violets were used a great deal by the Greeks and Romans who made them into wine, conserves, perfumes and cosmetics. They even ate fresh violet leaves in salads. Both the leaves and the flowers were candied and used as decorations. We still use candied violets to decorate confectionary.

The Greeks called this plant Ione. There is a legend that says that the God, Jupiter, fearing the jealousy of his wife, changed his beloved Ione into a white heifer. He then created violets for her to eat.

WOODRUFF

Classification: Perennial
Height: 1 foot
Conditions preferred: Sun or shade
Part of plant used and storage: Leaves, fresh, frozen or dried
Asperula odorata
Rubiaceae
Common name: Sweet woodruff

WOODRUFF

Records show that woodruff was used by the Benedictine monks during the ninth century as a seasoning and a medicament. This plant was mentioned in the Saxon leechbooks as well. Woodruff was popular during the Middle Ages because of its pleasant aroma, for woodruff, when cut, smells like new-mown hay. It was a very popular strewing herb, used for its insect repellent properties as well as its pleasant aroma. Branches were often cut and hung inside the dank smelling halls and castles as an air freshener.

Fresh woodruff leaves are used to flavor May wine bowls. Sometimes we see them frozen into an ice ring which is placed in the wine bowl as a decoration. During the middle ages the young shoots of this plant were used as a seasoning for food. Use woodruff cautiously because it contains coumarin, which is a blood thinner.

WORMWOOD

The 'ruff' part of the name of this herb comes from the French 'rovelle' meaning wheel. This name was given to the plant because of the whorl or wheel-like arrangement of its leaves. It is a very beautiful perennial and can be grown in either sun or shade.

WORMWOOD

Classification: Perennial
Height: to 4 feet
Conditions preferred: Sun or partial shade
Part of plant used and storage: Leaves, fresh
Artemisa absinthium
Compositae
Common names: Absinthe, Common wormwood

This shrub-like perennial is considered to be the second bitterest of all the herbs, rue being the first to have this honor. The name 'absinthium' is Greek and means destitute of delight, most probably given to the plant because of its flavor.

Wormwood was used by the Egyptians, Greeks and Romans as a medicament and for culinary purposes. It is a natural insect and animal repellent for moths, mice, etc.

We know wormwood mainly because it was once used in the making of absinthe. This is now illegal and today, absinthe is made with an extract of aniseed. Wormwood is still used to flavor many bitter liqueurs, including Vermouth. It is no longer used for cooking, as large doses of this herb can be harmful when taken internally.

COOKING

Preferred Ingredients
General Uses

RECIPES

Great Beginnings

Salads
Appetizers and Hors d'Oeuvres
Soups

Entrees

Fish
Poultry
Meats

Accompaniments

Butters, Sauces and Relishes
Vegetables
Starches

Desserts

Cakes
Pies and Tarts
Cookies
Creams, Mousses and Fruit Desserts

PREFERRED INGREDIENTS

We all have definite likes and dislikes when it comes to food. Many times these preferences are reflected in the products we select for use in cooking. Certain specific ingredients were used to develop the recipes in this book and since they can affect the quality of the finished product, I am listing some of my own personal preferences.

Butter used in all recipes is always unsalted or sweet butter. Salt is a preservative used by manufacturers in the making of butter to extend its shelf life and can often mask a bad or rancid flavor. Besides, salted butter often contains too much salt to be used for baked goods and pastries. It is better to use unsalted butter and then add only as much salt as is needed.

Flour used in all recipes is unbleached all purpose flour unless stated otherwise. My own preference is Heckers or Cerasota (the name depends on the part of the country).

Eggs are extra large farm fresh eggs, if possible. Please take this into account is substituting a different size.

Salt used for cooking purposes is a coarse grained kosher salt. I like the 'saltier' taste it gives to food. For baking, I do use regular table salt, as the smaller grains dissolve more evenly. How much salt and pepper to use in a recipe is a matter of personal taste. Specific amounts are usually not given in the recipes—add as little or as much as you like.

Pepper is always freshly ground as needed. I like to use Richard Olney's combination of three parts black peppercorns to two parts white peppercorns one part allspice berries (see page 50).

Oil used for cooking is always a bland salad-type oil. Peanut, corn or safflower oils could be substituted in most recipes. Be careful about substituting the stronger flavored oils such as olive, sesame, or those made from nuts.

I have a habit of pouring out and discarding most or all of the oil used to brown foods before continuing with the recipe. The reason is simple, we don't need to include the extra fat that would then be part of the finished dish. Both the calories and the oily flavor they would add are not necessary.

Herbs can be fresh, frozen or dried. Fresh is preferable, but not always available. It takes three times the amount of a fresh or frozen herb to equal the potency of a dried herb. When substitutions can be made in a recipe from fresh to dried, it is so listed. See page 22 for the shelf life of dried herbs.

A frozen herb can always be substituted in equal amounts for a fresh herb. Take into account the color of the finished dish and always try to add a complimentary fresh herb along with one that is frozen (see page 19). It is easier to chop frozen herbs while they are still firm rather than wait until they have defrosted and become limp and soggy.

Spices for the most part have a longer shelf life than herbs. See page 22 about storing and grinding spices. Seeds are usually toasted before they are ground to bring out their flavor and aroma.

Rice is always a long grain 'Carolina' type rice unless the recipe specifically states otherwise. I prefer to use a converted rice (Uncle Ben's). I never use precooked or instant rice. Rather than eat these poor excuses for what rice should be, have a fresh potato.

Stock can be canned or homemade. It is preferable to use homemade stocks for cooking, but canned may be substituted without any dire results, for the most part. The recipes in this book were written using single strength stocks. If the one you intend to use is concentrated, then dilute it first. Just be cautious when adding salt to your dishes, as most canned stocks tend to be very salty.

Wine used for cooking should be equally good enough for drinking. Use an inexpensive but decent white chablis or a red burgundy. Never use the so-called 'cooking wines' sold in many supermarkets—they will give a terrible flavor to your food.

Raisins should be plumped before cooking unless they are very soft. Soak them in a little warm water for about ten minutes, then squeeze dry and use. They will taste better if they are first softened.

Buttering and flouring pans. The amounts of butter and flour needed for this purpose are never included in the ingredient list of the recipes—just use whatever is necessary to coat the pans properly. **Oil** for oiling pans is also not included with the ingredient list, for the amount needed will depend on the size of the pan.

GENERAL USES

HERB AND SPICE BLENDS

For centuries, herbs and spices have been used in combination with one another. Each major cuisine has its own classic and unique way of blending and utilizing these mixtures.

American cuisine is considered to be a 'melting-pot' of the many styles of cooking brought here by people from all over the world. In our everyday cooking, we have adapted and used herb and spice combinations that can be traced to France, China, India, Spain, Mexico, Hungary and so on. The list is endless.

Many of these mixtures, such as chili or curry powder, can be bought ready-made. We have such a wealth of herbs and spices available to us here, that it is relatively easy to make many of our own blends when needed. This is purely a personal choice—I do both.

CHILI POWDER

Commercial chili powder is a blend of many spices and herbs and not just one single spice, as is often thought. Most mixes contain cumin, garlic, coriander and oregano along with several varieties of ground chili peppers (usually ancho from Mexico and hontake from Japan).

Although associated with Mexican cooking, this chili blend is not used in Mexico, just as curry powder is not used in India. The chili powder we know and use in the United States is a typical American invention and a Texan has been credited with first putting this mixture together early in the nineteenth century.

While Texas might claim full credit, the idea for chili powder did not originate there, for the Aztecs used a combination of oregano, cumin and hot peppers in their cooking several centuries earlier. The Aztec Indians may have originated chili powder, but Texas, as always, did it bigger and better.

CURRY POWDER

Commercial curry powder is a mixture of several spices, with both the ingredients and their proportions varying according to the manufacturer. They can range from a mild blend to one that is exceedingly hot. Curry powder is presumed to be an authentic Indian combination, although no self-respecting Indian cook would use a commercial pre-mixed blend of spices.

During the last century, many English families returned to England after a tour of duty in India. When they got home, they missed the spicy dishes to which they had grown accustomed and had learned to love while living there. Manufacturers, sensing this vacuum, began to produce a ready made spice blend named 'curry powder' (curry means sauce in the Indian language) that met with instant commercial success.

The list of ingredients found in curry powder is quite long. It can contain several or all of the following; cardamom, coriander, cumin, cloves, cassia or cinnamon, anise seed, fenugreek, turmeric, mustard, ginger, pepper, garlic, salt, fennel seeds, mace, nutmeg and ground chili seeds and powder.

For everyday cooking, commercially produced curry powder can be a very handy ingredient to have in the kitchen. Many of these blends are now made in India. I find Madras brand curry powder to be quite good if used properly. Curry powder must be stored in a light-proof and airtight container so that it will not deteriorate.

You have to be careful when cooking with curry powder not to allow the mixture to burn, or else the flavor of your finished dish will be ruined. Any blend of dried spices needs heat to bring out its true flavor and curry powder is no exception to this. The mixture should be added to a hot pan (along with onions, etc., according to the recipe) for just a minute. Then add some liquid and stir. The addition of a liquid at this point will keep the mixture from burning and developing an unpleasant bitter taste.

MASALA

A masala is a blend of spices which can be unique to a region or created to flavor a particular dish. Many cooks in India have their own (well guarded) recipes for these blends, often passed from one generation to the next. If you are trying to duplicate authentic Indian dishes, it is best to grind your own mixture or 'masala'. Both wet and dry masalas are used for cooking. A wet masala is

INGREDIENTS USED IN CURRY POWDER AND GARUM MASALA

a blend of spices ground to a paste with the addition of a liquid such as water and is usually used soon after blending.

A dry masala is in powder form and although often blended as it is needed, it can be made in large batches and stored for several weeks or even months. In the northern state of Kashmir, which borders on the Himalayas, dry spice blends are made during the summer months, when the ingredients are available. They are pressed and formed into round doughnut-like cakes that are stored for use in winter.

BOUQUET GARNI

Considered a staple in French cuisine, a bouquet garni is a small bunch of aromatic herbs used for cooking which is removed before the dish is served. The classic combination for a bouquet garni consists of a few sprigs of parsley, a bay leaf and some thyme tied together to form a small packet. It can be held together with just a piece of string or wrapped in cheesecloth and then tied. I usually forego the cheesecloth and just use string. This string allows for easy removal of the herbs once the dish has been cooked, because a bouquet garni is always discarded from the dish before serving.

Little bags of bouquet garni are available commercially, but you can easily make your own at home when needed. Occasionally other herbs, such as chervil, rosemary or a piece of celery stalk are added to a bouquet garni, depending on the dish to be cooked. Classically, however, the combination remains parsley, bay leaf and thyme.

FINES HERBES

Fines herbes is a mixture of finely chopped herbs, usually fresh, used to garnish a dish or added just near the end of its cooking time. The classic French combination of fines herbes consists of equal parts of parsley, chervil and tarragon, with the addition of chives sometimes.

Fines herbes are a part of a finished dish, as opposed to a bouquet garni which is always removed before serving. The purpose of a fines herbes combination is to impart a lovely fresh herbal flavor to the dish and therefore it is never cooked for very long. Both bouquet garni and fines herbes can be added to the same dish, although usually they are used separately.

FIVE SPICE POWDER

Five spice powder is a mixture of ground star anise, cinnamon, cloves, fennel seeds and peppercorns. Used mainly in Chinese cooking, it has a very pungent flavor with faintly sweet overtones. Prepared five spice powder blends can be found in many Chinese grocery stores. This mixture has a very long shelf life. Use with caution, it can overpower a dish quite easily.

HERB AND SPICE BUTTERS

An herb or spice butter is nothing more than a combination of butter with one or more herbs and/or spices. These seasoned butters can be stored in the refrigerator for several days or they can be frozen for a few months. Although they can be used for cooking, their purpose is rather to flavor foods at serving time.

A typical recipe for an herb butter would call for a quarter pound of softened butter to be mixed with a tablespoon or more of a chopped fresh herb or a teaspoon if the herb is dried. For a spice butter, use about a half-teaspoon of crushed seed to a quarter pound of butter.

Combinations of herbs and spices can be used in the same butter, along with the addition of garlic or shallots and even liqueurs. In any event, a few drops of lemon juice (or a lemony flavored herb) can be added to bring out the flavor of the herbs, along with salt and pepper to taste. Mix well to blend and store the butter in the refrigerator for at least three to four hours to allow the flavors time to mellow before using.

Place a dab on top of cooked vegetables right before serving or use them instead of a sauce with plain broiled fish or meats.

HERB SALTS

An herb salt is just what its name implies; a mixture of salt (usually sea salt) and an herb. To make your own blend, use one cup of non-iodized salt and mix it well with one cup of finely chopped fresh herbs or about one-third cup or more of a dried herb. You would always use less of a dried herb than one that is fresh in making these mixtures. The easiest way to do this is to chop the herb in a blender or food processor, then add the salt and combine right in the machine.

If you have used a fresh herb, spread this salt mixture out on a baking sheet and place it in a low oven for about one hour. Stir often, breaking apart any lumps that form with a spoon or your hand. Be careful not to let the mixture stick to the pan or burn. Cool, then store the herb salt in an air-tight glass container.

If you begin with a dried herb as opposed to one that is fresh, it is not absolutely necessary to oven-dry the mixture. Oven drying does tend, however, to bring out and enhance the flavor of the herb salt.

HERB VINEGARS

Home made herb (or spice) vinegar can add a very special and unique touch to salads and even cooked foods. Just one herb or a blend of herbs can be used to flavor the vinegar. I like to add a few cloves of garlic or some shallots to my vinegar as well.

There are two ways to make a flavored vinegar. For the first method, you start with a good quality wine vinegar and add fresh herbs directly into the bottle. Let it sit for a few weeks, shaking often, then strain and use. If the herb taste is not strong enough, the process can be repeated. This is the easy way, but I much prefer the next method.

This second method will take a little more work, but I find it produces a much stronger and more flavorful vinegar. You again begin with a good quality of wine vinegar (Desaux-fils is one of my favorites for this). Pour about one quart into a non-aluminum pot. You can also pour in any leftover dregs of wine which you happen to have around. Use dry, not sweet wine. Add a few cloves of slightly crushed garlic, or some shallots and a few handfuls of fresh herbs. Use just one or try a combination of those you like. Plain fresh tarragon, or tarragon and chervil, or thyme and chervil plus lemon balm or lemon verbena all work well for flavoring vinegar.

Bring the mixture to a boil, then simmer until it is reduced by at least one-third its volume. I reduce the liquid to one-half, as I like my vinegar very strong. Allow this mixture to cool and macerate at room temperature overnight, or even for a few days. Then strain and pour into airtight bottles and cork.

No matter which method you use, a few sprigs of fresh herbs in the bottles are always a nice touch for appearance sake. It will also serve to remind you exactly which herb or herbs you used to flavor the vinegar. Add the fresh sprigs to the bottles before sealing. At this point, label and date all of your bottles.

Although the vinegar can be used immediately, it will improve with age. Store for a few months, or even up to a year or two in a cool dark place, as you would fine wine.

INGREDIENTS USED IN FIVE-SPICE POWDER

Great Beginnings

SALADS

AVOCADO SALAD

1 tomato
1 ripe avocado
1 small onion, minced fine (1/4 cup)
1 small clove garlic, minced
salt, pepper
2 tablespoons wine vinegar
1/4 cup salad oil
1/2 teaspoon chopped fresh cilitrano

Cut the tomato in half and squeeze to remove as many seeds as possible.
Leaving the skin on, dice the tomato into small pieces.
Peel the avocado and cut it into the same size dice as the tomato.
Place the tomato and the avocado into a bowl along with the onion and the garlic.
Sprinkle with salt and pepper and pour in the vinegar and the oil.
Add the cilitrano and mix well to coat all the vegetables—I find this easiest to do with my hand.
Taste to correct the seasonings.
To serve, spoon the salad onto lettuce leaves or into hollowed tomato halves.
Serve chilled, or at room temperature.
The salad can be prepared an hour or two ahead of time and stored in the refrigerator. Any longer than this and the avocado will discolor.
Serves four as an appetizer or as a salad course.

CELERAIC SALAD

1 large knob celery root or celeraic
juice of 1/2 lemon
1 tablespoon mayonnaise
1 heaping tablespoon sour cream
1 heaping teaspoon Dijon mustard
salt, pepper
2 tablespoons chopped fresh parsley

Peel the celery root and cut it into fine julienne. A food processor fitted with a julienne or large grating disc is the easiest way to do this job.
Have the lemon juice ready in a bowl and mix the celery root with it immediately, or it will discolor.
Mix in the mayonnaise, sour cream and the mustard.
Season to taste with salt and pepper and stir in the chopped parsley.
Cover and place the salad into the refrigerator for a few hours to allow the flavors to blend and tenderize the celery root.
Spoon onto lettuce leaves and serve as an appetizer or as a salad course.
Serves four.

AVOCADO SALAD

MINTED CUCUMBER SALAD

2 large cucumbers
1/2 cup yogurt
1 tablespoon lemon juice
1 tablespoon chopped fresh mint
1 tablespoon chopped fresh parsley
salt, pepper

Peel the cucumbers and cut them in half, lengthwise. Using a spoon, remove all the seeds, then cut into thin slices.
Cover and refrigerate until ready to complete and serve.
Mix the yogurt with the lemon juice, mint and parsley. Add salt and pepper to taste.
Cover and refrigerate separately.
When ready to serve, mix the cucumbers and the dressing together. Taste to correct the seasonings. The reason you do not mix the cucumbers with the dressing ahead of time is that the dressing will become watery. If it must be mixed ahead, do not add salt until the last minute, this will help some.
The salad can be garnished with tomato wedges, if you like.
Serves four as an appetizer or salad course.

ENDIVE AND APPLE SALAD

3 or 4 Belgian endive
2 tablespoons white wine
2 tablespoons white wine vinegar
salt, pepper
2 tablespoons walnut oil
2 tablespoons salad oil
2 tablespoons heavy cream
1 apple
1 teaspoon lemon juice
2 tablespoons chopped walnuts
1 tablespoon raisins
2 tablespoons chopped fresh parsley

Slice the endive in half lengthwise and cut out the center core. Cut into thin julienne slices, lengthwise.
Soak the endive in cool water for thirty minutes. Drain well.
Pour the wine and the vinegar into a small bowl. Add some salt and pepper.
Whisk in the two oils and the heavy cream, beating until slightly thickened.
Peel, core and shred the apple. The julienne blade of a food processor is excellent for this. Or use a very coarse grater.
Mix immediately with the lemon juice.
Combine the drained endive, apple, nuts, raisins and the parsley with the salad dressing. Taste to correct the seasonings and mix well.
The salad can be refrigerated for up to one hour before serving.
Serve on lettuce leaves.
Serves four to six.

MINTED CUCUMBER SALAD

ENDIVE AND APPLE SALAD

ENDIVE AND BROCCOLI SALAD

ENDIVE AND BROCCOLI SALAD

2 large Belgian endive
1/4 cup white wine vinegar
1 tablespoon Dijon mustard
salt, pepper
1/2 cup salad oil
3 tablespoons heavy cream
1 cup cooked broccoli florets
4 mushrooms, sliced
1 tablespoon chopped shallots
3 tablespoons chopped fresh parsley

Slice the Belgian endive in half, lengthwise.
Cut out the center core, as it is very bitter. Then slice the endive into half inch rounds.
Soak the endive in a bowl of cool water for thirty minutes, then drain well.
Prepare the dressing by mixing together the vinegar, mustard, salt and pepper in a small bowl.
Slowly whisk in the oil. The dressing should thicken.
Then whisk in the cream. Taste to correct the seasonings.
Place the drained endive into a bowl along with the broccoli, mushrooms and shallots.
Add the parsley and the dressing and mix well.
The salad can be served immediately, or it can be refrigerated for an hour or two once tossed with the dressing.
Serve on lettuce leaves.
Serves four.

FENNEL AND PINEAPPLE SALAD

4 stalks fennel, bottom white part, only
1/2 of a fresh ripe pineapple
1/4 cup white wine vinegar
1 teaspoon sugar†
salt, pepper
1/4 cup salad oil
1/4 cup heavy cream
1 to 2 teaspoons Pernod
1/4 cup raisins
4 to 6 lettuce leaves
2 tablespoons toasted almond slices

Slice the fennel, crosswise, into very thin strips. A food processor fitted with a thin slicing disc is perfect for this.
Remove and place into a bowl.
Cut the half pineapple into thirds, lengthwise.
Remove the skin and the hard core.
Cut into very thin slices and add to the fennel.
This is best done by hand, as a processor tends to shred rather than slice the pineapple.
In a separate bowl, mix the vinegar, sugar, salt and pepper with the oil.
Beat until thick, then whisk in the heavy cream and the Pernod.
Pour this dressing over the fennel and the pineapple.
Add the raisins and mix well. Taste to correct the seasonings.
Spoon the salad onto the lettuce leaves, garnish

FENNEL AND PINEAPPLE SALAD

with the toasted almonds and serve.
The salad can be stored for an hour or two in the refrigerator.
This salad is especially good alone as an appetizer course. It also goes very well with fish or chicken.
Serves four as an appetizer course or six as a salad.

†You may need up to two teaspoons of sugar, this will depend on the sweetness of the pineapple. This should be a tart salad, so start with one teaspoon and add more to taste once assembled.

SPANISH FRUIT SALAD

1/4 cup currents
2 apples (tart)
1 cup seedless grapes
1/2 cup walnut halves
1 peach or nectarine, peeled and diced
1/4 cup sour cream
1 tablespoon mayonnaise
1 tablespoon lemon juice
1/8 teaspoon cinnamon

If the currents are hard, soak them in warm water for about fifteen minutes to soften. Drain and squeeze dry.
Do not peel the apples. Core and cut them into large dice.
Place the apples in a bowl with the currents, grapes, walnuts and diced peach.
In a small bowl, mix the sour cream with the mayonnaise, lemon juice and cinnamon.
Pour over the fruit and mix well.
Serve cold on lettuce leaves.
This salad can be refrigerated for a few hours, if necessary.
Serves four.

ROASTED PEPPER SALAD

10 or 12 banana or sweet peppers
3 tablespoons wine vinegar
2 tablespoons olive oil
1 tablespoon red wine
1 tablespoon chopped fresh parsley
1 tablespoon chopped fresh basil, or 1 teaspoon dried
1 tablespoon chopped fresh oregano, or 1 teaspoon dried
1 tablespoon minced garlic
salt, pepper
sliced tomatoes
sliced mozarella cheese

Arrange the peppers in a single layer in a flat pan. Place under a hot broiler and roast, turning, until the skins char and turn black. This should take about fifteen minutes.
The peppers can also be roasted on a barbeque.
Remove the pan from the heat, cover with a piece of aluminum foil and allow the peppers to rest for about twenty minutes.
Peel off the charred skins. Slit each pepper and

SPANISH FRUIT SALAD

remove the seeds and the core.
Save any juices that have accumulated in the roasting pan or from cutting the peppers to add to the marinade.
Place the vinegar, oil, wine, herbs, garlic and some salt and pepper into a glass or metal container. Mix and add the liquid from the peppers.
Add the peppers to the marinade and turn to coat them evenly.
Cover tightly and refrigerate for several hours before using.
The peppers can be stored for up to five days in the refrigerator.
A wonderful summer salad can be made by cutting fresh beefsteak tomatoes into thin slices and layering them alternately onto a plate with slices of mozarella cheese.
Place two or three roasted peppers alongside and a few spoons of the marinade on top and serve.
Best at room temperature.
Enough peppers for six salads.

WALNUT AND BIBB LETTUCE SALAD

2 heads Bibb lettuce†
1 ounce white wine vinegar
1 tablespoon Dijon mustard
salt, pepper
1 ounce walnut oil
1 ounce salad oil
1 hard boiled egg, chopped (optional)
1 cup walnut pieces

Wash and dry the lettuce leaves.
You can either break the leaves into bite-sized pieces or leave them whole if they are small. Refrigerate until serving time.
Mix together the vinegar, mustard and some salt and pepper in a small bowl.
Slowly whisk in the oils. This dressing should be thick.
The dressing can be prepared a few hours ahead of time, if necessary. Whisk again and check the seasonings before using.
Sprinkle the chopped egg (if using) and the walnuts over the lettuce.
Add the dressing, toss and serve immediately.
Serves four.

†One head of Boston lettuce can be substituted for the Bibb lettuce or a combination of both used.

A LOW CALORIE WALNUT VINAGRETTE

2 tablespoons white wine vinegar
2 tablespoons white wine
1 tablespoon walnut oil
1 tablespoon salad oil
4 walnut halves
1/2 cup lightly packed parsley leaves
1 teaspoon egg white
1 teaspoon Dijon mustard
salt, pepper

Place all of the ingredients into a food processor or blender and puree until thick and smooth.
The dressing can be prepared ahead of time.

WALNUT AND BIB LETTUCE SALAD

PASTA SALADS: PESTO AND WALNUT, SNOW PEA PODS AND SHRIMP, OLIVES AND CAPERS, CHICKEN AND BROCCOLI

Whisk well and check the seasonings before using. To serve, toss with Bibb or Boston lettuce as above.
The hard boiled egg and the walnuts can be eliminated from the salad, if you are counting calories. Tomato wedges or sliced mushrooms can be added for color and taste, if desired.
Serves four.

PASTA SALAD WITH CHICKEN AND BROCCOLI

2 cups cooked chicken
2 to 3 cups cooked broccoli florets
1/4 cup heavy cream
1/4 cup mayonnaise
juice of 1/2 lemon
salt, pepper
2 teaspoons chopped fresh tarragon or
 1/2 teaspoon dried
1/2 pound fettuccine noodles
1/2 cup toasted almond slices
12 cherry tomatoes (optional)

I prefer to use just chicken breast for this salad, but some dark meat could be used as well. Cut or pull the chicken meat into large shreds.
Separate the cooked broccoli into florets.
Mix the cream, mayonnaise, lemon juice, salt, pepper and the tarragon in a small bowl and have this dressing ready.
Cook the noodles in lots of boiling salted water until barely tender.
Drain well and mix with the dressing while the noodles are still hot.
Add the chicken, broccoli, almonds and cherry tomatoes (if using) and mix well.
Serve at room temperature.
This makes an excellent luncheon salad or summer-time dinner. Or use as an appetizer.
The salad can be stored in the refrigerator for a day or two. Wait to add the almonds until ready to serve, for they will stay crisper that way.
Serves six to eight as an appetizer course and even more if served with other dishes.

PASTA SALAD WITH SNOW PEA PODS AND SHRIMP

1/4 pound snow pea pods
6 or 7 sliced water chestnuts
2 scallions, cut into 1/4" rounds
1 carrot, cut into julienne
1 cup cooked shrimp, sliced†
4 teaspoons rice wine vinegar
2 teaspoons soy sauce
2 teaspoons sesame oil
1/4 cup salad oil
pinch salt
pinch sugar
Chinese chili oil or Tabasco to taste
1/2 pound fettuccine or Chinese egg noodles

Remove the strings from the snow pea pods. Cut them in half, lengthwise, on the diagonal.
Blanch for one minute in boiling salted water.

Refresh and drain well.
Slice the rest of the vegetables and the shrimp.
In a small bowl, mix the vinegar with the soy sauce, sesame and salad oils, salt and sugar. Add the chili oil to taste. I like to add at least one-quarter teaspoon.
Cook the noodles in lots of boiling salted water until barely tender. Drain well and toss with the dressing while they are still hot.
Mix the vegetables and the shrimp with the pasta and taste to correct the seasonings.
Served at room temperature, this makes a good luncheon dish as well as an appetizer.
The salad can be refrigerated overnight.
Serves six to eight as an appetizer, or even more if served along with other dishes.

†Cooked lobster meat or even diced cooked chicken can be substituted for the shrimp.

PASTA SALAD WITH OLIVES AND CAPERS

2 tablespoons chopped onion
1 tablespoon chopped gerkins
2 tablespoons chopped black olives
3 tablespoons diced green pepper
1 tablespoon chopped capers
1 clove garlic, minced
1/4 cup white wine vinegar
2 tablespoons olive oil
2 tablespoons salad oil
salt, pepper
1 pound thin egg noodles or spaghetti

Finely dice or chop all the ingredients as directed.
Place them into a small bowl and stir in the vinegar and the oils.
Add salt and pepper to taste.
Allow this dressing to sit for an hour or two at room temperature in order for the flavor to blend and mellow.
Cook the noodles in lots of boiling salted water until barely tender.
Drain well and toss with the dressing while the noodles are still hot.
Serve at room temperature.
The salad can be refrigerated for a day or two.
Serves eight as an appetizer, or more if served with other dishes.
Alternate: This dressing can be used on a tossed green salad as well as with pasta. Especially good on a crunchy lettuce like romaine.

PASTA SALAD WITH PESTO AND WALNUTS

1 pound spinach fettuccine
1 tablespoon olive oil
4 tablespoons pesto sauce, page 143†
1/4 cup chopped walnuts
1/4 cup pimentos, cut into julienne
1/4 cup grated Parmesan cheese
salt, pepper

Cook the pasta in lots of boiling salted water until barely tender.
Drain well and toss with the olive oil.
While the noodles are still hot, add the pesto and mix well.
Stir in the walnuts, pimentos and cheese.
Season to taste with salt and pepper.
This makes a nice summer lunch salad, as well as an appetizer course.
The pasta salad can be refrigerated for a day or two.
Serve at room temperature.
Serves eight as an appetizer or more if served with other dishes.

†If frozen, thaw before using.

SESAME PEANUT NOODLES

2 large cloves garlic, sliced
4 teaspoons ginger root, sliced
4 teaspoons soy sauce
3/4 teaspoon sugar
1/2 teaspoon salt, or more to taste
3/4 cup peanut butter
1/2 cup sesame paste†
2/3 cup water
3/4 teaspoon Chinese chili oil, or more to taste
1/4 teaspoon anise seed
3/4 cup chopped toasted peanuts
1 pound Chinese egg noodles††
2 tablespoons salad oil

To make the sauce, place the first eight ingredients into a blender or food processor and blend until smooth.
Add chili oil to taste, mix, then remove the sauce from the machine and place it into a bowl.
Stir in the anise seed and one-half cup of the chopped peanuts.
The sauce can be completed to this point and refrigerated for a few days or frozen. Allow to come to room temperature before using.
If the sauce seems too thick, thin with a little water.
Cook the noodles in lots of boiling salted water until they are barely tender.
Drain well and while still hot, toss with the salad oil.
Add the prepared sauce and mix well. Spoon into a serving dish and garnish the top with the remaining peanuts.
Serve at room temperature.
The finished noodles can be refrigerated for a day or two.
Serves eight as an appetizer or more if served along with other dishes.

†If sesame paste is not available, substitute two tablespoons of sesame oil and increase the amount of peanut butter to one cup.
††Any thin noodle can be used. Linguini also works well.

HORS D'OEUVRES AND APPETIZERS

COLD

ALMOND GARLIC DIP

1 1/2 cups mayonnaise
1/2 cup ground almonds
2 tablespoons dried bread crumbs or more, if needed
2 cloves garlic, minced
1 teaspoon lemon juice
3 tablespoons chopped fresh parsley
salt, pepper

Mix the mayonnaise with the almonds, bread crumbs, garlic, lemon juice and parsley in a bowl.
Stir in more bread crumbs, if needed, to make a nice thick dip.
Add salt and pepper to taste.
Use a spoon to blend the ingredients and not a food processor or blender. It will make a difference in the consistency and the taste of the dip.
Stored, tightly covered in the refrigerator, this dip will keep well for a day or two.
This recipe makes two cups of dip. Excellent with raw vegetables.

CHEESE SPREAD WITH WALNUTS AND BLACK OLIVES

6 ounces grated cheddar cheese
6 ounces grated Swiss cheese
6 ounces cream cheese
6 ounces butter, softened
1/4 cup Port wine
1/2 cup milk, or more if needed
1/2 cup chopped walnuts
1/2 cup chopped pitted black olives
1 teaspoon caraway seeds

Grate the cheddar and Swiss cheeses.
Using a food processor fitted with a steel knife, mix the grated cheese, cream cheese, butter and wine.
Process, using short on and off bursts, until all are well mixed.
Add the half cup of milk and process until smooth. You want a mixture that will spread easily, so do not be afraid to add an extra spoon or two of milk, if needed.
If the grated cheeses are very dry, they will absorb more milk.
If you do not have a food processor, you can use a mixer to make this spread.
Beat the butter and the cream cheese together until soft, then work in the grated cheese and the liquids.
If using a processor, remove the mixture and stir in the chopped nuts, olives and caraway seeds.
If using a mixer, the nuts, olives and caraway can be added directly to the bowl and mixed in.
Pack the spread into the crock or dish from which it will be served.
Cover and refrigerate for a few days to allow time for the flavors to mellow.
Serve at room temperature with crackers or thin slices of pumpernickel or French bread.
The cheese spread will keep well for a week or so, covered and refrigerated.
This recipe makes about three cups of cheese spread.

HERB CHEESE

6 ounces cream cheese, softened
1/4 cup sour cream
2 tablespoons shallots, chopped fine
1 very small clove garlic, minced
1/4 cup chopped fresh chives
1/4 cup chopped fresh parsley
1 1/2 teaspoons chopped fresh tarragon or 1/2 teaspoon dried
1 1/2 teaspoons chopped fresh thyme or 1/2 teaspoon dried
salt, pepper

Whip the cream cheese with the sour cream until light and fluffy.
Stir in the chopped shallots, garlic and the herbs.
Add salt and pepper to taste.
Do not combine this mixture in a food processor, as the herbs will turn the cheese green in color.
However, the herbs and the shallots can be chopped in a processor and then combined by hand.
This mixture will keep well in the refrigerator for a few days. Cover tightly.
Serve with crackers, thin rounds of bread or vegetable crudites.
Makes about one and one-half cups.

HERBED PORK AND SPINACH TERRINE

1 1/2 pounds fatty pork (2/3 meat, 1/3 fat)
6 ounces veal
2 ten ounce packages frozen spinach
1 cup parsley leaves, well packed
1 tablespoon fresh thyme
1 tablespoon fresh chervil
2 tablespoons fresh sage leaves
6 ounces chicken livers, diced fine
4 ounces smoked ham, cubed
2 or 3 cloves garlic, minced
1/4 cup dried bread crumbs
2 eggs
1/4 cup brandy
1/4 cup hazelnuts, coarsely chopped
1/2 teaspoon ground allspice
1/4 teaspoon grated nutmeg
6 juniper berries, crushed
lots of salt and pepper
3/4 pound sliced bacon, for lining mold

Grind the pork and the veal together, using a meat grinder or a food processor and reserve.
Cook the spinach in a pot of boiling salted water for a few minutes, then refresh under cold water. Squeeze dry, chop finely and set aside.
Finely chop the parsley along with the rest of the fresh herbs.
Mix all of the recipe ingredients together in a large bowl, except for the bacon.
To check the seasonings, form a little of this mixture into a small patty.
Heat a little oil in a frying pan and saute the patty on both sides until cooked.
Taste to check the seasonings. Remember that a cold meat mixture will need more seasonings than one that is hot. Make whatever corrections are necessary.
Butter a six cup terrine mold. Line the mold, crosswise, with the bacon slices, overlapping them slightly.
Pack the pate mixture into the mold, banging it down to eliminate any air pockets.
Fold the bacon slices over the top.
Cover the top with a double layer of heavy duty aluminum foil, sealing the edges well and place the terrine into a water bath.
Bake in a preheated 350 degree oven for one hour and thirty minutes, or until done.
The center of the meat should be hot when tested with a skewer and the juices should run yellow, not pink.
Remove the terrine from the water bath.
Once it reaches room temperature, place a weight on the top and refrigerate overnight.
The next day, unmold the terrine and wrap it well.
Store in the refrigerator for three to five days to allow the flavors time to mellow.
The terrine will keep well for one week in the refrigerator. Do not freeze, the texture changes and the taste becomes watery.
Serve in thin slices with a grainy mustard and cornichons.
This terrine will serve sixteen or more portions.

PHEASANT PATE

1 pheasant†
5 ounces veal
13 ounces fatty pork
1 medium onion
1 large clove garlic
1/2 pound boiled or baked ham
4 ounces cooked tongue
1/4 cup shelled and skinned pistachios
1 egg
3 tablespoons Cognac or brandy
2 teaspoons salt
1/2 teaspoon pepper
1/2 teaspoon ground allspice
1/4 teaspoon grated nutmeg
1 teaspoon dried thyme
3/4 pound sliced bacon

Skin the pheasant. Remove the meat from the breast and legs. Save the bones to make a game stock.
Grind the pheasant meat along with the veal, pork, onion and garlic.
Use a meat grinder, if possible, it will give the best texture to your finished product.
Cut the ham and the tongue into small dice.
Mix all the ingredients together in a large bowl, except for the bacon.
Saute a small patty of the meat mixture in a little oil, then taste to check the seasonings. Make whatever corrections are necessary.
Butter a two quart terrine. Line the mold with slightly overlapping slices of the bacon.
Fill the mold with the meat mixture, banging down to eliminate any air pockets. Fold the bacon slices over the top.
Cover the terrine with a double layer of heavy duty aluminum foil, sealing the edges well.
Place into a water bath and bake the pate in a preheated 350 degree oven for one hour and fifteen to thirty minutes, or until done. The pate should be hot all the way through and the juices yellow, not pink.
Remove the pate from the water bath.
Once it reaches room temperature, place a weight on top and refrigerate overnight.
Turn the pate out and wrap it well.
Allow it to mellow in the refrigerator for three to five days before slicing.
Serve with a grainy mustard and cornichons.
To serve, cut into thin slices. You should be able to get between thirty and forty slices.

†Duck or even rabbit meat can be substituted for the pheasant. You will need 14 ounces or about 1 1/2 cups meat.

CARAWAY ONION TART

Crust:
1 1/4 cups flour
1/4 teaspoon salt
7 tablespoons butter
1 teaspoon caraway seeds
2 1/2 tablespoons water
Filling:
3 slices bacon, diced
1 large onion, chopped
1/4 teaspoon dried marjoram
3 eggs
1/3 cup heavy cream
1/2 cup grated Swiss cheese
salt, pepper

First make the crust. Mix the flour with the salt in a bowl or a food processor.
Work in the butter until fine crumbs are formed, then stir in the caraway seeds.
Add the water and mix to form a dough. Wrap and chill for at least thirty minutes.
Roll out the dough and line a shallow ten inch tart pan, preferably with a removable bottom. Trim off the edges.
Chill the crust for another ten minutes.
Line the crust with a piece of aluminum foil and add baking weights.
Bake in a preheated 400 degree oven for fifteen minutes.
Remove the weights and the foil and continue to bake for another ten minutes.
Check while baking and prick the crust with a fork if any air bubbles begin to form.
Remove the crust and cool for a few minutes. Turn the oven down to 375 degrees.
To make the filling, saute the bacon and the onion in a frying pan over low heat until the bacon is browned and the onion soft. This should take about fifteen minutes.
Add the dried marjoram, stir and remove from the heat. Allow this mixture to cool a little.
Beat the eggs, just to mix, with the cream. Stir in the onion and bacon mixture and the cheese.
Season to taste with salt and pepper.
Pour the filling into the crust and bake in a 375 degree oven for thirty-five minutes, or until the crust is browned and the filling puffed and firm.
Serve warm or at room temperature.
This tart can be reheated. Warm in a 400 degree oven just until hot, about ten minutes.
Serves ten as an appetizer.

CARAWAY ONION TART

CHILI CHEESE PASTRIES

CHILI CHEESE PASTRIES

2 cups shredded cheddar cheese
4 tablespoons butter, softened
2 teaspoons Dijon mustard
2 teaspoons chili powder
1/2 teaspoon salt
2 teaspoons Worchestershire sauce
1 cup flour

Preheat the oven to 375 degrees.
Place all of the ingredients except the flour into a food processor fitted with a steel blade. Process until the mixture is fairly smooth.
Add the flour and continue to process, turning the machine on and off in short bursts until the flour is completely worked in.
Remove the dough from the machine.
This mixture can be combined by hand, but it is much easier to do in a processor.
Divide and roll the dough into forty-eight small balls. Place the balls onto an ungreased cookie sheet and flatten them with the tines of a fork to between one-quarter and one-third inch in thickness.
Bake the pastries for fifteen to seventeen minutes. The undersides should be lightly browned when they are done.
Cool for a few minutes, then remove the pastries from the baking sheet.
Serve while still warm.
These pastries can be frozen or refrigerated and reheated. Do not thaw first, just heat directly in the oven.
Makes forty-eight pastries, serve as an hors d'oeuvres or with soup.

FILO SAUSAGE ROLLS

1/2 pound sausage†
1 tablespoon oil
1/4 teaspoon dried rosemary
1 tablespoon chopped parsley
1/2 pound ricotta cheese
1 egg
salt, pepper
6 sheets filo dough
1/4 cup melted butter
2 tablespoons dried bread crumbs

Remove the casing and crumble the sausage into small pieces.
Heat the oil in a frying pan and add the sausage. Cook until well browned, stirring often.
Remove the meat from the pan and place it into a bowl, using a slotted spoon.
Discard the oil.
Mix the sausage with the rosemary, parsley, cheese and egg. Add salt and pepper to taste.
Allow this mixture to cool a little.
Spread out one filo sheet, short end towards you. Keep the rest of the dough covered while you work.
Brush the dough with melted butter and sprinkle with crumbs. Fold over from top to bottom. Brush with butter and cut into quarters.
Place one tablespoon of filling on the lower middle portion of each rectangle.
Roll the bottom up over the filling, fold in the sides and roll into a small cylinder.
Place onto a buttered baking sheet and brush the tops well with melted butter.
Continue until all are filled and rolled.

The pastries can be covered and refrigerated for several hours or baked immediately.
Bake in a preheated 400 degree oven for twenty-five to thirty minutes or until nicely browned. Serve hot.
The sausage rolls can be baked ahead and frozen. Do not thaw. Place in a 400 degree oven for about twenty minutes, or until hot.
Makes twenty-four small rolls.

†Sweet or hot sausage can be used for this recipe. I prefer the sweet, but either one will work.

HERBED BREAD FINGERS

6 to 8 slices bread
2 eggs
1 tablespoon heavy cream
1/4 teaspoon ground cinnamon
1/8 teaspoon grated nutmeg or mace
1 tablespoon chopped fresh tarragon
1 tablespoon chopped fresh parsley
1 tablespoon chopped fresh chervil†
salt, pepper
3 to 4 tablespoons butter

An egg bread, such as challah or brioche, works especially well for this recipe. Trim off the crusts and cut the bread into fingers, about four or five to the slice.
Mix the eggs in a flat pan with the cream, cinnamon, nutmeg and the fresh herbs. Season to taste with salt and pepper.
Dip the bread fingers in the egg mixture, turning to coat both sides and remove.
Heat two tablespoons of the butter in a frying pan. Add as many pieces of bread as will fit in one layer.
Brown slowly over a moderate heat, turning once. The bread should take about fifteen minutes to cook. Add more butter to the pan as needed.
The finished bread fingers can be refrigerated or frozen and reheated if necessary.
To reheat, place in a 425 degree oven on a rack for about five minutes, or until hot. If frozen, do not thaw, allow a few minutes longer in the oven.
Serve hot as an hors d'oeuvres or with soup.
Makes between twenty-four and thirty fingers, depending on the size of the bread slices.

†If not available, do not use the dried herb, just omit.

MUSHROOM AND CRABMEAT TRIANGLES

2 tablespoons butter
3 tablespoons chopped shallots
1/2 pound mushrooms, chopped fine
salt, pepper
pinch dried thyme
1/2 teaspoon curry powder
2 tablespoons flour
3 tablespoons sour cream
8 ounces crabmeat†
6 sheets filo
1/2 cup melted butter
3 to 4 tablespoons dried bread crumbs

Butter two baking sheets. Preheat the oven to 400 degrees.
Heat the 2 tablespoons of butter in a frying pan. Add the shallots and saute for a minute or two.
Add the finely chopped mushrooms, sprinkle with the salt, pepper and thyme and cook, stirring often, until all the moisture is gone.
Stir in the curry powder and then the flour. Cook for a half a minute, then remove the pan from the heat.
Mix in the sour cream.
Allow the mixture to cool a little, then mix in the crabmeat. This is easiest to do with your hands.
Taste to correct the seasonings.
Divide the filling into thirty-six portions and form into small disc shapes.
Spread out a sheet of filo horizontally. Keep the rest of the dough covered while working.
Brush the dough with melted butter and sprinkle with bread crumbs. Cut the sheet into six strips, from top to bottom (about two inches in width).
Place a round of filling on the bottom left side of the strip, then fold up as you would a flag into a triangular shape.
Place the triangles onto a buttered baking sheet and brush the tops with more melted butter.
Repeat until all of the filo and the filling is used.
The triangles can be baked immediately or covered and stored in the refrigerator for several hours.
Bake for fifteen to eighteen minutes, just until they are lightly browned.
Serve while hot.
The baked triangles can be frozen. Do not defrost. Bake in a 400 degree oven until hot, about ten to fifteen minutes.
Makes thirty-six triangles.

†A seven ounce package of frozen crabmeat can be substituted.

SAVORY EGG CUPS

2 hard boiled eggs
1 tablespoon melted butter
2 teaspoons chopped fresh parsley
2 teaspoons chopped fresh basil or 1/2 teaspoon dried
1 teaspoon chopped fresh marjoram or 1/4 teaspoon dried
pinch grated nutmeg
pinch ground allspice
salt, pepper
1 raw egg
1/4 cup heavy cream
24 slices thin white bread

MUSHROOM AND CRABMEAT TRIANGLES

SAVORY EGG CUPS

Chop the hard boiled eggs and place them into a bowl.
Add the rest of the ingredients, except for the bread, and mix well.
Do not use a food processor or blender, it will puree the mixture too finely.
Taste to correct the seasonings.
Flatten each bread slice with your hand or with rolling pin.
Cut out rounds, using a two and one-half inch round cookie cutter.
Thickly butter twenty-four miniature muffin tins.
Press the bread rounds into the tins to form small cups.
Fill each cup with one-half tablespoon of the filling. This should be enough to come to the top of the bread cup.
Bake the egg cups in a preheated 375 degree oven for twenty-five minutes, or until the bread is browned and the filling is set and lightly browned.
Remove and serve as an hors d'oeuvres while hot.
The filled cups can be frozen after they are baked.
Reheat, while frozen, in a 425 degree oven for fifteen minutes, or until they are hot.
This recipe makes twenty-four hors d'oeuvres.

SPICED SHRIMP IN RAMEKINS

1/2 pound raw shrimp
2 tablespoons + 1 teaspoon butter
1 clove garlic, minced
1/2 teaspoon grated ginger root
1/4 teaspoon dried thyme
1/8 teaspoon ground allspice
1/2 tablespoon chopped fresh parsley
1 teaspoon chopped fresh chives
1/2 tablespoon lemon juice
salt, pepper

Peel the shrimp and clean, removing the veins.
Cut into large dice and reserve.
Lightly butter four small ramekins.
Heat the two tablespoons of butter in a small frying pan.
Add the garlic and the ginger root and cook for just a few minutes.
Stir in the dried thyme and the allspice. Remove the pan from the heat.
Mix in the parsley, chives, lemon juice and the raw shrimp.
Add salt and pepper to taste.
Divide the shrimp mixture evenly into the ramekins.
Dot the tops with the teaspoon of butter.
The shrimp mixture can be refrigerated at this point for a few hours or even overnight. Cover well.
When ready to cook, preheat the oven to 350 degrees.
Bake the ramekins for about twelve to fifteen minutes, or just until the shrimp have turned white in color.
Serve immediately.
Serves four.

SPICED SHRIMP IN RAMEKINS

SOUPS

COLD

CUCUMBER DILL SOUP

3 cucumbers
1/2 small clove garlic
1/2 cup yogurt (4 ounces)
1 cup sour cream
3 tablespoons chopped fresh dill
salt, pepper
1/4 cup walnut pieces
1/4 cup raisins

Peel and seed all of the cucumbers.
Place two of the cucumbers along with the garlic, yogurt and sour cream into a food processor or blender.
Puree well and season to taste with salt and pepper.
Add two tablespoons of the chopped dill and mix just to blend.
Remove the soup from the processor.
Cut the third cucumber into small dice. Add it to the soup with the walnuts and the raisins. Chill until serving time.
The soup can be covered and refrigerated for a day or two. Do not add the walnuts more than an hour or so before serving, in order to keep them crisp.
Serve this soup very cold, garnished with the remaining tablespoon of dill.
Serves four.

GREEN GASPACHO

2 cucumbers
2 stalks celery
1 green pepper
1 small onion
3 cups yogurt (24 ounces)
1 very small clove garlic, optional
salt, pepper
1/3 cup + 1 tablespoon heavy cream
Garnish:
2 tablespoons chopped fresh parsley
1 or 2 tomatoes, peeled, seeded and diced

Peel and seed the cucumbers and cut them into large dice.
String and dice the celery.
Coarsley chop the green pepper and the onion.
Place the yogurt, cucumbers, celery, onion, green pepper and garlic along with some salt and pepper into a blender or food processor fitted with a steel blade. Process until well blended.
Add the cream and continue to process for about ten seconds.
Taste and correct the seasonings. This soup needs lots of salt and pepper.
Chill until ready to serve.
The soup will keep in the refrigerator several hours or overnight. Stir well before serving and check the seasonings again.
Spoon into small soup bowls or cups and garnish each with a little chopped parsley and diced tomato.
Serves six to eight portions.

COLD SPICED TOMATO SOUP

4 large tomatoes
1 half-inch slice onion
1/3rd of a green pepper
6 ounces tomato juice
6 tablespoons yogurt
2 tablespoons heavy cream
1/2 teaspoon chili powder
salt, pepper
1 tablespoon chopped fresh parsley

Peel, seed and dice the tomatoes, saving the juice.
Place all of the ingredients (including the juice from the tomatoes), except for the parsley, into a food processor or blender. If you are using a blender, you will probably have to do this in two batches.
Blend until all is finely pureed.
Chill the soup. It will keep well in the refrigerator for a few days.
Taste to correct the seasonings before serving.
Serve cold, garnished with the chopped parsley.
Serves four.

HOT

BEAN AND CABBAGE SOUP

1/2 cup dried lima beans
1 smoked ham hock
bouquet garni
6 cups water
1 large onion, diced
1 large carrot, diced
1 large clove garlic, minced
4 cups chopped cabbage
1 large potato, peeled and diced
2 cups beef stock
salt, pepper
1 tablespoon chopped fresh parsley

Presoak the beans in water overnight. Drain.
Place them into a stockpot along with the ham hock, bouquet garni and the six cups of water.
Bring to a boil, then skim off any white scum that may rise to the surface of the liquid.
Cover and simmer for one and one-half hours.
Cut the cabbage into quarters, then into half-inch sized slices and reserve.
Once the soup has cooked for the hour and a half, remove the bouquet garni from the pot and discard.
Add the onions, carrot, garlic, cabbage and potato along with the beef stock and some ground pepper.
Do not add any salt yet, as ham hock can often be very salty. Wait to add salt at the end, if needed.
Bring the soup to a boil, cover and simmer for forty-five minutes to one hour, or until all the vegetables are tender.
Remove the ham hock and allow it to cool a little. Discard the skin, bone and any fat or gristle. Dice the meat and return to the pot.
Heat and taste to correct the seasonings.
Stir in the parsley and serve.
This soup can be refrigerated for a few days and reheated, or it can be frozen.
Serves six to eight.

CABBAGE BORSHT

1 pound beef (chuck)
salt, pepper
1 to 2 tablespoons oil
1 large onion, chopped
1 leek, chopped
1 large carrot, diced
2 small white turnips, diced
1 fresh hot pepper, diced fine
1 large clove garlic, minced
2 cups shredded cabbage
1 cup peeled, seeded and diced tomatoes
1 teaspoon tomato paste
1 medium potato, peeled and diced
1 ten ounce package frozen lima beans
2 or 3 bay leaves
1 teaspoon sugar
4 cups beef stock
4 cups water
2 tablespoon wine vinegar

Trim all visible fat from the meat and cut it into one inch dice.
Sprinkle with salt and pepper.
Heat the oil in a large saucepan or a stockpot.
Add the beef and brown well.
Add the onion, leek, carrot, turnips and hot pepper to the pot and saute for a few minutes.
Add the garlic and the cabbage and cook for another minute or two.
Stir in the tomatoes, tomato paste, potato, beans, the bay leaves and the sugar.
Add the stock, water and some salt and pepper.
Bring the soup to a boil, cover and simmer for forty-five minutes to one hour, just until the meat and vegetables are tender.
Stir in the vinegar. Taste to correct the seasonings, adding more salt and pepper if needed.
Serve with black bread and butter.
This soup both freezes and reheats well.
Serves eight.

CHESTNUT AND CARDAMOM BISQUE

1 pound fresh chestnuts
2 tablespoons butter
1 large onion, chopped
1 carrot, diced
1 stalk celery, chopped
salt, pepper
pinch ground allspice
3/4 teaspoon ground cardamom
1 small potato, peeled and diced
4 cups chicken stock
1 cup light cream
2 cups water or more if needed

Cut an X in the top of the chestnuts with a sharp paring knife.
Bake them in a 375 degree oven for about thirty minutes, or until they split open.
Or cook in a microwave oven for five to six minutes at high power.
Cool for just a few minutes, then peel. Chestnuts are easier to peel while they are still hot.
Heat the butter in a saucepan.
Add the onions, carrots and celery, sprinkle with a little salt and pepper and cook for about five minutes.
Add the allspice, cardamom, the potato and the chestnuts.
Stir in the chicken stock and bring the soup to a boil.
Cover and simmer for about an hour and thirty minutes, or until the vegetables and the chestnuts are very tender.
By this time, most of the liquid will have been absorbed by the vegetables.
Cool a little, then puree in a blender, a food mill or a food processor.
Stir in the cream, then thin with the water until the bisque is of a proper consistency.
This should be a thick soup, I find two cups of water to be about the right amount.
The soup can be refrigerated for a few days or it can be frozen. Thaw before reheating.
Heat until the soup reaches the boiling point.
Taste to correct the seasonings and serve hot.
Serves six. This is a rich soup and small portions are best.

CHESTNUT AND CARDAMOM BISQUE

GREEN GASPACHO

CHICK PEA SOUP

CHICK PEA SOUP

1 tablespoon butter
1 medium onion, chopped fine
1 clove garlic, minced
1 teaspoon dried marjoram
pepper and salt (if needed)
4 cups chicken stock
1 cup water
1 can (2 cups) chick peas, drained
2 ounces small noodles, uncooked
2 tablespoons chopped fresh parsley

Heat the butter in a saucepan.
Add the onion and saute for a few minutes.
Add the garlic, the marjoram and a little pepper (no salt).
Pour in the stock and the water and stir.
Add the chick peas and the noodles.
Bring the soup to a boil, then cover and simmer until the noodles are cooked, stirring once or twice. This should take only about ten minutes.
Taste to correct the seasonings, adding salt at this point, if needed (canned chick peas tend to be salty).
Stir in the parsley and serve hot.
Serves six to eight.
Alternates:
A diced potato can be substituted for the noodles. Increase the cooking time by about ten minutes, or until the potato is tender.

CHICKEN CORN SOUP

2 tablespoons butter
1 large onion, chopped fine
1 stalk celery, chopped fine
1 carrot, chopped fine
salt, pepper
4 slices bacon
1/2 teaspoon dried thyme
1 or 2 bay leaves
3 cups chicken stock
1 cup diced cooked chicken
1 large potato, peeled and diced fine
2 cups creamed corn (canned)
1 tablespoon chopped fresh parsley

Place the butter, onion, celery and carrot into a saucepan.
Sprinkle with some salt and pepper and saute the vegetables for about five minutes, stirring occasionally.
While the vegetables are cooking, saute the bacon in a separate pan until lightly brown. Or cook in a microwave oven.
Drain well, dice finely and reserve.
Add the thyme and the bay leaf to the vegetables.
Stir in the stock.
Add the diced chicken, potato, the creamed corn and the cooked bacon.
Mix well and bring the soup to a boil.
Cover the pan and simmer for twenty minutes, or until the vegetables are tender.
Remove the bay leaves, stir in the parsley and taste to correct the seasonings.
Serve hot.
This soup can be reheated or even frozen.
Serves six to eight.

LEEK AND SORREL SOUP

2 tablespoons butter
3 cups sliced leeks, including greens
1 1/2 cups tightly packed sorrel leaves†
2 large potatoes, peeled and diced
3 cups chicken stock
1 1/2 cups water
salt, pepper
1/2 cup sour cream
1 1/2 cups half and half
1 to 2 tablespoons chopped fresh chives or parsley

Melt the butter in a large saucepan or stockpot.
Add the leeks and saute them for about five minutes.
Cut the fresh sorrel leaves into julienne. Add them to the pot and cook for a few minutes, stirring often, until they are just wilted.
If you are using frozen sorrel, there is no need to defrost, just add it along with the stock and the water.
Add the potatoes, stock and water, and some salt and pepper.
Bring the soup to a boil, then simmer for one hour, stirring occasionally.
The leeks and potatoes should be very tender by this time.
Cool a little, then puree the soup, using a blender, food processor or food mill.
Stir in the sour cream and the half and half.
Heat and taste to correct the seasonings, adding more salt and pepper as needed.
This soup can be refrigerated for a few days and reheated. It also freezes well.
Serve hot with a sprinkling of parsley or chives on top.
Serves eight.

†Equal to six tablespoons blanched sorrel or three ice cube sized portions.
See 'sorrel', page 56 for an explanation.

RED LENTIL SOUP

1 cup dried red lentils
4 cups water
1 1/2 teaspoons ground cumin
2 teaspoons ground coriander
2 tablespoons butter or oil
1/2 teaspoon ground turmeric
1 medium onion, chopped
2 cloves garlic, minced
2 or 3 hot peppers, diced
1 cup tomatoes, peeled and diced

1 zucchini, diced
1 cup diced eggplant
1 small potato, diced
1 tablespoon salt, or more as needed
2 tablespoons wine vinegar
1 teaspoon chopped fresh cilitrano

Wash and pick over the lentils to remove any stones or debris.
Place them in a pot with the water. Cover and simmer until they are tender.
This should take about one and one-half hours.
Puree, using a food mill in order to remove the skins. Or use a food processor or blender and strain.
Heat the butter in a frying pan. Add the ground cumin, coriander and the turmeric and cook, stirring, for a minute or two.
Add the onion, garlic and peppers and cook over low heat for about ten minutes, or until they are very soft, stirring often.
Puree in a food processor or blender.
Place the strained lentil puree and the spice puree (wet masala) into a pot.
Add the tomatoes, zucchini, eggplant and the potato.
Stir in the salt and one tablespoon of the vinegar.
Bring the soup to a boil, cover and simmer for forty-five minutes to one hour, or until the vegetables are very tender.
Stir in the cilitrano and the second tablespoon of vinegar, if needed. The soup should be very spicy and somewhat tart.
Serve hot.
This soup can be refrigerated for a day or two and reheated. You may have to add some water, as it tends to thicken upon standing. Or it can be frozen.
Defrost before heating.
Serves six to eight.
If using cumin and coriander seeds, toast them first in a 375 degree oven for ten to fifteen minutes, or use a microwave oven at high power for three minutes. Cool and grind before adding to the pan. A food processor or blender will not grind them finely enough for use in this soup.

MUSHROOM BISQUE

7 or 8 dried mushrooms
3 1/2 cups water
2 tablespoon butter
1 large onion, sliced
1 leek, white only, sliced
1 pound fresh mushrooms
1/4 cup + 2 tablespoon Madeira
3 cups water
3 cups chicken stock
salt, pepper
pinch cayenne pepper
1/4 cup heavy cream
1 or 2 teaspoons chopped fresh chervil or parsley

Soak the dried mushrooms in one-half cup of the water for at least thirty minutes.
Remove the mushrooms and squeeze dry, reserving the soaking liquid.
Slice the dried mushrooms and set aside.
Heat the butter in a large saucepan or a stockpot. Add the sliced onions and leeks and saute until they are soft.
Reserve three or four of the fresh mushrooms for garnish. Chop the rest into small pieces.
Add both the fresh and dried mushrooms to the pot.
Cook, stirring often, until the mushrooms have given up their liquid.
Add the quarter cup of Madeira and stir well.
Pour in the soaking liquid from the dried mushrooms (be careful not to add any grit that may be present in the bottom of the dish), the water and the chicken stock.
Season with salt, pepper and a pinch of cayenne.
Bring the soup to a boil, cover and simmer for thirty minutes.
Cool a little, then puree in a food processor or blender.
The soup can be frozen at this point or refrigerated for a day or two.
When ready to serve, heat the soup.
Stir in the heavy cream and the remaining two tablespoons of Madeira.
Bring to a boil and simmer for a few minutes, then taste to correct the seasonings.
Cut the reserved mushrooms into thin slices.
Serve the soup in bowls, garnished with a few mushroom slices and a sprinkling of fresh chervil or parsley.
This recipe serves eight.
Alternate: The heavy cream can be eliminated, if calories are important.

TOMATO CHOWDER

2 tablespoons butter or oil
1 large onion, chopped
1 green pepper, diced
1 carrot, diced
1 stalk celery, diced
salt, pepper
2 cloves garlic, minced
28 ounce can Italian plum tomatoes or crushed tomatoes
1/2 teaspoon sugar
pinch cayenne pepper
2 tablespoons chopped fresh parsley
1 tablespoon chopped fresh basil†
1 tablespoon fresh oregano
1 1/2 cups beef or chicken stock
1 1/2 cups water
1 large potato, peeled and diced
1/2 cup lima beans, fresh or frozen
1/2 cup diced fresh string beans
1/2 cup peas, fresh or frozen
1/4 pound raw shrimp, diced (1/2 cup)
1/4 pound crabmeat (1/2 cup)
1/2 cup white wine

Heat the butter or oil in a large saucepan or a stockpot.
Add the onion, green pepper, carrot and celery.
Sprinkle with salt and pepper and cook for five minutes, stirring often.
Add the garlic, tomatoes, sugar, cayenne pepper and the herbs.
Bring the mixture to a boil, then cover and simmer for thirty minutes.
Pour in the stock and the water.
Add the potatoes and lima beans, raw string beans and fresh peas. If using frozen peas, add later.
Bring the soup to a boil, cover and simmer for twenty minutes.
Add the shrimp, crabmeat and the wine.
If using frozen peas, add now.
If the string or lima beans are already cooked, do not add until this point, as well.
Simmer for five minutes.
Taste to correct the seasonings and serve.
This soup can be refrigerated overnight and reheated or it can be frozen.
Serves eight.

†Dried basil or oregano can be substituted. Use one teaspoon of each.

RED LENTIL SOUP

TOMATO CHOWDER

Entrees

FISH

FILLETS OF SOLE, FARCI

FILLET OF FLUKE WITH BASIL

2 medium to large fillets of fluke†
salt, pepper
2 tablespoons chopped shallots
2 tomatoes, peeled, seeded and diced
1 small clove garlic, minced
2 tablespoons chopped fresh basil
1 tablespoon chopped fresh parsley
1 tablespoon lemon juice
2 tablespoons dried bread crumbs
2 tablespoons butter, softened

This recipe is best when made in summer with ripe tomatoes and garden fresh basil.
Rinse and dry the fish fillets. Cut them into four individual serving sized portions.
Place the fish, skinned side down, onto a buttered baking dish and sprinkle with a little salt and pepper.
In a bowl, combine the shallots, tomatoes, garlic, basil, parsley, lemon juice, bread crumbs and softened butter.
Mix well and add salt and pepper to taste.
Spread this topping evenly over the fish.
The fish can be prepared to this point and refrigerated for a few hours. Remove thirty minutes before baking.
Bake the fish in a preheated 375 degree oven for about twenty-five to thirty minutes, or until the fish is tender.
The amount of time needed will depend upon the thickness of the fish. The suggested time is for fillets that are about an inch thick.
Serve immediately.
Serves four.

†Any fillets of fish that are thick enough can be used for this recipe. Excellent with sea trout, striped bass, red snapper, halibut, etc.

FLUKE WITH TOMATOES AND MUSTARD

1 1/2 pounds thick fluke
salt, pepper
4 tablespoons butter, softened
1 tablespoon lemon juice
2 tablespoons Dijon mustard
1 tablespoon chopped fresh dill weed
2 tomatoes, sliced thin
2 teaspoons dried bread crumbs

Cut the fish into individual serving sized pieces. To serve four, you will need approximately two fillets that weigh three-quarters of a pound each or one very large fillet.
Use a thick fish. Fillet of sole or baby flounder are too thin for this style of preparation and will fall apart when you try to lift them out of the pan.
Rinse and dry the fish. Sprinkle with salt and pepper.
Mix the softened butter with the lemon juice, mustard and dill.
Spread this seasoned butter evenly on the tops of the fish fillets with a knife.
Place the fillets into a buttered baking pan.
Cover the buttered fish with overlapping slices of tomato.
Sprinkle the tops of the tomatoes with salt, pepper and the bread crumbs.
The fish can be covered and refrigerated at this point for a few hours.
Bake in a preheated 375 degree oven for twenty-five to thirty minutes (about five minutes longer if cold), just until the fish is fork tender. The tomatoes will hardly have changed in appearance.
Serve immediately.
Serves four.

FISH FILLETS WITH JULIENNED VEGETABLES

2 large or 4 small fillets of fish†
salt, pepper
flour for dredging
1 1/2 tablespoons oil
2 1/2 tablespoons butter
1 carrot, cut into julienne
1 stalk celery, cut into julienne
white of 1 leek, cut into julienne
1/4 cup white wine
2 tablespoons heavy cream
1 tablespoon chopped fresh parsley

Rinse and dry the fish.
Sprinkle the fillets with salt and pepper and dredge them lightly in the flour.
Heat the oil with one and one-half tablespoons of the butter in a frying pan.
Add the fish and saute until browned on both sides and cooked through.
This should take about five minutes per side, depending on the thickness of the fish.
Remove the fish to a serving plate and keep warm.
Discard the fat from the pan.
Add the fresh butter along with the julienned carrot, celery and leek.
Sprinkle with salt and pepper.
Pour in the white wine and immediately cover the pan.
Cook the vegetables for two minutes without removing the lid.
Uncover the pan and pour in the cream.
Taste to correct the seasonings and stir in the chopped parsley.
When hot, spoon the vegetables and the sauce over the fish and serve.
Serves four.

†Almost any fillet of fish will work for this recipe. Try sea trout, striped bass, red snapper, fluke, flounder, sole or even salmon.

FISH WITH A SORREL SAUCE

2 large bluefish or shad fillets or 4 small salmon steaks
salt, pepper
3 tablespoons butter
juice of 1/2 lemon
1 medium onion, chopped
1 cup fresh sorrel, cut into julienne and packed down†
1/2 cup white wine
1/2 cup fish or chicken stock
2 tablespoons sour cream
1/2 teaspoon flour

Rinse and dry the fish and place onto a broiling pan (skin side down if using fillets). Sprinkle with salt and pepper.
Melt one tablespoon of the butter and mix it with the lemon juice. Brush on top of the fish.
Broil under a medium heat until the fillets are well browned, about fifteen to twenty minutes. Thick fish steaks take a little longer and need to be turned once.
Prepare the sauce while the fish is cooking.
Heat the remaining butter in a saucepan. Add the onions, sprinkle with salt and pepper and cook for a few minutes, until they are golden.
Add the sorrel and cook, stirring, until wilted.
Pour in the wine and the stock and mix well.
Reduce the sauce by half over high heat.
Mix the sour cream with the flour and stir in. Taste to correct the seasonings.
Serve the sauce hot over the broiled fish. It should be tart enough to cut the oily taste of the bluefish, shad or salmon.
Serves four.

†Or use four tablespoons of frozen or blanched sorrel.

SEA TROUT WITH A GREEN PEPPERCORN SAUCE

1 large or two medium fillets of sea trout†
1 tablespoon heavy cream
2 tablespoons sour cream
1/2 teaspoon green peppercorns, crushed
1/2 teaspoon salt
1 tablespoon chopped fresh parsley
1/2 teaspoon dried marjoram

Rinse and dry the fish.
Cut into individual serving sized pieces and place them, skin side down, into a buttered baking dish, as close to each other as possible.
Mix together the rest of the ingredients in a bowl. Spread this sauce over the fish in an even layer.
The fish can be completed to this point, covered and refrigerated for an hour or two, if necessary.
Bake in a preheated 375 degree oven until tender. The length of time will depend upon the thickness of the fish. It will take anywhere from twenty to thirty minutes, or even longer if the fish is very thick.
Test with a fork after twenty minutes.
Serves four.

†Other fish can be substituted for the sea trout. The sauce works well with fluke, red snapper, halibut, etc.

SEA TROUT WITH MUSHROOMS AND SCALLIONS

4 small fillets of sea trout†
salt, pepper
flour for dredging
1 1/2 tablespoons oil
4 1/2 tablespoons butter
10-12 mushrooms, sliced
1/2 teaspoon dried thyme
1/2 cup Vermouth
6 scallions, cut into 1/4" slices
1/4 cup toasted almond slices

Rinse and dry the fish.
Sprinkle the sea trout with salt and pepper and dredge lightly in the flour.
Heat the oil with one and one-half tablespoons of the butter in a frying pan and saute the fish until browned on both sides and tender.
The fillets should take about five minutes to cook on each side, depending upon their thickness.
While the trout is cooking, heat two tablespoons of the butter in a separate frying pan.
Add the mushrooms, sprinkle with salt, pepper and the thyme.
Cook until the mushrooms have given up their liquid and are almost dry, stirring occasionally.
Pour in the Vermouth and stir, scraping the bottom of the pan well.
If for any reason, the fish is not ready, stop at this point and finish the topping once the fish is done.
Add the scallions to the topping and cook for about thirty seconds, just until they are hot.
Add the remaining tablespoon of butter, remove the pan from the heat and swirl until the butter is melted.
Place the fish onto a serving platter, spoon the mushroom mixture over the top, sprinkle with the toasted almonds and serve immediately.
Serves four.

†Or use 2 large fillets of sea trout, cut into half. Other fish fillets can be used as well. Try red snapper, striped bass, flounder, etc.

FILLET OF SOLE WITH SHRIMP AND ARTICHOKES

8 small fillets of sole†
salt, pepper
8 raw shrimp, shelled and cleaned
6 mushrooms, sliced
2 tablespoons chopped shallots

STRIPED BASS WITH GREEN PEPPER, FENNEL AND TOMATOES

1 package frozen artichoke hearts, thawed and drained
1/2 cup white wine
1/2 cup water
1 teaspoon lemon juice
2 1/2 tablespoons butter
2 tablespoons flour
1 cup half and half
1 cup grated Swiss cheese
1/4 cup grated Parmesan cheese
1/2 teaspoon Dijon mustard

Rinse and dry the fish fillets. Sprinkle with salt and pepper.
Place them, skin side up, on a flat surface.
Set a shrimp on the narrow end of each fillet and roll, lengthwise, into cylinders (skinned side in).
Butter the bottom of an ovenproof pan just large enough to hold all the fish rolls in one layer.
Place the mushrooms and the shallots into the bottom of the pan. Set the fish rolls on top.
Scatter the artichoke hearts around the fish.
Pour in the wine, water and lemon juice.
Dot the tops of the fish rolls with a half tablespoon of the butter.
Cover the pan with a piece of buttered waxed paper and then a lid.
Place the pan on top of the stove and bring the liquid to a boil, then bake the fish in a preheated 350 degree oven for ten to fifteen minutes, or until just cooked. The fish should have turned white in color, but still be quite firm.
It will cook again when reheated with the sauce, so be careful not to overcook at this point.
Remove the pan from the oven and carefully drain off and reserve all the liquid.
While the fish is cooking, you can start the sauce.
Heat two tablespoons of butter in a saucepan. Stir in the flour and cook for one minute.
Slowly stir in the half and half. Cook for a minute or two and set aside until the fish is finished cooking.
Once the fish has finished cooking, add the drained liquid to the waiting sauce base and stir well.
Bring it to a boil and reduce over high heat to half the volume.
Remove the pan from the heat and stir in the two cheeses and the mustard.
Add salt and pepper to taste.
Pour this sauce over the fish rolls.
The dish can remain at room temperature for a half hour or so, or it can be refrigerated at this point (well covered) for a few hours, if necessary.
Bake in a 375 degree oven for about twenty minutes (about five minutes more, if refrigerated), or until the sauce is hot and bubbling.
Serve immediately. Good with a rice pilaf.
Serves four, two rolls per person as an entree, or eight as an appetizer.

†If only larger fillets are available, use one per person instead of two (or cut in half for serving). Use four shrimp, one per roll.

SHRIMP WITH ASPARAGUS

FILLETS OF SOLE FARCI

8 four-ounce fillets of sole†
salt, pepper
2 cups fresh spinach leaves, pressed down††
2 tablespoons ricotta cheese
1 tablespoon grated Parmesan cheese
1/2 tablespoon chopped fresh parsley
3 tablespoons butter, melted
2 teaspoons lemon juice
1 teaspoon toasted dried bread crumbs
Sauce Beurre Blanc

Cook the spinach in boiling salted water for a minute or two. Refresh under cold water, drain and squeeze dry.
Or cook in a microwave oven with no additional liquid other than the water which clings to the leaves for one or two minutes at high power. Refresh and squeeze dry also.
Chop the cooked spinach finely.
To make the filling, mix the spinach with the two cheeses, parsley and some salt and pepper.
Rinse and dry the fish fillets. Sprinkle with salt and pepper.
Place half of the fillets, skinned side up in front of you.
Spread a quarter of the filling over the center of each of the fillets, leaving one-half inch from the edge clear on all sides.
Place the remaining fillets, skinned side down, on top of the filling and press to seal the edges.
Melt the butter with the lemon juice. Spread about one-third into the bottom of a low sided baking dish.
Place the filled fillets into the pan.
Brush the rest of the lemon butter on top.
Sprinkle with the bread crumbs.
The fish can be covered and refrigerated at this point for a few hours, if necessary.
Bake the fish in a preheated 375 degree oven for twenty-five to thirty minutes (the time will depend on the thickness of the fish), or until done.
The color of the flesh should be white and the fish should feel firm to the touch when ready.
Serve immediately with the Beurre Blanc sauce on the side.
Serves four.

†Or use four larger (eight ounce) fillets. They will take five to ten minutes longer to bake. You would have to cut the larger ones in half for serving.
††Frozen spinach leaves can be substituted. You will need enough to make one-quarter cup of spinach which has been cooked, squeezed dry and chopped.

SAUCE BEURRE BLANC

3 tablespoons butter
3 tablespoons chopped shallots
salt, pepper
3/4 cup white wine
6 tablespoons heavy cream
1 1/2 teaspoons lemon juice

Heat one and one-half tablespoons of the butter in a saucepan.
Add the shallots, sprinkle with salt and pepper and saute for one minute.
Pour in the wine and cook to reduce the liquid by half.
Add the heavy cream and the lemon juice. Cook for three to four minutes.
Taste to correct the seasonings.
The sauce can be completed to this point and allowed to sit at room temperature for about a half-hour. Reheat before proceeding.
Remove the pan from the heat, add the rest of the butter and swirl until melted. Serve immediately.
Serves four. You only need a little bit, this is a very rich sauce.

STRIPED BASS WITH GREEN PEPPER, FENNEL AND TOMATOES

2 large or 4 small fillets of striped bass†
salt, pepper
flour for dredging
1 1/2 tablespoons oil
4 1/2 tablespoons butter
1 large onion, sliced thin
1 large green pepper, sliced thin
1 large stalk fennel, sliced thin
1/2 teaspoon dried thyme
1/2 cup white wine
1/2 cup chicken or fish stock
1 tomato, sliced thin

Rinse and dry the fish.
Sprinkle the fillets with salt and pepper and dredge them lightly in the flour.
Heat the oil with one and one-half tablespoons of the butter in a frying pan.
Saute the fish until browned on both sides and tender.
This will take about four to five minutes on each side, depending on the thickness of the fillets.
Remove the fish to a serving platter and keep warm until the topping is finished.
While the fish is cooking, make the topping by melting two tablespoons of butter in a separate frying pan.
Add the onion and cook, stirring, for one minute.
Add the green pepper and fennel.
Sprinkle with salt, pepper and the thyme.
Continue to cook, stirring, for two minutes.
Pour in the wine and the stock and mix well.
Cook over high heat for five to six minutes, until the liquid is well reduced.
Add the sliced tomato and cook for a half a minute, just to heat.
Taste to correct the seasonings.
Add the remaining tablespoon of butter, remove the pan from the heat and swirl until melted.
Spoon the topping over the fish and serve

immediately.
Serves four.

†Other fish can be substituted for the striped bass. Try red snapper, flounder, fluke, sea trout, sole, etc.

RED SNAPPER, MEXICAN STYLE

1 large onion, cut into rings
2 green peppers, cut into rings
4 small or 2 large fillets of red snapper
salt, pepper
juice of 1 lime
Sauce:
2 tablespoons olive oil
1 medium onion, chopped
2 cloves garlic, minced
2 cups tomatoes, peeled, seeded and diced†
2 teaspoons tomato paste
1 fresh hot pepper, seeded and diced††
1 tablespoon fresh oregano or 1 teaspoon dried
1 or 2 bay leaves
12 pitted black olives, halved
salt

Lightly oil the bottom of a baking pan.
Place the onion and pepper rings into the pan.
Wash and dry the fish.
Set the fillets on top of the vegetables.
Sprinkle with salt and pepper and squeeze the lime juice over the fish.
Next make the sauce.
Heat the oil in a saucepan. Add the onion and cook until golden.
Then add the garlic and continue to cook for another half minute.
Stir in the tomatoes, tomato paste, the hot pepper, bay leaves and olives.
Add salt to taste.
Bring the sauce to a boil and cook over a medium heat for about ten minutes, or until the sauce thickens. If using canned tomatoes, allow about fifteen minutes.
Remove the bay leaves and spread the sauce evenly over the fish fillets.
The fish can be prepared to this point, covered and refrigerated for an hour or two, if necessary.
Bake in a preheated 375 degree oven for twenty to twenty-five minutes, or until the fish is just tender.
The addition of the lime juice helps to cook the fish more quickly.
Serve immediately.
Serves four.

†Two cups of canned Italian plum tomatoes can be substituted.
††Canned chili peppers can be substituted for fresh hot peppers. Use about one-quarter cup, diced.

SHRIMP WITH ASPARAGUS

1 pound raw shrimp
1 pound fresh asparagus
1 eight-ounce can water chestnuts
1 large onion, sliced thin
2 or 3 cloves garlic, minced
3 tablespoons oil
Marinade:
1 teaspoon cornstarch
1 teaspoon oil
pinch salt
pinch sugar
Sauce:
1 teaspoon cornstarch
1/3 cup chicken stock
1/3 cup water
2 tablespoons soy sauce
1 tablespoon rice wine or Sherry
1 tablespoon Chinese oyster sauce
pinch sugar
pinch pepper

Peel and remove the veins from the shrimp. Rinse well and mix with all of the marinade ingredients. Refrigerate until needed.
If the asparagus is thick, peel the stalks. Cut the stalks into one inch slices on the diagonal. Keep the tips separate from the stalks.
Drain the water chestnuts and cut them into thin slices.
Mix together all of the sauce ingredients in a bowl and reserve.
When ready to cook, heat the oil in a large frying pan or wok.
Add the onion and the garlic and stir-fry for one half a minute.
Add the shrimp, along with its marinade and cook, stirring, for another minute.
Then add the asparagus stalks and cook, stirring, for a half a minute.
Add the water chestnuts and the asparagus tips.
Pour in the sauce and continue to cook for an additional two to three minutes.
Cook only until the shrimp are white and the sauce thick. The asparagus should remain very crisp.
Serve immediately.
Serves four as a main course or more if served with other dishes as part of a Chinese meal.
Alternate: Broccoli can be substituted for the asparagus. The stalks will take an additional minute or two to cook.

HOT AND SOUR SHRIMP

1 pound raw shrimp
1 1/2 teaspoons cornstarch
1 tablespoon rice wine or Sherry
1/2 tablespoon fresh ginger
2 cloves garlic

2 fresh hot peppers
6 scallions
2 carrots
1/2 bunch broccoli (about 3 cups cut)
3 tablespoons oil
Sauce:
1/4 cup rice wine vinegar
2 tablespoons soy sauce
1 teaspoon sugar
1/2 teaspoon cornstarch
1 tablespoon water

Shell, rinse and remove the veins from the shrimp.
Mix the shrimp with the cornstarch and the rice wine in a small bowl and set aside.
Ready the vegetables.
Crush the ginger root and mince the garlic finely.
Seed the hot peppers and cut into small dice.
Chop the scallions into one-quarter inch pieces, keeping the greens and whites separate.
Peel and slice the carrots into thin rings, on the diagonal.
Separate the broccoli florets from the stalks. Peel the stalks and cut them into thin slices on the diagonal.
Mix the rice wine vinegar with the soy and the sugar to make the sauce and reserve.
In a separate bowl, combine the cornstarch and the water.
Heat the oil in a large wok or frying pan.
Add the shrimp and stir-fry for about two minutes, just until they turn white.
Remove the shrimp with a slotted spoon and reserve.
Add the white part of the scallions, garlic, ginger and hot peppers to the wok or frying pan. Cook, stirring, for a half-minute.
Add the carrot and broccoli stems and cook, stirring, for one to two minutes.
Return the shrimp and add the broccoli florets to the pan.
Pour in the sauce and stir-fry for a minute or two.
Bring the sauce to a hard boil, stir in the cornstarch thickening and cook for another thirty seconds. Add the scallion greens.
Serve immediately.
Serves four as a main course, or more if served along with other dishes as part of a Chinese meal.

SHRIMP WITH TARRAGON

1 1/2 pounds raw shrimp
3 tablespoons butter
3 tablespoons chopped shallots
8 medium mushrooms, sliced
salt, pepper
1 1/2 tablespoons brandy
3/4 cup heavy cream
2 tablespoons chopped fresh parsley
1 tablespoon chopped fresh tarragon

Peel, rinse and remove the veins from the shrimp.
Heat the butter in a frying pan, add the shallots and saute for a minute or two.
Add the mushrooms and sprinkle with salt and pepper.
Cook until most of the liquid given off by the mushrooms is evaporated.
Add the shrimp to the pan and saute, stirring, until they turn white. This will only take a few minutes, do not overcook.
Pour in the brandy and the cream.
Stir in the parsley and the tarragon.
Cook just until the sauce thickens, this should take just a few minutes.
Taste to correct the seasonings and serve immediately.
Serve with rice or noodles.
Serves four as a main course or eight as an appetizer.

SHRIMP WITH TARRAGON AND HERBED RICE WITH PINE NUTS

SHRIMP AND CRABMEAT CASSEROLE

3/4 pound raw shrimp
2 tablespoons butter
2 tablespoons chopped shallots
5-6 mushrooms, sliced thin
salt, pepper
1/4 cup white wine
1 teaspoon lemon juice
1/2 pound cooked crabmeat
4 water chestnuts, sliced thin (2 oz.)
2 tablespoons dried bread crumbs
2 tablespoons grated Parmesan cheese
Sauce:
1 1/2 tablespoons butter
1 1/2 tablespoons flour
1 cup milk
salt, pepper
pinch grated nutmeg
1/2 cup grated Swiss cheese

First make the sauce. Heat the butter in a saucepan.
Stir in the flour and cook for a minute or two.
Gradually add the milk to the pan, stirring constantly.
Season with salt, pepper and the nutmeg.
Simmer the sauce for about ten minutes, stirring occasionally.
Mix in the grated cheese, remove the pan from the heat and set aside.
Peel, rinse and remove the veins from the raw shrimp. Cut them in half lengthwise and reserve.
Heat a tablespoon and a half of butter in a frying pan. Add the shallots and cook for a minute or two.
Add the mushrooms, sprinkle with salt and pepper and cook until they have given up their liquid and are dry, stirring occasionally.
Add the sliced shrimp and cook, stirring, for one minute.
Pour in the wine and the lemon juice and continue to cook, stirring often, until the shrimp are white. This should take from two to three minutes.
Add the crabmeat and cook for another minute.
Spoon the contents of the pan (including any liquid) into a bowl.
Add the water chestnuts and the sauce.
Mix carefully so as not to break apart the shrimp and the crabmeat. Taste to correct the seasonings.
Spoon this mixture into a shallow buttered casserole† and sprinkle the top with the bread crumbs and the Parmesan cheese. Dot with the remaining butter.
The dish can be completed to this point, covered and refrigerated for a few hours or overnight. Remove from the refrigerator thirty minutes before baking. It can also be frozen, do not thaw before cooking.
Bake the casserole, uncovered, in a preheated 400 degree oven for about twenty-five minutes, or until the top is lightly browned and the sauce bubbling. If frozen, allow an extra ten to fifteen minutes.
Serves four as a main course or eight as an appetizer.

†The shrimp and the crabmeat can be placed into eight individual buttered ramekins for use as an appetizer. Baking time will be just about the same.

CHICKEN CACCIATORA

POULTRY

ARROZ CON POLLO

one 3 1/2 pound chicken
salt, pepper
flour for dredging
2 tablespoons olive oil
2 tablespoons salad oil
1 large onion, chopped
2 large cloves garlic, minced
1 teaspoon cumin seed, toasted and ground
1/2 teaspoon ground allspice
1 tablespoon chopped fresh oregano or 1 teaspoon dried
1 cup peeled, seeded and diced tomatoes†
1 or 2 hot peppers, seeded and diced††
1 cup (raw) rice
2 cups chicken stock
1/4 cup diced pimento

Cut the chicken into eighths.
Sprinkle with salt and pepper and dredge the pieces lightly in the flour.
Heat both the oils in an oven-proof pan that has a tight fitting lid.
Add the chicken pieces and brown on both sides.
Remove and reserve the chicken.
Drain off and discard all but one tablespoon of the oil.
Add the onion to the pan, sprinkle with salt and pepper and saute for a minute or two.
Stir in the garlic and cook for another half-minute.
Then add the rice, stirring to coat all the grains with the oil.
Mix in the cumin, allspice and oregano.
Add the tomatoes and the hot peppers.
Pour in the stock and bring the liquid to a boil.
Stir again and return the chicken to the pan.
Cover and bake in a preheated 375 degree oven for thirty to thirty-five minutes.
Remove the pan from the oven and allow it to sit for five minutes without taking off the lid.
Garnish with the diced pimento and serve immediately.
Serves four.

†One cup canned Italian plum tomatoes can be substituted for the fresh.
††The amount of peppers will depend on the kind used (for example one serrano versus two jalapeno peppers). Canned chili peppers can be substituted for the fresh. Or if you do not want a hot dish, use a frying or bell pepper.

BARBEQUED CHICKEN WITH CURRY AND THYME

one 3 1/2 pound chicken
salt, papper
4 tablespoons butter
2 tablespoons honey
1 tablespoon lemon juice
1 1/2 teaspoons curry powder
1/4 teaspoon dried thyme

Split the chicken into halves, or quarters, if you prefer.
Sprinkle with salt and pepper.
Combine the rest of the ingredients in a small saucepan and heat until the butter is melted. Or heat in a microwave oven for one minute.
Stir well and add salt and pepper to taste.
Set or ready a barbeque to a medium heat. When hot, cook the chicken for fifteen minutes, turning once.
Then begin to baste with the sauce.
Continue to cook the chicken, turning often and basting each side two or three times with the sauce.
The chicken should take an additional twenty-five minutes to cook (forty minutes, total).
I like to turn the heat up to high during the last ten minutes of cooking time to get the skin nice and brown.
This chicken can also be roasted in an oven.
Coat both sides with the sauce first, then roast in a 425 degree oven for fifteen to twenty minutes, bone side up.
Baste both sides with the sauce, turn and continue to roast for another twenty minutes, or until the meat is tender and the skin nice and crisp.
Serves four.

CHICKEN CACCIATORA

one 3 1/2 pound chicken
salt, pepper
flour for dredging
3 tablespoons oil
1 large onion, chopped
10-12 mushrooms, sliced
2 cloves garlic, minced
2 cups canned Italian plum tomatoes, chopped
2 teaspoons tomato paste
2 tablespoons chopped fresh basil
1 tablespoon chopped fresh oregano, or
1 teaspoon dried
pinch sugar
pinch cayenne pepper
1/2 cup white wine
1/2 cup chicken stock

Cut the chicken into eighths. Sprinkle with salt and pepper and dredge the pieces lightly in the flour.
Heat the oil in a large frying pan.
Add the chicken and brown well on both sides.
Remove the meat from the pan and reserve.
Pour off and discard all but one tablespoon of the oil.
Add the onions and saute for a few minutes until they are golden.
Add the mushrooms, sprinkle with salt and pepper and cook, stirring occasionally, until they are dry.
Add the garlic to the pan and cook for another half minute.
Stir in the chopped tomatoes and the tomato paste.
Then add the herbs, sugar and cayenne pepper.
Pour in the wine and the stock, scraping the bottom of the pan well.
Return the chicken and bring the sauce to a boil.
Cover and simmer for about twenty to twenty-five minutes, or until the chicken is tender, turning once or twice.
If there is too much sauce, remove the lid and boil hard for a few minutes.
Taste to correct the seasonings and serve.
Serves four.

CHILI CHICKEN

one 3 1/2 pound chicken
6 tablespoons butter
2 teaspoons Dijon mustard
1 teaspoon paprika
1/4 teaspoon cayenne pepper (optional)
1 teaspoon chili powder
1 teaspoon salt
corn flake crumbs to coat

Cut the chicken into eighths and remove all skin and visible fat.
Rinse and dry well.
Melt the butter in a small saucepan and add the mustard, paprika, cayenne pepper, chili powder and the salt.
Mix well, heat to the boiling point, then remove the pan from the heat.
Or use a microwave oven. Melt the butter on high power for one minute. Add the rest as above and cook on high for thirty seconds.
Place the corn flake crumbs into a shallow bowl or a plate for coating.
Line a low-sided pan with aluminum foil. Lightly oil the foil.
One at a time, dip the chicken pieces into the spiced butter mixture, turning to coat well on all sides.
Lift out and place onto the crumbs, turn and press lightly to coat.
Transfer the finished chicken to the foil.
Continue until all the pieces are coated.
The chicken can be refrigerated for a few hours at this point, if necessary.
Bring to room temperature or allow an extra five to ten minutes in the oven.
Bake the chicken in a preheated 400 degree oven for thirty-five minutes, or until the meat is tender and the coating is well browned.
Do not turn the chicken while cooking.
Serve while hot.
Serves four.

CHICKEN SAUTEED WITH FRESH HERBS

one 3 1/2 pound chicken
salt, pepper
flour for dredging
2 to 3 tablespoons oil
2 tablespoons butter
3 tablespoons chopped shallots
8 large mushrooms, sliced
1/2 teaspoon paprika
1 cup chicken stock
1/2 cup white wine
1 tablespoon chopped fresh parsley
1 tablespoon chopped fresh chervil
1/2 tablespoon chopped fresh chives
1 teaspoon chopped fresh tarragon

Cut the chicken into eighths. Sprinkle with salt and pepper and dredge the pieces lightly in the flour.
Heat the oil in a large frying pan. Add the chicken and saute until brown on both sides. Remove the chicken and reserve.
Discard any oil remaining in the pan.
Add one tablespoon of the butter and the shallots to the pan. Cook for one minute.
Then add the mushrooms and sprinkle with salt and pepper. Continue to cook, stirring, for a few minutes, until the mushrooms are dry.
Stir in the paprika and cook for only a half minute.
Pour in the stock and the wine, scraping well to deglaze the bottom of the pan.
Bring the sauce to a boil and return the chicken to

CHICKEN SAUTEED WITH FRESH HERBS AND CURRY- RICE TOMATOES

the pan. Cover and simmer for about twenty minutes, or until the chicken is tender, turning once.
You will need a scant cup of liquid left in the pan for the sauce. If there is more, remove the lid and boil hard for a minute or two until reduced.
Remove the chicken to a serving platter.
Stir the chopped fresh herbs (fines herbes) into the sauce.
Remove the pan from the heat and add the remaining butter, stirring until the butter is melted. Taste to correct the seasonings.
Pour the sauce over the chicken and serve.
This recipe serves four.

CHICKEN WITH LEMON AND GARLIC

one 3 1/3 pound chicken
salt, pepper
flour for dredging
2 to 3 tablespoons oil
1 tablespoon butter
2 tablespoons chopped shallots
2 cloves garlic, minced
1/2 teaspoon chopped fresh rosemary or a large pinch dried
2 cups chicken stock
juice of 1 lemon

Cut the chicken into eighths. Sprinkle with salt and pepper and dredge the pieces lightly in the flour.
Heat the oil in a frying pan. Add the chicken and brown well on both sides.
Remove and reserve the meat.
Discard the oil remaining in the pan.
Add the butter and the shallots to the pan and cook for a minute or two.
Add the garlic and the rosemary and continue to cook for another minute.
Pour in the stock and deglaze the pan by scraping the bottom well.
Then add the lemon juice and some salt and pepper.
Return the chicken to the pan, cover and simmer for about twenty minutes, or until the meat is tender, turning once.
Place the chicken on a serving plate and keep warm.
Boil the sauce hard until it is reduced to about two-thirds cup.
Taste to correct the seasonings, pour over the chicken and serve.
Serves four.

CHICKEN WITH A MUSTARD SAUCE

one 3 1/2 pound chicken
salt, pepper
flour for dredging
2 to 3 tablespoons oil
2 tablespoons chopped shallots
2/3 cup white wine
2/3 cup chicken stock
water, as needed
1/4 cup yogurt or sour cream
1 tablespoon Dijon mustard
2 teaspoons lemon juice
1 tablespoon chopped fresh parsley
1 tablespoon chopped fresh dill

Cut the chicken into eighths.
Sprinkle with salt and pepper and dredge the pieces lightly in the flour.
Heat the oil in a large saute pan that has a lid.
Add the chicken and brown well on both sides.
Remove the meat and reserve.
Discard all but a teaspoon of oil from the pan.
Add the shallots and cook for a minute or two.
Deglaze the pan with the wine and the stock.
Return the chicken, cover and simmer until tender, turning once.
The chicken should take about twenty minutes to cook. Add water, if needed, to keep the meat from sticking.
While the chicken is cooking, mix together the yogurt, mustard and lemon juice in a small bowl and reserve.
Remove the chicken from the pan and place onto a serving plate.
You need about one half to three-quarters cup of liquid in the pan in order to finish the sauce, as it will be fairly thick. If there is not enough liquid remaining, add some water and bring the sauce to a boil. If too much, boil down.
Whisk in the mustard mixture, add the fresh herbs and taste to correct the seasonings.
When the sauce is hot, pour over the chicken and serve.
Serves four.

LEMON CHICKEN PILAF

one 3 1/2 pound chicken
salt, pepper
flour for dredging
2 to 3 tablespoons oil
3 tablespoons butter
1 large onion, chopped
6 mushrooms, sliced thin
2 cloves garlic, minced
1 cup (raw) rice
grated rind of 1 lemon
1/2 teaspoon dried thyme
1 bay leaf
1/2 cup white wine
1 1/2 cups chicken stock
1 tablespoon lemon juice
2 tablespoons chopped fresh parsley

Cut the chicken into eighths.
Sprinkle with salt and pepper and dredge the pieces lightly in the flour.
Heat the oil in an oven-proof skillet that has a tight fitting lid.
Brown the chicken pieces on both sides, then remove and reserve.
Discard any oil remaining in the pan.
Add the butter and the onion to the pan and cook until golden.

CHICKEN BREASTS IN A GREEN SAUCE AND RICE WITH COCONUT AND RAISINS

Add the mushrooms, sprinkle with salt and pepper and continue to cook for a few minutes, until the mushrooms have given up their liquid and are dry.
Stir in the garlic and the rice. Mix well to coat all of the grains of rice with the butter.
Add the lemon rind, thyme and bay leaf.
Pour in the wine, stock and lemon juice. Stir, scraping the bottom of the pan well.
Allow the liquid to come to a boil, stir again and place the chicken pieces back into the pan in a single layer, if possible. If not, place the dark meat on the bottom of the pan and the white meat on top.
Cover the pan with a lid and place into a preheated 375 degree oven for thirty to thirty-five minutes. Both the chicken and the rice should be tender by this time.
Remove the pan from the oven and allow it to sit for five minutes before taking off the cover.
Taste to correct the seasonings, stir in the parsley and serve.
Serves four.

POULET a l'ANCIENNE

one 3 1/2 pound chicken
salt, pepper
flour for dredging + 1/2 teaspoon
2 to 3 tablespoons oil
1 tablespoon butter
2 tablespoons chopped shallots
3 slices bacon, diced
12 small pearl onions, peeled
24 small whole mushrooms, or 12 medium cut in halves
1 1/2 cups white wine
1 cup chicken stock
bouquet garni
2 tablespoons sour cream
2 tablespoons chopped fresh parsley

Cut the chicken into eighths.
Sprinkle with salt and pepper and dredge the pieces lightly in the flour.
Heat the oil in a frying pan and brown the chicken well on both sides. Remove and reserve.
Discard all the oil remaining in the pan.
Place the butter, shallots and diced bacon into the pan and saute until the bacon is lightly browned.
Add the pearl onions and the mushrooms and continue to cook for a few minutes, stirring often.
Pour in the wine and the stock, scraping the bottom well to deglaze the pan.
Add the bouquet garni, bring the liquid to a boil and return the chicken to the pan.
Cover and simmer for about thirty minutes, or until the chicken and the vegetables are tender.
Discard the bouquet garni.
Place the chicken onto a serving plate and keep warm while finishing the sauce.
Reduce the sauce over high heat until just about one cup of liquid remains.
Mix the sour cream with the half-teaspoon of flour and stir this into the sauce.
Taste to correct the seasonings.
If the chicken has cooled down too much, it can be returned to the pan at this point for just a minute until hot. If still warm enough, spoon the sauce over the top, garnish with the parsley and serve.
Serves four.

MOGUL CHICKEN

one 3 1/2 pound chicken
4 tablespoons butter
2 large onions, chopped
2 large cloves garlic, sliced
2 teaspoons sliced fresh ginger root
2 teaspoons salt
1 teaspoon ground black peppercorns
1/4 teaspoon cayenne pepper (optional)†
1 1/2 teaspoons ground cardamom
1 teaspoon ground cinnamon
1/2 teaspoon grated nutmeg
1/2 teaspoon ground turmeric
1/2 cup + 2 tablespoons water
1 or 2 bay leaves
1 cup yogurt

Cut the chicken into eighths. Remove all skin and visible fat.
Use a frying pan large enough to hold all the chicken pieces in one layer, if possible.
Melt the butter and add the onions. Cook over low heat until they are very tender. This should take about ten minutes.
While the onions are cooking, make a wet masala by placing the garlic, ginger root, salt, pepper, cayenne, cardamom, cinnamon, nutmeg and tumeric into a food processor (or blender) along with the half-cup of water. Puree well and set aside until needed.
Once the onions are cooked, add this wet masala, or paste, along with the bay leaves to the frying pan. Cook over low heat, stirring often, for five to six minutes. This will remove the raw taste of the spices from the finished dish.
Slowly stir in the yogurt, a few spoons at a time. Cook, stirring constantly for a minute or two between each addition.
Mix in the remaining two tablespoons of water.
Add the chicken pieces to the pan. Cover with a lid and simmer for fifteen minutes.
Turn the chicken pieces over, cover and simmer for another ten to fifteen minutes, or until the meat is tender.
If the sauce seems too liquid, boil hard for a minute or two to reduce a little. You do, however, want a lot of sauce with this chicken.
The dish can be reheated.
Serves four. Serve with a rice pilaf.
Alternate: Puree the cooked onion along with the masala if you would like a very smooth sauce. Personally, I prefer the bits of onion.

†This is a very aromatic but mild dish. Add the cayenne pepper if you prefer a degree of hotness.

SPANISH CHICKEN WITH RICE AND PEPPERS

one 3 1/2 pound chicken†
salt, pepper
flour for dredging
1 tablespoon oil
1 tablespoon butter
1 small onion, chopped
1 small clove garlic, minced
pinch saffron, crushed
1/2 teaspoon dried basil
pinch cayenne pepper
1/2 cup (raw) rice
1 large tomato, diced
1/2 cup fresh or frozen peas
1/4 cup white wine
1/2 cup chicken stock
1 tablespoon chopped fresh parsley

Cut the chicken into eighths. Sprinkle with salt and pepper and dredge the pieces lightly in the flour.
Heat the oil and the butter in an ovenproof pan or casserole.
Add the chicken and brown the pieces lightly on both sides.
Remove and reserve.
Add the chopped onion to the pan and cook for a few minutes.
Stir in the garlic.
Then add the green pepper, basil, saffron and the cayenne pepper to the pan.
Stir in the rice, mixing well to coat all the grains with the butter and oil.
Add the tomatoes and peas, then pour in the wine and the stock.
Add some salt and pepper.
Return the chicken to the pan and bring the liquid to a boil.
Cover and place into a preheated 375 degree oven for thirty-five to forty minutes, or until the chicken and the rice are done.
Taste and add more salt and pepper if needed.
Sprinkle with the chopped parsley and serve.
Serves four.

†Four whole chicken legs can be used instead. Cut them in half before cooking.

CHICKEN BREASTS IN A GREEN SAUCE

4 double chicken breasts
salt, pepper
flour for dredging
3 to 4 tablespoons oil
Green Sauce:
1 twelve ounce can tomatillo verde
2 ounces shelled pumpkin seeds
1 small onion, coarsely chopped
2 cloves garlic
4 large lettuce leaves
2 tablespoons chopped fresh cilitrano
1/2 teaspoon cumin seeds, toasted
2 fresh hot peppers†
1/2 teaspoon salt

First prepare the green sauce. Drain and discard the liquid from the can of tomatillos.
Place all of the sauce ingredients into a food processor and blend until well pureed.
If using a blender, you will have to divide the mixture into two batches.
The sauce can be prepared ahead and kept in the refrigerator for a few hours, if necessary. The fresher it is, the better it will taste.
Skin and bone the chicken breasts. Pound them a little to flatten.
Sprinkle with salt and pepper and dredge them lightly in the flour.
Heat the oil in a large frying pan and saute the breasts over moderate heat for about five minutes on each side. They should be crusty on the outside and tender inside in this amount of time.
Remove the chicken to a serving plate.
Discard all but a scant tablespoon of the oil remaining in the pan.
Add the green sauce and heat gently, just until the sauce comes to a boil.
Spoon over the chicken breasts and serve.
Serves four. Good with a rice pilaf.
Alternate: This sauce is also excellent with sauteed shrimp or thin veal tenders.

†Increase or decrease the amount of hot peppers used to taste. This should be a very hot sauce.

CURRIED CHICKEN BREASTS

4 small double chicken breasts†
salt, pepper
flour for dredging
2 to 3 tablespoons oil
2 tablespoons butter
1 apple, peeled, cored and diced††
1 medium onion, chopped
3 tablespoons coarsley chopped walnuts
2 tablespoons raisins, plumped
2 teaspoons Madras curry powder
1/2 teaspoon ground cardamom
1/2 teaspoon ground cinnamon
3 or 4 slices diced mango (optional)
1/2 cup chicken stock
2 tablespoons honey
1/4 cup yogurt
1 to 2 tablespoons toasted sliced almonds

Skin and bone the chicken breasts. Pound them a little to even them out.
Sprinkle with salt and pepper and dredge them lightly in the flour.

Heat the oil in a frying pan and saute the breasts for about four minutes on each side, until they are browned and tender. Remove and reserve.
Discard the oil from the pan.
Add the butter, apple and onions to the pan. Cook for a few minutes, until they are tender and begin to color.
Add the walnuts and the raisins and cook for another minute or two.
Stir in the curry powder, cardamom and cinnamon.
Add the mango, if using and pour in the stock, scraping well to deglaze the pan.
Stir in the honey and the yogurt.
Simmer for a few minutes, then taste to correct the seasonings.
Add the chicken back to the pan and cook just until the meat is hot.
Serve garnished with the toasted almond slices.
Serves four.

†If the chicken breasts are very large, one per person is enough. Cook five minutes per side. The same amount of sauce will be sufficient.
††If preparing ahead of time, place the diced apple in water with a little lemon juice added to keep it white.

CHICKEN BREASTS WRAPPED IN FILO

2 whole chicken breasts
salt, pepper
flour for dredging
2 to 3 tablespoons oil
2 tablespoons butter
2 tablespoons chopped shallots
8 medium mushrooms, sliced
2 tablespoons brandy
1 teaspoon chopped fresh tarragon or a pinch dried
1 teaspoon chopped fresh thyme or a pinch dried
1 teaspoon chopped fresh parsley
4 slices mozzarella cheese
4 slices Swiss cheese
4 slices gruyere cheese†
8 sheets filo
1/4 cup melted butter
2 tablespoons dried bread crumbs

Split the chicken breasts in half. Skin and bone them (save the bones for stock). Sprinkle with salt and pepper and dredge them lightly in the flour. Heat the oil in a frying pan and saute the chicken breasts for just two minutes on each side. You only want to lightly brown the chicken, it will finish

CHICKEN BREASTS WRAPPED IN FILO

SAUTEED CHICKEN BREASTS WITH PEPPERS AND PEAS

cooking later. Remove from the pan and cool a little.

Discard the oil remaining in the pan. Add the two tablespoons of butter and the shallots and saute for a minute or two.

Add the mushrooms, sprinkle with salt and pepper and cook until they are almost dry.

Pour in the brandy and add the herbs. Continue to cook until there is no liquid remaining in the pan. Set aside to cool a little.

Place the cheese into four separate piles so that each stack contains one slice of each kind of cheese used.

Spread out one sheet of filo vertically in front of you. Keep the rest of the dough covered while you work.

Brush with melted butter and sprinkle with a little of the crumbs.

Cover with a second sheet of filo and brush with a little more butter.

Place one stack of cheese onto the lower center portion of the filo.

Spoon one quarter of the mushrooms on top of the cheese.

Make sure the chicken is dry (blot with a paper towel if necessary) and place one piece on top of the mushrooms.

Fold the bottom of the filo up and over the chicken, then fold in both the sides and roll, forming a rectangle.

Place the packet, seam side down, onto a buttered baking sheet. Brush the top well with melted butter.

Repeat with the other three pieces of chicken and the rest of the ingredients.

The chicken can be loosely covered with a towel and refrigerated for several hours at this point, or it can be cooked immediately.

Place the baking sheet into a preheated 425 degree oven (no cover) and bake for about twenty-five to thirty minutes, or until the filo is well browned.

Serve immediately.

Serves four.

†Or use four thicker slices of Swiss cheese and skip the gruyere. I like the flavor combination of all three, but use whatever you prefer.

CHICKEN BREASTS, HUNGARIAN STYLE

2 large double chicken breasts
salt, pepper
flour for dredging + 1/2 teaspoon
2 tablespoons oil
1 medium onion, chopped fine
8 mushrooms, sliced
1 large clove garlic, minced
1 green pepper, seeded and diced
1 tomato, peeled, seeded and diced

1/2 teaspoon tomato paste
1 teaspoon paprika
1/2 teaspoon dried marjoram
pinch cayenne pepper
1/2 cup white wine
1/2 cup chicken stock
1/4 cup sour cream

Split the chicken breasts in half, leaving the bone in and the skin on.
Sprinkle with salt and pepper and dredge them lightly in the flour.
Heat the oil in a frying pan.
Saute the chicken for a few minutes on each side, until lightly browned.
Remove and reserve.
Discard all but one tablespoon of oil from the pan.
Add the chopped onion, cook for a minute or two, then add the mushrooms.
Sprinkle with a little salt and pepper and continue to cook until the mushrooms are dry.
Add the garlic, then the green pepper and diced tomato to the pan, stirring well.
Mix in the tomato paste, paprika, marjoram and cayenne pepper.
Pour in the wine and the stock, stirring well to deglaze the bottom of the pan.
Return the chicken to the pan, cover and simmer until tender, turning once.
This should take no more than ten to twelve minutes for chicken breasts.
Mix the sour cream with the flour and stir this into the sauce.
Continue to cook for a minute or two, then taste to correct the seasonings and serve.
Serves four.
I prefer this dish made with chicken breasts. However, chicken legs can be used as well. Use four whole legs and increase the cooking time by five to ten minutes.

SAUTEED CHICKEN BREASTS WITH PEPPERS AND PEAS

2 double chicken breasts
3 large red peppers
salt, pepper
flour for dredging
3 tablespoons oil
1 large onion, chopped
10 to 12 mushrooms, sliced
2 cloves garlic, minced
1/2 teaspoon dried thyme
1/2 teaspoon dried oregano
1/2 cup cooked peas†
1/2 cup white wine
1/4 cup chicken stock
1 tablespoon lemon juice
1 tablespoon butter
1 tablespoon chopped fresh parsley

Skin and bone the chicken breasts.
Cut each breast into six or eight pieces.
Cut the red peppers into large dice the same size as the cut up chicken breasts and reserve.
Sprinkle the chicken with salt and pepper and dredge the pieces lightly in the flour.
Heat the oil in a large frying pan.
Add the chicken and cook over medium heat, stirring often, until the meat is lightly browned and tender. This should take about four to five minutes.
Remove the chicken and reserve.
You want about a tablespoon of oil to remain in the pan. Discard any excess.
Add the onions and cook for a minute or two.
Then add the mushrooms and continue to cook until they have given up most of their liquid.
Stir in the garlic, thyme and oregano and cook for a half a minute.
Add the peppers and peas and sprinkle with a little salt and pepper.
Immediately deglaze the pan with the wine, stock and lemon juice, scraping the bottom well.
Return the chicken to the pan and cook for about three minutes. The peppers should still be very crisp.
Remove the pan from the heat and add the butter and the parsley.
Swirl until the butter is melted.
Taste to correct the seasonings and serve.
Serves four.

†Frozen peas can be used. Thaw only, do not cook. Diced cooked string beans work equally well in this recipe.

CHICKEN BREASTS SAMANTHA

4 double chicken breasts
salt, pepper
flour for dredging
3 tablespoons oil, or more as needed
8 thick slices mozzarella cheese
2 tablespoons butter
1/4 cup chopped shallots
8 mushrooms, sliced†
1/2 teaspoon dried thyme
1/2 teaspoon dried oregano
1/2 cup white wine
1/2 cup chicken stock
2 tablespoons brandy
1 tablespoon chopped fresh parsley

Skin and bone the chicken breasts.
Pound them with a mallet until they are flattened, as you would veal tenders.
Sprinkle with salt and pepper and dredge the breasts lightly in the flour.
Heat the oil in a large frying pan.
Add as many breasts as will fit at one time without overlapping.
Brown well on both sides, remove and place onto an ovenproof pan. (I like to use a baking sheet lined with a piece of aluminum foil, it saves cleaning a second pan.)

Continue until all the breasts are done, adding more oil to the pan, if needed.
Pounded chicken breasts need only a few minutes to cook and should be quite tender inside by the time the outside is browned.
Once all the chicken is browned, top each piece with a thick slice of cheese.
Place the pan into a preheated 375 degree oven.
Remove from the oven when the cheese is melted.
While the cheese is melting, begin the sauce.
Discard any oil remaining in the pan.
Add a tablespoon and a half of butter along with the shallots.
Cook for one minute.
Add the mushrooms, sprinkle with salt and pepper and saute until they have given up their liquid and are dry.
Add the thyme and the oregano.
Deglaze the pan with the wine, stock and the brandy.
Cook for a few minutes, until the sauce is well concentrated in flavor.
While the sauce is reducing, place the chicken onto a serving plate.
Taste the sauce to correct the seasonings.
Add the parsley and the remaining butter.
Remove the pan from the heat and swirl until the butter is melted.
Spoon the sauce over the chicken and serve.
Serves four, two pieces of chicken per person.

†If fresh shitake mushrooms are available, they are wonderful in this dish. Just be careful when cooking them, as they are much drier than regular mushrooms.

SESAME CHICKEN

6 tablespoons sesame seeds
6 tablespoons toasted unsalted peanuts
1/2 cup whole wheat flour (divided)
4 double chicken breasts
salt, pepper
1 or 2 eggs
1 or 2 teaspoons water
3 to 4 tablespoons oil
1 1/2 tablespoons sesame oil

Toast the sesame seeds in a 375 degree oven for ten to fifteen minutes. Or use a microwave oven for three to four minutes on high power, stirring once halfway. Cool them a little.
Place the peanuts along with one-third cup of the whole wheat flour into a food processor or blender. Grind until fairly fine.
Add the sesame seeds and one-quarter teaspoon salt and process together for about ten seconds.
Remove and place the mixture into a flat pan or dish.
Skin and bone the chicken breasts. Pound them a little to flatten and even them out.
Sprinkle with salt and pepper and dredge the breasts lightly in the remaining whole wheat flour.
Mix the egg with a teaspoon of water. Begin with one egg, if you need more egg wash, then use the second one. One at a time, dip the breasts into the egg wash, then coat with the sesame mixture.
Place the coated chicken breasts onto a sheet of waxed paper once they are finished.
The chicken can be refrigerated for up to a few hours at this point. The coating will adhere better if the chicken breasts are refrigerated for about thirty minutes before they are cooked.
Heat the two oils in a large frying pan. Add the chicken and saute over a moderately high heat for about five minutes on each side, until the crust is nicely browned and the chicken is tender.
Sesame chicken is good served either hot or cold.
Serves four.

CHICKEN WITH PEANUTS

2 whole chicken breasts
2 tablespoons rice wine or sherry
1 tablespoon soy sauce
1 teaspoon sesame oil
2 teaspoons egg white
1 teaspoon sugar
3 tablespoons cornstarch
3 to 4 tablespoons oil
1 cup raw peanuts†
5 slices ginger root, lightly crushed
5 large cloves garlic, lightly crushed
7 or 8 dried chili peppers
1 green pepper, diced
1 red pepper, diced
2 carrots, cut into julienne
4 tablespoons Hoisin sauce
8 scallions, cut into half-inch pieces
1 cup snow pea pods, strings removed

Skin and bone the chicken breasts. Cut the meat into one inch dice.
Place the chicken into a small bowl and add the rice wine, soy sauce, sesame oil, egg white and sugar.
Mix well to coat the meat, then stir in the cornstarch. Reserve until needed.
Add the oil to a large frying pan or wok.
Add the raw peanuts and stir-fry for a minute or two, just until the nuts are lightly browned.
Remove, using a slotted spoon and reserve.
Add the sliced ginger, garlic and dried peppers to the oil.
Cook and stir for a few minutes, pressing hard on the garlic and ginger to release their flavors into the oil. The peppers will turn black.
Be careful, the fumes can be very pungent.
Remove and discard the garlic, ginger and peppers, using a slotted spoon to keep as much of the flavored oil in the pan as possible.
Add the chicken to the pan and stir-fry for two minutes, until the meat turns white in color.
Add the green and red peppers along with the carrot. Cook, stirring, for two minutes.
Pour in the Hoisen sauce and mix well.

Add the scallions, the peanuts and the snow pea pods. Stir-fry for a half minute, just to heat, and serve immediately.
This dish serves four as a main course, or more if served with other dishes as part of a Chinese dinner.

†Toasted unsalted peanuts can be used. Do not cook them separately as you would the raw ones. Skip this step and add them in with the carrots and the peppers.

CHICKEN LIVERS WITH MUSHROOMS

7 or 8 dried mushrooms
1/2 cup warm water
1 1/2 pounds chicken livers
salt, pepper
flour for dredging
3 tablespoons oil
3 slices bacon, diced
1 large onion, chopped
2 cloves garlic, minced
1/2 teaspoon dried thyme
1/2 cup chicken stock
1/2 cup dry Marsala
1 teaspoon tomato paste
1 tablespoon chopped fresh parsley

Soak the dried mushrooms in the water for at least thirty minutes. Squeeze dry and slice the mushrooms, reserving the liquid.
Rinse and dry the livers, removing any green spots and membranes.
Sprinkle with salt and pepper and dredge them lightly in the flour.
Heat the oil in a large frying pan.
Add the livers and cook, turning, over high heat, for one minute only, just until they are browned.
Remove with a slotted spoon and reserve.
Discard the oil from the pan.
Add the bacon, onion and dried mushrooms and cook for a few minutes over medium heat, until the bacon begins to crisp and the onions turn golden.
Add the garlic and the thyme to the pan and cook for another half-minute.
Deglaze the pan with the stock, wine and reserved mushroom liquid.
Stir in the tomato paste.
Cook the sauce over high heat for a few minutes, so that it is reduced by about one-third. Taste to correct the seasonings.
Add the livers back to the pan and simmer them for just a few minutes. You want them to remain pink inside, since they taste better this way.
Sprinkle with the chopped parsley and serve immediately.
Serves four.

CHICKEN BREASTS SAMANTHA

SESAME CHICKEN, SWEET AND SOUR EGGPLANT, SNOW PEA PODS WITH ALMONDS

CHICKEN LIVERS STROGANOFF

1 1/2 pounds chicken livers
salt, pepper
2 to 3 tablespoons oil
2 tablespoons butter
1 large onion, chopped
6 to 8 mushrooms, sliced
1 large clove garlic, minced
1 teaspoon paprika
1/2 cup white wine
1/2 cup chicken or beef stock
1/2 cup sour cream
1 teaspoon flour
1 tablespoon chopped fresh dill
2 tablespoons toasted sliced almonds

Rinse and dry the livers well, removing any green spots or membranes.
Sprinkle with salt and pepper.
Heat the oil in a large frying pan.
Add the livers and saute them over high heat, for just a minute on each side, in order to brown them.
Remove with a slotted spoon and reserve.
Discard any oil remaining in the pan.
Add the butter and the onions to the pan. Saute for a few minutes, until the onions are golden.
Add the mushrooms and sprinkle with salt and pepper. Cook until the mushrooms have given up their liquid and are dry.
Mix in the garlic and cook for thirty seconds, then stir in the paprika.
Pour in the wine and the stock, scraping the bottom of the pan well.
Cook the sauce for about five minutes in order to reduce and concentrate the flavors.
Mix together the sour cream and the flour and stir into the sauce.
Add back the chicken livers and cook for just a few minutes. Be careful not to overcook the livers. They taste better when still pink inside.
Stir in the chopped dill.
Spoon onto a serving plate and sprinkle with the toasted almonds. Serve immediately.
Serves four.

CORNISH HENS WITH GREEN PEPPERCORN BUTTER

2 cornish hens
2/3 teaspoon green peppercorns
4 tablespoons butter, softened
2 tablespoons chopped fresh parsley
1/4 cup fresh bread crumbs
pinch ground cinnamon
1 teaspoon Dijon mustard
1 tablespoon chopped shallots
salt, pepper
1 tablespoon oil

Cut the cornish hens in half, lengthwise. With your fingers, loosen the skin from the flesh, leaving it attached at the back, the bottom of the leg and the wing.
Crush the green peppercorns and chop them finely.
Combine the softened butter with the green peppercorns, parsley, bread crumbs, cinnamon, mustard and shallots.
Mix well and add salt and pepper to taste.
Divide in quarters and press this seasoned butter between the flesh and the skin of the hens as evenly as possible.
Lightly oil the bottom of a low sided roasting pan.
Place the hens in the pan, skin side up.
Sprinkle with salt and pepper and rub the skins with a very light coating of oil.
The hens can be refrigerated for an hour or two at this point, or they can be roasted immediately.
Place into a preheated 425 degree oven and roast for about thirty-five minutes, or until the hens are tender and the skin is brown and crisp.
Serves four, one-half hen per person.
This herb butter is also excellent with chicken. The amount given in this recipe is enough for one three to three and one-half pound broiler. Cut in half for roasting, then into quarters for serving.

ROAST DUCK WITH LINGONBERRIES

two 4 1/2 to 5 pound ducks
1 large onion, coarsely chopped
4 cloves garlic, lightly crushed
8 parsley sprigs
salt, pepper
water as needed
Sauce:
3 tablespoons butter
2 tablespoons sugar
2 tablespoons wine vinegar
1/2 teaspoon Madras curry powder
1 cup duck stock
2 tablespoons heavy cream
salt, pepper
1/4 cup canned lingonberries, with juice

Rinse and dry the ducks. Fold back the wing tips.
Sprinkle the inside cavities with salt and pepper and place half the onion, garlic and parsley into each.
Sprinkle the skin with salt and pepper.
You can truss the ducks or not. It does not make too much difference, unless you plan to present them whole to your company before carving.
Place the ducks, breast side down, into a roasting pan. Fill the pan with about an inch of water.
Roast the ducks in a preheated 425 degree oven for one hour.
Remove the pan from the oven and drain off most of the liquid.
Turn the ducks breast side up and continue to roast, basting as necessary, for about forty-five minutes or until the meat is tender and the ducks are nicely browned.
Remove from the oven and allow the ducks to rest for about ten minutes before carving.
While the ducks are roasting, prepare the sauce.
Place two tablespoons of the butter, along with the sugar and the vinegar into a small saucepan.
Heat until the mixture takes on a light brown color, stirring occasionally.
Be careful not to burn the sugar, as you will spoil the taste of the sauce. In case you do, discard and begin again.
Stir in the curry powder and cook for a few seconds.
Then stir in the stock and the cream. Bring the sauce to a boil and add salt and pepper to taste.
The sauce can be completed to this point and finished while the ducks are resting.
When ready to serve, bring the sauce to a boil again and add the lingonberries. Cook for a half a minute, just to heat.
Turn off the heat and add the remaining butter.
Swirl the pan until the butter is melted, this will thicken the sauce.
To serve the ducks, cut into quarters. Or remove the breasts and the legs and just serve them alone, it all depends on how fancy you want to be. I like to chew on the bones.
Spoon some of the sauce over the ducks and serve the rest in a sauceboat.
Serves four to six, depending upon appetites.

DUCK STOCK†,

giblets and necks from two ducks
2 tablespoons oil
1 onion, chopped
1 stalk celery, chopped
1 carrot, chopped
2 tablespoons flour
1 cup white wine
3 cups water or chicken stock
2 teaspoons tomato paste
1/2 teaspoon dried thyme
1 bay leaf
3 fresh parsley sprigs
salt, pepper

Chop the necks and giblets (not the livers) from the ducks.
Heat the oil in a saucepan. Add and cook the necks and giblets, stirring occasionally, until they are well browned.
Add the chopped onion, celery and carrot to the pan. Cook for about five minutes, stirring occasionally.
Sprinkle the meat and vegetables with the flour and stir it in well.
Deglaze the pan with the white wine, scraping the bottom well. Stir in the water or stock and the tomato paste.
Bring the liquid to a boil and skim off any foam or scum that rises to the top of the stock.
Add in the thyme, bay leaf, parsley sprigs and salt

and pepper.
Cover, leaving the lid ajar and simmer the stock for one and one-half to two hours.
Strain the stock, pressing the vegetables well to remove all the liquid.
Cool and remove any fat that forms on the surface of the stock.
The stock can be refrigerated for a few days or it can be frozen.
Use this stock as a base to make a sauce for roast duck.
This recipe makes about one and one-half cups of stock.

†Reprinted from "COOKING FOR THE '80's"

A RAISIN AND ONION SAUCE FOR ROAST DUCK

2 dozen pearl onions†
1/4 cup raisins
1 cup water
1 1/2 tablespoons butter
1 1/2 tablespoon Cognac
1/4 cup Madeira
3/4 cup duck stock, page 112
salt, pepper

Place the onions, raisins and water into a saucepan along with one tablespoon of the butter.
Cook slowly without a lid until the water evaporates and the onions are glazed.
By the time the water is gone, the onions usually are tender. If not, add a little more water and continue to cook until they are done.
Pour in one tablespoon of the Cognac.
Add the Madeira and scrape the bottom of the pan well to deglaze.
Add the duck stock and simmer until the sauce is reduced by one-third. Taste to correct the seasoning.
The sauce can be prepared to this point and refrigerated for up to a day or two before serving.
When ready to serve, heat the sauce to the boiling point.
Stir in the remaining Cognac and check the seasonings again.
Remove the pan from the heat and add the rest of the butter. Swirl the pan until the butter is melted, then serve.
Enough sauce for two roasted ducks.
See the previous recipe for roasting ducks.

†Frozen pearl onions can be used, if necessary, but the fresh ones will make a better tasting sauce. They will not take as long to cook as fresh onions, nor are they as sweet.
Use one cup of frozen onions, but decrease the amount of water to just one-half cup. Add one-half teaspoon sugar to the mixture to help carmelize the sauce. You may also want to add an extra spoon or two of Madeira at the end to help make up the flavor difference.

DUCK WITH BAMBOO SHOOTS

3 to 4 tablespoons oil
2 tablespoons minced garlic
2 tablespoons minced ginger root
2 green peppers, sliced thin
1 eight-ounce can bamboo shoots, sliced†
12 ounces cooked duck, shredded
8 scallions, cut into one inch lengths
Sauce:
2 tablespoons soy sauce
2 tablespoons Sherry
3 tablespoons oyster sauce
1/2 cup duck or chicken stock
1 teaspoon cornstarch
2 tablespoons water

Mix the soy sauce, Sherry, oyster sauce and the stock in a small bowl and set aside.
Stir the cornstarch into the water and reserve.
Heat the oil in a frying pan or wok.
Add the garlic and the ginger and cook for one minute, stirring constantly.
Add the green pepper and stir-fry for a half a minute.
Stir in the bamboo shoots, the duck and the scallions.
Pour in the prepared sauce and stir-fry for two minutes.
Make sure that the sauce is boiling, then stir in the cornstarch thickening.
Cook for another thirty seconds, or until the sauce thickens.
Serve immediately.
Serves four as a main course or more when served along with other dishes as part of a Chinese dinner.

†A can of water chestnuts can be substituted for the bamboo shoots if necessary.

DUCK WITH BAMBOO SHOOTS

OUTDOOR MARKET, INDIA

MEATS

BRAISED BEEF WITH CUMIN AND CORIANDER

2 pounds beef for stew (chuck)
2 teaspoons cumin seed
2 teaspoons coriander seed
salt, pepper
2 to 3 tablespoons oil
1 large onion, chopped
3 or 4 cloves garlic, minced
2 teaspoons paprika
1 1/2 cups white wine
1 1/2 cups beef stock

Trim the meat of all visible fat and cut it into one-inch cubes.
Toast the cumin and the coriander seeds in a 375 degree oven for ten to fifteen minutes or in a microwave oven for three minutes on high power. Let cool a little, then grind. If you are using ground cumin and coriander, just skip this step.
Sprinkle the meat with salt and pepper.
Heat the oil in a large pan.
Add the meat and brown well on both sides, then remove and reserve.
Drain and discard all but a tablespoon of the fat.
Add the onion to the pan and saute for a few minutes, until golden.
Add the garlic, then the cumin, coriander, paprika and some salt and pepper.
Deglaze the pan with the wine and the stock, scraping the bottom well.
Bring the sauce to a boil then return the meat.
Cover the pan and simmer until the meat is tender, stirring occasionally.
This should take one to one and one-half hours, depending on the cut of the meat used.
The sauce will have reduced greatly when finished.
Serve with rice, noodles or a potato.
This dish can be reheated. Add a little water, if necessary, to keep the meat from sticking to the pan. It can also be frozen. Defrost before reheating.
Serves four.
Alternate: Three pounds of lamb shoulder can be substituted for the beef in this recipe. Reduce the cumin, coriander and paprika to one teaspoon each. Use chicken instead of beef stock and reduce the liquid to half (3/4 cup each of white wine and chicken stock).

BRAISED BEEF WITH CUMIN AND CORIANDER, SESAME NOODLES AND JULIENNE OF CARROTS WITH MINT

BEEF STEW WITH LEEKS AND POTATOES

2 pounds beef for stew (chuck)
salt, pepper
2 to 3 tablespoons oil
1 large onion, chopped
white of 1 large or 2 small leeks, chopped
2 large cloves garlic, minced
1/2 teaspoon dried caraway thyme†
1/2 teaspoon dried savory
2 cups beef stock
2 large potatoes, peeled and sliced
water, as needed
1 tablespoon chopped fresh parsley

Trim the beef well and cut into one inch cubes. Sprinkle with salt and pepper.
Heat the oil in a large saute pan. Add the beef and brown well on all sides.
Remove the meat and reserve.
Discard most of the oil from the pan.
Add the onions and the leeks and saute for a few minutes, until they are soft.
Stir in the garlic, thyme, savory, salt and pepper.
Pour in the stock, scraping the bottom of the pan well.
Return the meat to the pan. Cover and simmer for about forty-five minutes, or until the meat is almost tender, stirring occasionally.
Add the potatoes to the pan. Cover and continue to cook for about twenty minutes, stirring often, until the potatoes are done. Add water as needed to keep the potatoes from sticking to the pan.
Taste to correct the seasonings, stir in the parsley and serve.
The stew can be reheated or even frozen, but the potatoes will tend to fall apart. It will still taste fine, but it will look messy.
Serves four.

†Regular thyme can be used instead.

BEEF KABOBS

2 pounds beef, cut into cubes
1 cup water
1 tablespoon butter
12 large mushrooms
salt
1 large onion
1 or 2 green peppers
6 slices bacon
Marinade:
1/2 cup salad oil
1/4 cup tarragon wine vinegar
3 tablespoons lemon juice
2 tablespoons Dijon mustard
2 tablespoons soy sauce
1 large clove garlic, minced
1 large onion, sliced
1/2 teaspoon salt
pepper to taste

Combine all of the marinade ingredients in a bowl. Stir well, cover and refrigerate for a few hours in order to blend the flavors.
The marinade can be made the day before it is to be used. Refrigerate, covered, until needed.
Place the cubed beef into the marinade, turning well to coat all the meat.
Cover the dish and allow the meat to marinate at room temperature for about four hours or refrigerate overnight.
Bring the water to a boil. Add the butter, mushrooms and a pinch of salt.
Simmer for about three minutes, just long enough to partially pre-cook the mushrooms.
Allow them to cool in the cooking liquid.
Cut the onion into quarters and separate the pieces.
Slice the green peppers into large dice.
Cut the bacon strips in half, crosswise, and fold them over once.
Remove the meat from the marinade and dry a little for easier handling.
Assemble the kabobs on skewers by alternating pieces of meat, onion, green pepper, bacon and mushrooms.
The skewers can be prepared early in the day and refrigerated until ready to cook.
To cook outdoors, heat a barbeque and grill the kabobs, turning, for about fifteen minutes. The beef will be rare. Cook a few minutes longer if you prefer your meat more well done.
The kabobs can also be cooked under a broiler or pan sauteed in a little oil.
Enough to fill four large or six small kabobs.
Serve with a rice pilaf.
The marinade will hold for two or three days in the refrigerator and can be re-used once during that time.
Serves four.

STEAK WITH A GREEN PEPPERCORN SAUCE

4 tenderloin or sirloin strip steaks, cut about one inch thick
salt, pepper
3 to 4 tablespoons oil
1/4 cup Cognac or brandy
1/4 cup water
1/2 cup heavy cream
1 tablespoon green peppercorns, lightly crushed
1/2 cup sour cream
1 teaspoon flour

Trim off any extra fat from the steaks. Sprinkle with salt and pepper.
Heat the oil in a frying pan.
Add the steaks and cook them for four minutes on each side over high heat.
The steaks will be rare. Cook a minute or two longer if you like your meat more well done.
Remove the steaks to a serving plate and keep warm.

Discard any oil remaining in the pan.
Add the Cognac, water, heavy cream and lightly crushed green peppercorns, scraping well to deglaze the bottom of the pan.
Mix the sour cream with the flour and stir this into the sauce.
Add salt and freshly ground black pepper to taste.
Simmer the sauce for a minute or two. If it gets too thick, do not be afraid to add another spoon or two of water.
Pour the sauce over the steaks and serve.
Serves four.
If your steaks are very large, you may want to increase the amount of sauce.
This recipe is enough for four moderate sized steaks.

BROILED STEAK WITH A MUSTARD AND GARLIC TOPPING

4 rib steaks, three-quarters to one inch thick each
3 large cloves garlic, minced
3 tablespoons Dijon mustard
2 tablespoons chopped fresh parsley
1 teaspoon salt
1/2 teaspoon ground black peppercorns
2 tablespoons shallots, chopped fine
2 tablespoons dried bread crumbs

Trim the steaks well, removing most of the exterior fat.
Mix together the garlic, mustard, parsley, salt, pepper and shallots in a small bowl and reserve.
This topping can be prepared early in the day. Cover tightly and refrigerate until needed.
Turn your broiler to medium-high. Place the steaks in a broiling pan.
When the broiler is hot, grill the steaks on one side for eight to ten minutes for rare meat. Grill a few minutes longer if you prefer your meat more well done.
Remove the pan from the broiler and turn the steaks over.
Spread them evenly with the garlic and mustard topping and sprinkle with the bread crumbs.
Return the steaks to the broiler for five minutes, or until the topping is nicely browned. Serve immediately.
Serves four.

BEEF AND VEGETABLES IN AN OYSTER SAUCE

10 to 12 dried Chinese mushrooms
1/2 cup warm water
1 pound thinly sliced flank steak
2 dozen snow pea pods
3 to 4 tablespoons oil
1 medium onion, sliced thin
2 cloves garlic, minced
1 1/2 teaspoons minced ginger root
2 carrots, cut into julienne
2 green or red peppers, sliced thin
8 ounces water chestnuts, sliced thin

Marinade:
1 teaspoon soy sauce
2 tablespoons oyster sauce
2 teaspoons rice wine or Sherry
1/4 teaspoon pepper
2 teaspoons cornstarch

Sauce:
1 teaspoon soy sauce
1 teaspoon rice wine or Sherry
pinch sugar
2 tablespoons oyster sauce
1/4 cup reserved mushroom liquid

Soak the dried mushrooms in the water for thirty minutes.
Remove and squeeze dry, reserving a quarter of a cup of the liquid.
Cut off and discard the hard tips of the mushrooms. Slice into thin strips.
Cut the beef into strips two inches long by one-half inch wide and place into a bowl.
Add the marinade ingredients to the meat and mix well. Let sit while you chop and prepare the rest of the ingredients.
String the snow pea pods and cut them in half on the diagonal.
Mix all of the sauce ingredients together in a small bowl and reserve.
Heat two tablespoons of the oil in a wok or a large frying pan.
Add the meat and stir-fry for two to three minutes, just until browned.
Remove and reserve.
Pour the rest of the oil into the pan.
Add the sliced onion, garlic and ginger. Stir-fry for one minute.
Add, in order, the dried mushrooms, carrots, and the green or red pepper.
Cook for one minute, then add the water chestnuts and the snow pea pods.
Return the meat to the pan, cook thirty seconds.
Pour in the sauce, bring it to a boil and serve immediately.
This recipe will serve four as a main dish, or more along with other dishes as part of a Chinese meal.

SZECHWAN BEEF WITH PEPPERS

1 pound flank steak, sliced thin
1 1/2 green peppers
1 1/2 red peppers
6 scallions
2 carrots, cut into julienne
1 large onion, sliced thin
3 to 4 cloves garlic, minced
1 teaspoon crushed ginger root
3 to 4 tablespoons oil

Marinade:
2 teaspoons cornstarch
pinch sugar
1/4 teaspoon pepper
2 tablespoons soy sauce
2 tablespoons rice wine or Sherry
2 teaspoons oil

BEEF KABOBS

BROILED STEAK WITH A MUSTARD AND GARLIC TOPPING AND OVEN BROWNED POTATO SLICES

SZECHWAN BEEF WITH PEPPERS

CHILI WITH BEANS

Sauce:
1 teaspoon cornstarch
4 teaspoons rice wine or Sherry
2 tablespoons soy sauce
2 teaspoons black bean sauce with chili paste
1 teaspoon sugar
1 teaspoon vinegar
1/4 cup water
1 teaspoon sesame oil

Cut the beef into strips one half inch wide by two to three inches in length and place into a bowl.
Add the marinade ingredients to the meat and mix well. Let sit while you ready the rest of the ingredients.
Cut the peppers into quarters and then into slices one-half inch wide.
Cut the scallion greens into one inch pieces. Chop the whites into quarter inch dice.
Mix all the sauce ingredients together in a bowl and reserve.
Heat two tablespoons of the oil in a wok or frying pan.
Add the meat and stir-fry until browned. Remove with a slotted spoon and reserve.
Add the remaining oil to the pan along with the garlic, ginger and whites of the scallions. Stir-fry for one minute.
Add the onion, green and red peppers and the carrots. Stir-fry for one minute.
Add the scallion greens and stir-fry for another half minute.
Return the meat to the pan.
Pour in the sauce and cook, stirring, for another minute or two.
Serve immediately.
This dish will serve four as a main course, or more if served with other dishes as part of a Chinese dinner.

CHILI WITH BEANS

1 tablespoon oil
1 medium onion, chopped
1/2 pound ground beef
2 large cloves garlic, minced
salt, pepper
1 1/2 teaspoons chili powder
1/2 teaspoon ground cumin
1 teaspoon dried oregano
1/2 teaspoon paprika
1/4 teaspoon cayenne pepper†
2 cups plum tomatoes, peeled and diced
1 tablespoon tomato paste
pinch sugar
2 cups canned kidney beans, with liquid
2 cups canned pinto beans, with liquid
2 tablespoons corn meal

Heat the oil in a large saute pan. Add the onion and cook for a few minutes, until golden.
Add the beef and the garlic and sprinkle with salt and pepper.
Cook, stirring to break apart the meat, until it is lightly browned.
Add the chili powder, cumin, oregano, paprika and cayenne pepper to the pan.
Cook for one minute, then stir in the tomatoes, tomato paste and the sugar.
Stir in both kinds of beans along with any liquid in the cans.
Bring the mixture to a boil and add salt to taste.
Cover and simmer for about one hour and fifteen minutes, stirring occasionally.
Mix in the cornmeal and continue to simmer for about ten minutes, stirring often. The cornmeal serves to mellow the taste of the chili and acts as a thickener.
Taste to correct the seasonings and serve with boiled rice, corn chips and shredded Monterey Jack cheese, if you like.
The chili reheats well and can also be frozen.
Serves four.

†More cayenne pepper can be added if you prefer a very hot chili.

SPICED MEAT LOAF

1 pound ground beef (chuck)
1 small onion, chopped fine
1 clove garlic, minced fine
1/2 teaspoon ground coriander
1/4 teaspoon ground cumin
1/4 teaspoon cayenne pepper
1/2 teaspoon salt
pinch grated nutmeg
pinch ground cardamom
1 teaspoon tomato paste
1 egg
1/2 cup dried bread crumbs

Place all the ingredients into a bowl and mix together well. This is easiest done with your hands.
Form the meat mixture into a loaf shape about eight inches long.
Place onto an oiled baking pan with low sides.
I prefer to use a baking pan instead of traditional meat loaf pan. The fat can drain off more easily while cooking and the finished loaf will be crustier.
Score the top of the loaf lightly on the diagonal in both directions.
The meat loaf can be baked immediately or covered and refrigerated for a day.
Bake in a preheated 375 degree oven for about fifty minutes, or until the meat is well cooked and the outside crust is nice and brown.
Allow the meat loaf to rest for about ten minutes, then slice and serve.
Good plain or with a tomato sauce.
The cooked meat loaf will keep for several days in the refrigerator.
It can also be frozen.
Leftovers are good cold or hot. If reheating, I

prefer to cut the meat loaf into slices and saute them in a little butter or oil until hot and crunchy. Serves four.

MOUSSAKA

1 large eggplant
2 eggs
1/2 cup yogurt or sour cream
1/2 cup grated Parmesan cheese†
1/4 cup dried bread crumbs
Sauce:
2 tablespoons oil
1 large onion, chopped
6 or 8 mushrooms, sliced
2 cloves garlic, minced
1 pound ground beef or lamb
salt, pepper
1 cup plum tomatoes, peeled and chopped
1 teaspoon tomato paste
1/4 cup chopped fresh parsley
1 teaspoon dried oregano

First prepare the sauce. Heat the oil in a frying pan. Add the onions and cook until they are golden.
Add the mushrooms and continue to cook, stirring occasionally, until they are dry.
Add the garlic, then the beef. Sprinkle with salt and pepper and cook, stirring to separate the meat, until it is browned. This should take about five minutes.
Add the chopped tomatoes, tomato paste, parsley and oregano.
Cook for about fifteen minutes, stirring often. The sauce should be thick.
Taste to correct the seasonings.
The meat sauce can be prepared to this point and refrigerated for a day or two, or it can even be frozen.
You can peel the eggplant or leave the skin on, as you prefer.
Cut the eggplant into quarter-inch thick slices, lengthwise.
Layer half the slices in a large buttered casserole. Spread with half of the meat sauce.
Layer the rest of the slices in the casserole, then cover them evenly with the remaining sauce.
Mix together the eggs and the yogurt. Pour this evenly over the top.
Sprinkle with the grated cheese and the bread crumbs.
The casserole can be prepared early in the day, covered and refrigerated. It can also be frozen, if necessary.
Bake in a preheated 350 degree oven for sixty to sixty-five minutes (about ten minutes longer if cold), until the eggplant is tender and the topping browned.
Serves four to six.
Alternate:
Peel and cut the eggplant into one inch dice. Steam until barely cooked.
Drain well and stir into the meat mixture. Cover with the topping and bake for about fifty minutes.

†Or use half Swiss and half Parmesan cheese.

BEEF TONGUE WITH A RAISIN SAUCE

1 fresh beef tongue
water to cover
1 large onion, chopped
1 large carrot, chopped
2 stalks celery, chopped
1 or 2 teaspoons salt
1 large clove garlic
5 or 6 sprigs fresh parsley
3 or 4 sprigs fresh thyme, or 1/2 teaspoon dried
10 peppercorns, crushed
6 allspice berries, crushed
Raisin Sauce

Place the tongue into a large pot and fill with cold water to cover.
Bring the water to a boil and skim the surface of the water to remove any scum that forms.
Boil for five or ten minutes and skim again.
Add the rest of the ingredients (except for the raisin sauce) and simmer until the meat is tender. This can take anywhere from two and one-half to three and one-half hours, depending on the size of the tongue. Add water as needed to keep the meat immersed.
Lift out the tongue and let it cool until it can be handled.
Remove all the skin as well as the gristle and fat found at the back portion.
Strain and save the cooking liquid for preparing the sauce or use as a base for a meat soup.
The tongue can be sliced and reheated directly in the raisin sauce. Or use some of the cooking liquid.
One beef tongue usually serves six.
Alternate:
Two calves tongues can be substituted. They are much smaller and do not take nearly as long to cook. Both beef and calves tongue are good served with the raisin sauce.

RAISIN SAUCE

1/2 cup orange juice
4 teaspoons lemon juice
1 tablespoon cornstarch
1/4 cup dark brown sugar
1/2 cup cooking liquid from tongue†
1/2 cup water
1 teaspoon Dijon mustard
1/8 teaspoon cinnamon
1/2 cup raisins

Place all of the ingredients except the raisins into a food processor or blender.
Puree well and pour into a saucepan.
Add the raisins. Heat the sauce, stirring

BEEF TONGUE WITH A RAISIN SAUCE

occasionally, until it is thick.
Serve hot with sliced tongue.
The sauce can be reheated and even frozen.
This recipe will make about one and one-half cups sauce, enough for one beef tongue.

†Beef stock can be substituted for the cooking liquid.

VEAL CUTLETS WITH HAZELNUTS

8 veal cutlets
salt, pepper
flour for dredging
3 to 4 tablespoons oil
2 tablespoons chopped shallots
1 tablespoon ground hazelnuts
1/2 cup white wine
1/2 cup chicken stock
2 tablespoons Cognac or brandy
1 tablespoon chopped fresh parsley
1 1/2 teaspoons chopped fresh tarragon or 1/2 teaspoon dried
1/2 tablespoon butter

Pound the veal cutlets until they are very thin and sprinkle with salt and pepper.
Dredge lightly in the flour.
Heat the oil in a frying pan.
Saute the veal cutlets for a minute or two on each side, until lightly browned. If they are very thin, this is enough cooking time.
As they finish cooking, remove the cutlets to a platter and keep warm.
Continue until all the cutlets are cooked, adding more oil to the pan, if needed.
Discard all but about a teaspoon of oil from the pan.
Add the shallots and cook for one minute.
Add the ground hazelnuts and cook, stirring for another minute.
Deglaze the pan with the wine, stock and Cognac.
Cook over high heat until the sauce is reduced by half, stirring often.
Stir in the parsley and the tarragon and taste to correct the seasonings.
Remove the pan from the heat and add the butter.
Swirl until it is melted, then pour the sauce over the veal and serve immediately.
Serves four.

VEAL WITH LEMON

8 veal cutlets
salt, pepper
flour for dredging
3 tablespoons oil, or more if needed
1 medium onion, chopped
1 tablespoon butter
10 mushrooms, sliced
1 clove garlic, minced
1/2 cup Vermouth or white wine
1/2 cup veal or chicken stock
2 tablespoons lemon juice
1/2 tablespoon chopped fresh parsley
1/2 tablespoon chopped fresh tarragon†

Pound the veal until the slices are very thin.
Sprinkle with salt and pepper and dredge them lightly in the flour.
Heat the oil in a large frying pan and brown the cutlets for just a minute or two on both sides.
Remove and reserve the meat.
Continue until all the cutlets are browned, adding more oil to the pan if needed, to keep the veal from sticking.
When finished, discard any oil remaining in the pan.
Add the butter and the onion and saute for a few minutes until golden.
Add the mushrooms, sprinkle with salt and pepper and cook until they are dry.
Stir in the garlic and cook for a half a minute longer.
Deglaze the pan with the wine, stock and lemon juice, scraping the bottom well.
Reduce the liquid to half over high heat.
Add the fresh herbs to the pan and return the veal.
Simmer for a few minutes, turning, just until the veal is hot and tender.
Taste to correct the seasonings and serve.
Serves four.
Alternate:
Turkey breast can be substituted for the veal in this recipe. Do not reduce the sauce by half, but add the turkey back to the pan after deglazing and simmer for five or six minutes, turning, until tender.

†One-half teaspoon dried tarragon can be substituted for fresh. Add before deglazing the pan.

VEAL CUTLETS WITH HAZELNUTS AND CARROTS a LA VARENNE

VEAL WITH SAGE, HAM AND MUSHROOMS

4 large loin or rib veal chops
salt, pepper
flour for dredging
2 to 3 tablespoons oil
1 small onion, chopped
1 ounce diced boiled ham
1 large clove garlic, minced
6 mushrooms, sliced
4 or 5 fresh sage leaves, chopped
1/2 cup chicken stock
1/4 cup beef stock†
1/2 cup peas

Trim the chops of any visible fat. Sprinkle with salt and pepper and dredge them lightly in the flour.
Heat the oil in a frying pan. Add the chops and brown well on both sides.
Remove and reserve.
Discard all but a scant tablespoon of oil from the pan.
Add the onion and the ham and cook for a few minutes, until the onion is golden.
Add the mushrooms and continue to cook for another few minutes, until the mushrooms give up most of their liquid.
Add the garlic and the sage leaves, then deglaze the pan with the chicken and beef stock.
Return the meat to the pan, cover and simmer until the veal is tender, about twenty to thirty minutes.
If using fresh peas, add to the pan after fifteen minutes.
If using frozen, defrost and add just a few minutes before the veal is done.
Taste to correct the seasonings and serve with buttered noodles.
Serves four.

†All chicken stock can be used, but the combination will make a better tasting sauce.

VEAL WITH MUSHROOMS AND TARRAGON

4 thick loin or rib veal chops
2 to 3 tablespoons oil
salt, pepper
flour for dredging + 1/2 teaspoon
2 tablespoons butter
3 tablespoons chopped shallots
16 mushrooms, sliced (about 3 cups)
2/3 cup white wine
2/3 cup chicken stock
1/4 cup heavy cream
2 tablespoons sour cream
2 tablespoons chopped fresh tarragon

Sprinkle the veal chops with salt and pepper and dredge them lightly in the flour.
Heat the oil in a frying pan and add the chops. Cook until they are lightly browned on both sides, then remove and reserve.
Pour out and discard the oil.
Add the butter to the pan, then the shallots and cook for a minute or two.
Add the mushrooms, sprinkle with salt and pepper and continue to cook until the mushrooms have given up all their liquid.
Pour in the wine and the stock, stirring well to deglaze the bottom of the pan.
Return the chops and cover the pan. Simmer, turning a few times, until the meat is tender. This should take about fifteen minutes.
Remove the chops to a serving plate and keep warm.
Add the heavy cream to the sauce and stir well.
Mix the sour cream with the half teaspoon of flour, then stir this mixture into the sauce.
Cook for just a minute to heat well.
Stir in the fresh tarragon and taste to correct the seasonings.
Pour the sauce over the chops and serve immediately.
Serves four.
Alternates:
If fresh tarragon is not available, substitute a teaspoon or two of the dried, adding it to the pan before the wine and the stock. Sprinkle with a spoon or two of chopped fresh parsley at the end for color.
Chicken breasts (skinned and boned) can be substituted for the veal chops. Decrease the cooking time by about five minutes.

STUFFED VEAL CHOPS

4 thick rib veal chops
2 tablespoons chopped pistachios, skins removed
1 tablespoon chopped fresh parsley
1 tablespoon grated Swiss cheese
1/2 tablespoon raisins
1 tablespoon chopped shallots
salt, pepper
3 tablespoons oil
flour for dredging
1/2 cup white wine
1/2 cup veal or chicken stock
1 teaspoon lemon juice

Trim all visible fat from the veal chops. Cut a lengthwise pocket in the meaty portion of each chop.
Chop together the nuts, parsley, cheese, raisins and shallots. Use a large chefs knife or a food processor. Add some salt and pepper.
The stuffing mixture will be dry.
Divide into four portions and stuff some of the filling into the pocket of each chop.
Press down along the edges with your fingers to seal the chops.
The veal can be prepared to this point and refrigerated for a few hours until time to cook.

Heat the oil in a frying pan.
Sprinkle the chops with salt and pepper and dredge them lightly in the flour.
Brown on both sides, then remove and reserve the chops.
Pour out and discard any oil remaining in the pan.
Deglaze the pan with the wine and the stock, scraping the bottom well.
Add the lemon juice and return the chops to the pan.
Cover and simmer the chops for about twenty minutes, or until they are tender, turning once.
Taste the sauce to correct the seasonings and serve.
Serves four.

HUNGARIAN VEAL STEW

1 1/2 pounds veal for stew†
salt, pepper
2 to 3 tablespoons oil
2 slices bacon, diced
1 medium onion, sliced thin
10 to 12 mushrooms, sliced thin
1 large clove garlic, minced
1 teaspoon paprika
1/2 teaspoon dried marjoram
1 teaspoon tomato paste
2 tablespoons brandy
3/4 cup chicken or beef stock

Trim off any visible fat and cut the veal into one inch cubes.
Sprinkle with salt and pepper.
Heat the oil in a frying pan and brown the veal on all sides.
Remove and reserve the meat.
Discard any oil remaining in the pan.
Place the diced bacon and the onion into the pan.
Cook for a few minutes, until the onion is golden.
Add the mushrooms, sprinkle with salt and pepper and continue to cook until they are almost dry.
Add the garlic, cook for a half a minute, then stir in the paprika and the marjoram.
Cook for a few seconds, then add the tomato paste, brandy and stock. Scrape well to deglaze the bottom of the pan.
Add the veal back to the pan, cover and simmer until the meat is tender, stirring occasionally. This should take about forty to forty-five minutes.
Add a little water, if needed, to keep the meat from sticking.
Taste to correct the seasonings and serve. Good served with noodles.
Serves four.

†Or use whole loin, rib or shoulder veal chops. Loin or rib chops will take only about fifteen to twenty minutes to cook. Shoulder chops will take thirty minutes. The shoulder chops are more economical than loin or rib chops and I think taste better in this dish.

VEAL SHANKS WITH DRIED MUSHROOMS

12 dried Italian or Polish mushrooms
1 cup warm water
2 veal shanks, sawed into two inch pieces, crosswise
salt, pepper
3 tablespoons oil
2 ounces double smoked bacon, diced†
1 large onion, chopped
2 large cloves garlic, minced
1 teaspoon dried thyme
2/3 cup white wine
2/3 cup chicken stock
2 tablespoons brandy
1 tablespoon glace de viande or demi-glace (optional)
1 tablespoon butter
1 tablespoon chopped fresh tarragon or parsley

Soak the dried mushrooms in the cup of water for thirty minutes.
Squeeze dry, reserving the liquid. Cut the mushrooms into thin slices.
Sprinkle the veal shanks with salt and pepper and dredge them lightly in the flour.
Heat the oil in a pan large enough to hold all the meat in one layer.
Add the veal and saute until well browned on both sides.
Remove the meat and reserve.
Discard the oil remaining in the pan.
Add the diced bacon and the onion to the pan and saute for a few minutes, until the onion turns golden.
Stir in the garlic, dried mushrooms and the thyme.
Pour in the wine, the stock and the reserved mushroom liquid. Scrape well to loosen any residue that sticks to the bottom of the pan.
Add the brandy and the demi-glace, if using.
Return the veal to the pan. Cover and simmer for one hour, turning the meat once.
Add water, if needed, to keep the meat from sticking as it cooks.
Remove the veal from the pan and place on a serving plate.
You want a fairly thick sauce, so if there is a lot of liquid in the pan, boil down a little. Usually in this amount of time it is just about right.
Taste to correct the seasonings.
Add the butter and the tarragon to the sauce in the pan. Remove from the heat and swirl until the butter is melted.
Pour over the veal and serve.
The veal can be reheated. You may need to add a little water to keep it from sticking. It also freezes well.
This recipe will serve four to six portions, depending upon the size of the shanks.

†Regular bacon can be substituted for double smoked. Use four slices.

VEAL SHANKS SOUBISE

2 veal shanks, sawed into two inch pieces, crosswise
salt, pepper
flour for dredging
3 to 4 tablespoons oil
2 large onions, sliced (3 cups)
1/4 teaspoon grated nutmeg
1 1/2 cups chicken stock
3 tablespoons raw rice
2 bay leaves
3 tablespoons heavy cream

Sprinkle the veal shanks with salt and pepper and dredge them lightly in the flour.
Heat the oil in a pan large enough to hold all the meat in one layer.
Add the veal and brown well on both sides.
Remove the meat and reserve.
Discard all but one tablespoon of oil from the pan.
Add the sliced onions, sprinkle with a little salt, pepper and nutmeg.
Saute for a few minutes, until golden.
Pour in the stock, stirring well to deglaze the bottom of the pan.
Mix in the rice, add the bay leaves and return the veal to the pan.
Cover and simmer for forty-five minutes to one hour, or until the veal is tender, turning once.
Remove the meat and discard the bay leaves from the pan.
Cool the sauce for a few minutes, then puree in a food processor or blender.
Stir in the heavy cream. Taste to correct the seasonings.
Place the veal shanks back into the pan (or a serving casserole) and pour the sauce over them.
The recipe can be completed to this point and the casserole covered and refrigerated for up to two days. Allow to come to room temperature before reheating.
The veal can also be frozen. Reheat while still frozen, just double the time needed.
Heat the casserole (covered) in a preheated 375 degree oven for thirty to forty minutes, or until both the veal and the sauce are very hot.
Serves four to six portions, depending upon the size of the shanks.

STUFFED VEAL CHOPS

VEAL SHANKS WITH DRIED MUSHROOMS

CALVES LIVER WITH APPLES AND SPINACH CASSEROLE

CALVES LIVER WITH HERBS

4 slices calves liver, cut one-half inch thick
salt, pepper
flour for dredging
2 tablespoons oil
4 tablespoons butter
1 tablespoon chopped shallots
1/4 cup white wine
1/4 cup chicken stock
2 tablespoons Sherry wine vinegar
1 tablespoon chopped fresh savory or 1 teaspoon dried
2 tablespoons chopped fresh chives
2 tablespoons chopped fresh parsley

Remove any outer membrane from the liver. Rinse and dry the slices well.
Sprinkle the liver with salt and pepper and dredge lightly in the flour.
Heat the oil along with two tablespoons of the butter in a large frying pan.
Add the liver and cook for two minutes on each side. The slices should remain pink in the center, do not overcook.
Remove to a serving plate when done and keep warm.
Discard most of the fat remaining in the pan.
Add the shallots and cook for one minute. If using dried savory, add now.
Pour in the wine, the stock and the vinegar, scraping well to remove any residue stuck to the bottom of the pan.
Cook this sauce over high heat until reduced by half.
Add all of the fresh herbs and the remaining butter. Remove the pan from the heat and swirl until the butter is melted.
Taste to correct the seasonings.
Pour the sauce over the liver and serve immediately.
Serves four.
Alternate: Chicken livers can be substituted for the calves liver. Use one and one-half pounds for four people. The cooking time will be just a minute or two longer.

CALVES LIVER WITH APPLES

4 tablespoons butter
1/4 teaspoon ground cinnamon
large pinch grated nutmeg
2 small apples, peeled, cored and cut into 1/2 inch thick slices
2 tablespoons sugar
2 tablespoons wine vinegar
1/2 cup Madeira
1/2 cup chicken stock
1 tablespoon demi-glace or glace de viande
salt, pepper
4 thick slices calves liver
flour for dredging
2 to 3 tablespoons oil

First prepare the sauce. Melt three tablespoons of the butter in a frying pan.
Add the cinnamon, nutmeg and the apple slices. Saute, turning occasionally, for about five minutes. You want the apple slices to cook, but still remain firm.
Remove them with a slotted spoon and reserve.
Add the sugar and the vinegar to the pan and cook just until the mixture thickens and begins to turn brown.
Pour in the Madeira, stock and demi-glace, scraping the bottom of the pan well.
Season to taste with salt and pepper.
Continue to cook to reduce the volume of the sauce to half while preparing the liver.
Remove any outer membrane from the liver. Rinse and dry well.
Sprinkle the liver slices with salt and pepper and dredge them lightly in the flour.
Heat the oil in a separate frying pan.
Saute the liver over high heat for just about three minutes on each side, then remove and place onto a serving plate.
Do not overcook, the liver tastes best when still pink inside.
Add the apples back to the pan containing the sauce and cook just until they are hot. This should take only a minute.
Add the remaining butter to the sauce, remove from the heat and swirl the pan until the butter is melted.
Pour the sauce over the liver and serve.
Serves four.
Alternate: The liver can be broiled instead of sauteed. Omit the flour, but do rub the meat with a thin coating of oil to keep it moist while cooking.

BROILED LAMB CHOPS WITH CUMIN AND MUSTARD SEED

12 baby rib lamb chops, well trimmed†
1 teaspoon white mustard seeds
1/2 teaspoon toasted cumin seed
1 large clove garlic, chopped
1 teaspoon paprika
1/2 teaspoon salt
1/4 teaspoon pepper
2 tablespoons oil

Place all of the ingredients, except for the lamb, into a spice grinder and grind to a paste.
A blender or food processor can be used, pulse on and off and stir down frequently until a paste is formed. Or crush with a mortar and pestle.
Spread both sides of the chops with a very thin coating of this mixture.
The meat can be cooked immediately or allowed to sit for a half hour or so at room temperature. The longer it sits, the more spices it will absorb.
Place the chops under a hot broiler and cook for four to five minutes on each side. The chops should be lightly pink at the center at this point. If you prefer your lamb well done, continue to broil for another minute or two.
The lamb chops can also be cooked on a barbeque. They will take about the same amount of time.
Serve immediately.
Serves four, three small chops per person.

†Or use eight loin lamb chops and serve two per person.

RACK OF LAMB WITH TARRAGON

1 rack of lamb†
2 tablespoons butter, melted
1 clove garlic, minced fine
2 teaspoons Dijon mustard
1/2 teaspoon lemon juice
1 tablespoon chopped fresh parsley
1 1/2 teaspoons chopped fresh tarragon or 1/2 teaspoon dried
salt, pepper
1 tablespoon oil
2 tablespoons dried bread crumbs

Have your butcher crack the back side of the rack bones, but leave the rack in one piece. This will make it easier for you to cut it into chops for serving.
Mix the butter, garlic, mustard, lemon juice, parsley and tarragon together in a bowl. Add salt and pepper to taste and reserve until needed.
Trim off as much visible fat from the rack as possible. Sprinkle with salt and pepper and coat very lightly with the oil.
Place the rack, bone side up, into a lightly oiled roasting pan with low sides.
Roast in a preheated 425 degree oven for twenty minutes.
Remove the pan from the oven and turn the rack bone side down. Allow it to cool for a few minutes.
Spread the herb butter evenly over the top of the rack, then sprinkle with the bread crumbs.
The lamb can be held at room temperature for about a half hour at this point, if necessary.
Turn the oven to 450 degrees.
When hot, return the meat to the oven and roast for another fifteen to twenty minutes.

RACK OF LAMB WITH TARRAGON

The lamb should still be pink at the center and the crumb topping lightly browned. If you prefer your meat well done, roast for another five minutes.
Remove the rack from the oven and allow the lamb to rest for five to ten minutes. Cut into chops and serve.
One rack of the lamb will serve two or three, depending upon appetites.
Double the recipe to serve four.

†I prefer to use rib chops, but loin lamb chops, if left in a rack, can be prepared this way as well.

LAMB STEWS

I perfer to use lamb with some bone for stewing and find the shoulder portion to be best. Neck is also excellent, but as it is mostly bone, you may want to increase the amount of meat called for in all the recipes by about one pound. A combination of shoulder and neck meat will also make a wonderful tasting stew.

BRAISED LAMB WITH SCALLIONS AND GARLIC

3 pounds lamb shoulder, cut for stew
salt, pepper
2 tablespoons oil
8 large scallions, cut into quarter inch rounds
6 to 8 cloves garlic, sliced thin
1 cup white wine
1 cup beef or chicken stock
1 or 2 dried hot peppers
1 piece star anise (optional)
water, as needed

Have your butcher cut or saw the lamb into one and one-half inch cubes.
Trim off all visible fat and sprinkle the meat with salt and pepper.
Heat the oil in a large saute pan, add the meat and brown well on all sides.
Add the scallions and garlic to the pan and cook for a minute or two.
Pour in the wine and the stock, stirring well to deglaze the bottom of the pan.
Add the dried hot pepper and the star anise, if using.
Cover and simmer for one hour or until the meat is tender, stirring every fifteen minutes.
Add water, if needed, to keep the meat from sticking.
Remove the dried pepper and the star anise and taste to correct the seasonings.
There should be just a light coating of sauce on the meat.
If there is not enough liquid, add a little water. If the sauce is too liquid, boil hard for a minute or two to reduce.
Serve hot with potatoes, rice or noodles.
This dish can be reheated. Add water, if needed to keep the meat from sticking. It can also be frozen. Thaw before reheating.
Serves four.

LAMB SAUTEED WITH LEMON AND ROSEMARY

3 pounds lamb shoulder, cut for stew
salt, pepper
2 to 3 tablespoons oil
1 large onion, chopped
2 large cloves garlic, minced
1/2 teaspoon dried rosemary
1/2 cup white wine
1/2 cup chicken or beef stock
2 tablespoons lemon juice
water, as needed
1 tablespoon chopped fresh parsley

Have your butcher saw or cut the meat into one and one-half inch cubes.
Trim off all visible fat.
Sprinkle the lamb with salt and pepper.
Heat the oil in a large saute pan. Brown the meat on all sides and remove.
Add the onion to the pan, sprinkle with salt and pepper and saute for a minute or two.
Add, in order, the garlic, rosemary, wine, stock and lemon juice. Scrape well to deglaze the pan.
Return the lamb, cover and simmer for one hour, or until the meat is tender, stirring occasionally.
Add water, if needed, to keep the meat from sticking while cooking.
When finished, there should be just a light coating of sauce on the meat.
Taste to correct the seasonings, stir in the parsley and serve.
This dish can be reheated. Add water, if needed, to keep from sticking. It can also be frozen. Thaw before reheating.
Serves four.

LAMB STEW WITH EGGPLANT

3 pounds lamb shoulder, cut for stew
salt, pepper
2 to 3 tablespoons oil
1 large onion, chopped
1/2 teaspoon cumin seeds
1/2 teaspoon dill seeds
2 large cloves garlic, minced
1 cup chicken or beef stock
1 eight ounce can plum tomatoes, with juice
1 teaspoon tomato paste
water, as needed
1 medium eggplant
1/4 cup sour cream†
1/2 teaspoon flour
2 teaspoons chopped fresh dill weed

Have your butcher saw or cut the meat into one and one-half inch cubes.
Trim off all visible fat.
Sprinkle the meat with salt and pepper.
Heat the oil in a large saute pan and brown the meat on all sides.
Remove and reserve the meat.

Discard all but a scant tablespoon of fat from the pan.
Add the onion, sprinkle with salt and pepper and saute for one minute.
Add the cumin and dill seeds and cook, stirring, for about two minutes.
Stir in the garlic, then add the stock, scraping well to deglaze the bottom of the pan.
Coarsley chop the tomatoes and add them along with their juice to the pan.
Stir in the tomato paste.
Return the lamb, cover and simmer for forty-five minutes, or until the meat is just about tender.
Stir occasionally to keep from sticking, adding water if necessary.
While the lamb is cooking, peel and cut the eggplant into one inch cubes.
Sprinkle with salt and allow to sit for about thirty minutes. Then rinse and drain well.
After the lamb has cooked for forty-five minutes, add the eggplant to the pan.
Continue to cook, stirring occasionally, for about ten minutes, or just until the eggplant is tender.
Mix the sour cream with the flour and stir this carefully into the stew along with the fresh dill weed.
Taste to correct the seasonings and serve.
If reheated, the eggplant will fall apart. The stew will taste fine, but not look as well. Do not freeze.
Serves four.

†Yogurt can be substituted for the sour cream. If so, eliminate the flour.

LAMB STEW WITH ORZO

3 pounds lamb shoulder, cut for stew
salt, pepper
2 to 3 tablespoons oil
2 large onions, chopped
3 cloves garlic, minced
2 cups canned Italian plum tomatoes
1 teaspoon dried thyme
1 teaspoon dried oregano
1 teaspoon dried savory
pinch cayenne pepper
3/4 cup white wine
water, as needed
1 cup orzo (rice shaped noodles)

Have your butcher saw or cut the meat into one and one-half inch cubes.
Trim off all visible fat.
Sprinkle the meat with salt and pepper.
Heat the oil in a large saute pan and brown the lamb cubes on all sides.
Carefully pour all but a scant tablespoon of fat out of the pan.
Add the onions and cook for a few minutes, until they are golden.
Stir in the garlic and cook for one more minute.
Chop the plum tomatoes coarsely and add them, along with any liquid in the can, to the pan.
Crumble and stir in all of the dried herbs and the cayenne pepper. Add a little salt.
Pour in the wine and scrape well to deglaze the bottom of the pan.
Bring the liquid to a boil, cover and simmer until the lamb is almost tender, about forty to forty-five minutes.
Make sure there is about a cup and a half of liquid in the pan at this point, adding water if needed.
Add the noodles to the pan.
The stew can be finished on top of the stove or in the oven. I prefer to do so in the oven, as the noodles will cook more evenly and not stick to the bottom of the pan.
Bring the liquid to a boil, stir, then cover the pan.
Either cook on top of the stove over a low heat for fifteen minutes, stirring two or three times. Add more water, if needed, to keep the noodles from sticking.
Or place the pan in a preheated 375 degree oven for fifteen minutes. It is not necessary to stir the noodles if they are finished in the oven.
Taste to correct the seasonings, mix well and serve.
This dish both reheats and freezes well.
Serves four.

LAMB STEW WITH POTATOES

3 pounds of lamb for stew
salt, pepper
3 tablespoons oil
1 large onion, sliced
2 cloves garlic, minced
1 teaspoon dried thyme
1 teaspoon dried oregano
1 bay leaf
1 1/2 cups chicken or beef stock
1 tablespoon tomato paste
2 large potatoes, peeled and sliced
water, as needed
1 tablespoon chopped fresh parsley

Have your butcher saw or cut the meat into one and one-half inch cubes.
Trim off all visible fat.
Sprinkle the meat with salt and pepper
Heat the oil in a large frying pan.
Add the lamb and saute, over high heat, turning, until the meat is browned on both sides.
Remove the meat and reserve.
Pour off and discard all but one tablespoon of the fat.
Add the onion to the pan and saute until golden.
Add the garlic and continue to cook for another minute.
Add the thyme, oregano and the bay leaf.
Pour in the stock, add the tomato paste and stir well, scraping up any residue from the bottom of the pan.
Bring the sauce to a boil and add salt and pepper to taste.
Return the lamb to the pan, cover and simmer for

LAMB STEW WITH EGGPLANT

LAMB STEW WITH ORZO

LAMB STEW WITH POTATOES

INDIAN BRAISED LAMB AND BASMATI RICE WITH SAFFRON

about thirty-five to forty minutes, or until the lamb is almost tender. Stir once or twice while cooking.
Add the sliced potatoes, cover and simmer the stew for another twenty minutes, or until both the lamb and potatoes are tender.
Check from time to time and add water to the pan as needed to keep the meat and potatoes from sticking.
Taste to correct the seasonings, sprinkle with the chopped parsley and serve.
The stew can be reheated or even frozen if necessary. The potatoes will fall apart when they are reheated, but the stew will taste good anyway.
Serves four.

LAMB STEW WITH WHITE BEANS

3 pounds lamb shoulder, cut for stew
salt, pepper
2 tablespoons oil
3 slices bacon, diced
1 large onion, chopped
2 cloves garlic, minced
1 teaspoon dried savory
1/2 cup white wine
1/2 cup chicken stock
one 15 1/2 ounce can great northern beans†
1 tablespoon chopped fresh parsley

Have your butcher saw or cut the meat into one and one-half inch cubes.
Trim off all visible fat.
Sprinkle the meat with salt and pepper.
Heat the oil in a large saute pan and brown the meat on all sides.
Remove the meat and reserve.
Carefully discard any fat remaining in the pan.
Add the diced bacon, the onions and a little salt and pepper to the pan.
Cook for a few minutes, until the onions turn golden and the bacon begins to color.
Add the garlic and the savory and cook for a half a minute longer.
Deglaze the pan with the wine and the stock, scraping the bottom well.
Return the meat, cover and simmer for forty minutes, stirring occasionally.
Add the beans, along with their liquid, to the stew.
Cover and simmer for another twenty minutes, or until the meat is tender.
If there is a lot of liquid in the pan, remove the cover and boil hard for a few minutes.
Taste to correct the seasonings, stir in the parsley and serve.
Serves four.

†Almost any type of bean can be used. I like great northern beans, but lima beans or white kidney beans work equally well.

INDIAN BRAISED LAMB

1 teaspoon cumin seeds
1/2 teaspoon fenugreek seeds
3 pounds cubed lamb, shoulder or leg
salt, pepper
3 tablespoons oil
1 large onion, chopped
2 large cloves garlic, minced
2 teaspoons ginger root, chopped fine
1/4 teaspoon cayenne pepper
2 teaspoons lemon juice
1/2 cup chicken stock
2/3 cup yogurt
water, as needed

Toast the cumin and fenugreek seeds in a 375 degree oven for about ten minutes or in a microwave oven (high power) for three minutes. Cool a little, then crush.
Use a mortar and pestle, a blender, or my preference for grinding spices, a small electric coffee mill.
If using pre-ground spices, skip this step.
Trim any visible fat from the meat and cut into one and one-half inch cubes.
Sprinkle the meat with salt and pepper.
Heat the oil in a large pan. Add the lamb and brown on all sides.
Remove and reserve the meat.
Add the onion to the pan and cook for a few minutes.
Stir in the garlic and the ginger and cook for another minute.
Add the ground cumin and fenugreek, the cayenne pepper and the lemon juice.
Cook and stir for two to three minutes, being careful not to allow the spice mixture to burn.
Pour in the chicken stock and scrape the bottom of the pan well.
Slowly stir in the yogurt, a few spoons at a time. Wait until the yogurt is absorbed before adding more.
Add the lamb back to the sauce. Cover and simmer for forty-five minutes to one hour, or until the lamb is tender, stirring a few times while cooking.
If the sauce looks too dry, add a few spoons of water to keep the meat from sticking.
Taste to correct the seasonings and serve with a rice pilaf or potatoes.
This dish both reheats and freezes well.
Serves four.

LAMB SHANKS WITH LENTILS

4 large or 8 small lamb shanks†
salt, pepper
3 to 4 tablespoons oil
3 slices bacon, diced
1 large onion, chopped
2 cloves garlic, minced
1 teaspoon dried oregano

2 tomatoes, peeled, seeded and diced
2 cups chicken stock
1 tablespoon lemon juice
1 1/2 teaspoons tomato paste
1 cup lentils, rinsed well and drained
water, as needed
1 tablespoon chopped fresh parsley

Sprinkle the lamb shanks with salt and pepper.
Heat the oil in a large pan and brown the shanks well on all sides.
Remove the meat and reserve.
Drain off and discard all but one tablespoon of the oil, if there is more than this left.
Add the bacon and onions and cook until the onions are golden and the bacon just begins to brown.
Add the garlic, cook for another minute, then stir in the oregano and the tomatoes.
Stir in the stock, lemon juice, tomato paste and some salt and pepper.
Return the lamb shanks to the pot.
Bring the liquid to a boil, cover and then simmer for about forty-five to fifty minutes.
Stir in the lentils.
Cover and continue to cook for another hour, or until both the lentils and the meat are tender.
Add water, if needed, during this time to keep the lentils from sticking.
Taste to correct the seasonings, stir in the chopped parsley and serve.
This dish can be reheated and also freezes well.
Serves four.

†Instead of using shanks, this recipe can be made in to a stew using lamb shoulder or neck. Use three pounds of shoulder or four pounds of neck.
Add the lentils at the same time you return the lamb to the pot and cook both for one hour, or until tender.

LEMON ROASTED LEG OF LAMB

1 small leg of lamb, bone in
salt, pepper
1 to 2 tablespoons oil
1 medium onion, chopped
2 cloves garlic, sliced
1 teaspoon dried lemon verbena†
water, as needed
1/4 cup brandy
1/2 cup white wine
1/4 cup chicken stock

Have your butcher saw the shank portion off the leg of lamb and save it for braising.
Season the lamb with salt and pepper. Rub all over with the oil.
Place the onion, garlic and lemon verbena into the bottom of a shallow roasting pan which has been coated lightly with oil.
Add a half cup of water and place the meat into the pan.
Roast in a preheated 425 degree oven, turning the meat once or twice.
Add water to the pan as the roast cooks to keep the vegetables from sticking and burning.
I find that one hour and fifteen minutes is just about the right amount of time for a small leg to cook so that it is still pink inside. Roast longer if you prefer your meat more well done.
Remove from the oven and place the lamb on a carving board.
Cover to keep warm and allow the meat to rest at least fifteen minutes while you prepare the sauce.
Drain off any fat from the roasting pan and place the pan on the stove.
Stir in the brandy, wine and stock.
Bring the liquid to a boil, scraping the bottom of the pan well.
Cook to reduce by half.
Strain the sauce, removing as much fat as possible and pour it into a sauceboat.
Carve the meat into thin slices. Serve with the sauce on the side.
Serves six or more.

†Lemon balm or lemon thyme can be substituted for the verbena. Or use regular thyme and add lemon juice to taste to the sauce (about one tablespoon).

LEG OF LAMB WITH AN APRICOT STUFFING

one 7 to 8 pound leg of lamb
salt, pepper
2 tablespoons oil
1/2 cup white wine
1/2 cup chicken stock
water, as needed
Stuffing:
2 tablespoons butter
2 tablespoons chopped shallots
3 ounces dried apricots, cooked and chopped
1 tablespoon raisins, chopped
1/4 teaspoon ground cinnamon
1/2 cup fresh whole wheat bread crumbs
1 tablespoon chopped fresh parsley
2 tablespoons chopped walnuts
salt, pepper

Have your butcher saw the shank portion off the leg of lamb and save it for braising.
Bone and butterfly the leg of lamb, or have your butcher do this.
Make the stuffing. Heat the butter in a small pan.
Add the shallots and saute for a few minutes.
Mix in the bread crumbs and continue to cook, stirring, for a few minutes.
Remove the pan from the heat and mix in the rest of the stuffing ingredients.
Set aside to cool a little.
Spread out the lamb, boned side up, removing as much visible fat as possible.
Sprinkle with salt and pepper.

Pat the stuffing onto the lamb in a thin even layer, leaving an inch clear around the edges.
Roll and tie the leg securely. Sprinkle the outside of the roast with salt and pepper.
The lamb roast can be refrigerated for several hours at this point, if necessary. Bring to room temperature before continuing.
Heat the oil in a shallow roasting pan (on top of the stove).
Brown the lamb on all sides in the hot oil.
Remove the meat and discard any remaining fat.
Deglaze the pan with the wine and the stock, scraping loose any brown bits stuck to the bottom.
Return the lamb to the pan and place it into a preheated 375 degree oven.
Roast for about one and one-half hours, until the lamb is tender. We like ours to still be a little pink at the center.
Turn the lamb occasionally and add water to the pan as needed to keep the meat from sticking.
Remove the lamb and place it onto a platter (leave the liquid in the pan).
Cover and allow it to rest for about fifteen to twenty minutes before carving.
Meanwhile, prepare the sauce. Place the roasting pan back on top of the stove.
Add one and one-half cups water and cook and stir until the sauce takes on a nice color and is reduced to about one cup.
Strain the sauce and remove as much of the fat as possible. I like to serve this sauce in one of those dishes that has a pouring spout coming from the bottom, thus eliminating the need for degreasing.
Carve the meat into slices and serve with the sauce on the side.
Serves six to eight, depending on the size of the leg of lamb.

SPINACH, PARSLEY AND PINE NUT STUFFING

1 ten-ounce box frozen spinach, or 1 pound fresh
2 tablespoons butter
1 small onion, chopped
2 tablespoons pine nuts
2 cloves garlic, minced
salt, pepper
pinch grated nutmeg
1 teaspoon lemon juice
2 tablespoons chopped fresh basil
1/2 cup chopped fresh parsley
2 tablespoons grated Parmesan cheese

Cook the spinach in boiling salted water for a few minutes.
Refresh under cold water, squeeze dry and chop.
Heat the butter in a frying pan. Add the onions and the pine nuts and saute until the nuts are lightly toasted.
Add the garlic, spinach, salt, pepper and nutmeg to the pan. Cook for another minute, then remove from the heat and cool a little.
Stir the lemon juice, basil, parsley and the grated cheese into the cooked spinach mixture.
Season to taste with salt and pepper.
The stuffing can be prepared a day ahead of time and refrigerated separately from the meat.
Use this stuffing for the leg of lamb recipe found on page 135 instead of the apricot. Follow the recipe for cooking instructions for the leg of lamb.
Alternate: Either stuffing can be used for a shoulder of lamb as well as the leg.

SWEET AND PUNGENT PORK

PORK WITH APRICOTS

4 thick rib or loin pork chops†
12 dried apricot halves
salt, pepper
flour for dredging + 1/2 teaspoon
2 tablespoons chopped shallots
1 tablespoon ginger root, slivered
1 cup white wine
1 cup chicken or beef stock
2 tablespoons apricot brandy
2 tablespoons sour cream
1 tablespoon chopped fresh parsley

Trim any visible fat from the pork chops.
Cut a lengthwise pocket in each and stuff with two dried apricot halves apiece (the rest are used for the sauce).
Cut the remaining apricot halves into slivers and reserve.
Sprinkle the chops with salt and pepper and dredge them lightly in the flour.
Heat the oil in a frying pan.
Brown the chops on both sides and remove.
Pour out and discard all but a scant tablespoon of the oil.
Add the shallots and the slivered ginger root to the pan.
Cook for a minute or two, then deglaze the pan with the wine, stock and brandy, scraping the bottom well.
Add the slivered apricots to the pan and return the chops.
Cover and simmer for about thirty-five minutes, or until the chops are tender, turning once or twice.
Remove the chops to a serving plate.
Boil the sauce hard until reduced to just one cup.
Mix the sour cream with the half teaspoon of flour and stir this into the sauce.
Add the chopped parsley and taste to correct the seasonings.
Pour the sauce over the chops and serve.
Serves four.

†Eight thin rib or loin chops can be used instead of four thick ones. Cut a pocket in each but stuff with only one apricot half per chop. Reduce the cooking time to twenty to twenty-five minutes and serve two chops per person.

PORK WITH APRICOTS

PORK CHOPS STUFFED WITH PRUNES AND WALNUTS

4 double rib pork chops†
2 tablespoons diced prunes (about 4)
1 tablespoon coarsely chopped walnuts
1 tablespoon dried bread crumbs
1 tablespoon butter, softened
1/8 teaspoon ground allspice
salt, pepper
flour for dredging
2 to 3 tablespoons oil
1/3 cup Madeira
2/3 cup beef or chicken stock

Trim the chops of all visible fat. Cut a lengthwise pocket in each.
In a small dish, mix the prunes, walnuts, bread crumbs, butter and allspice until well combined.
Divide into four portions and stuff the pocket of each chop with the filling.
Press the edges of the chops together well with your fingers to seal.
The chops can be prepared to this point and refrigerated for a few hours before cooking.
Sprinkle the chops with salt and pepper and dredge them lightly in the flour.
Heat the oil in a frying pan.
Brown the chops well on both sides and remove.
Discard any oil remaining in the pan.
Deglaze the pan with the Madeira and the stock, scraping the bottom of the pan well.
Bring the liquid to a boil.
Return the chops to the pan, cover and simmer for about thirty-five minutes, or until the chops are tender, turning once.
The sauce should reduce to just a light glaze. If not, remove the lid and boil hard for a minute or two.
Serves four.

†Eight single rib chops can be used instead of four doubles. You will need one and one-half times the filling recipe to stuff eight of the smaller chops. Reduce the cooking time to about twenty to twenty-five minutes.

PORK CHOPS WITH AN ONION AND SAGE STUFFING

4 thick rib or loin pork chops
1 tablespoon butter
1 medium onion, chopped
1 clove garlic, minced
8 to 10 fresh sage leaves, chopped†
3 tablespoons soft whole wheat bread crumbs
1 tablespoon chopped fresh parsley
flour for dredging
3 tablespoons oil
1 cup beef or chicken stock
1/2 cup white wine
2 tablespoons brandy

Trim the chops of all visible fat. Cut a lengthwise pocket in each.
Heat the butter in a small frying pan. Add the onion and saute until very soft.
Add the garlic and cook for another minute.
Stir in the sage, parsley and bread crumbs. Add salt and pepper to taste.
Allow the mixture to cool a little.
Divide the filling into four portions and stuff some into the pocket of each chop. Press down on the edges well with your fingers to seal.
The chops can be prepared to this point and refrigerated for a few hours before cooking.
Sprinkle the chops with salt and pepper and dredge them lightly in the flour.
Heat the oil in a frying pan.
Brown the chops well on both sides and remove.
Discard any oil remaining in the pan.
Deglaze the pan with the stock, wine and brandy, scraping the bottom well.
Bring the liquid to a boil.
Return the chops to the pan. Cover and simmer for about thirty-five minutes, or until the chops are tender, turning once.
Remove the chops to a serving plate.
Boil the sauce hard to reduce until just a scant cup remains.
Strain the sauce over the chops and serve.
Serves four.

†About one teaspoon chopped fresh sage. Or use a healthy pinch of dried sage.

SWEET AND PUNGENT PORK

1 pound boneless pork loin
2 tablespoons soy sauce
1 tablespoon rice wine or Sherry
1/4 teaspoon pepper
1/2 teaspoon sugar
4 tablespoons oil, or more if needed
1 tablespoon cornstarch
Sauce:
1 cup canned pineapple chunks, with juice
1 tablespoon soy sauce
1/2 cup water
1/4 cup sugar
1/2 cup rice wine vinegar
1 tablespoon oil
1 small onion, sliced thin
1/2 green pepper, sliced thin
1 carrot, cut into julienne
1 tablespoon cornstarch

Cut the pork loin into thin julienne strips.
Place in a small bowl and mix with the soy, Sherry, pepper and sugar.
Reserve until ready to cook.
Heat the oil in a frying pan or wok.
Mix the marinated pork with the cornstarch and cook, stirring often, over a medium heat until the meat is browned and tender.
This should take about five minutes.

While the pork is cooking, prepare the sauce.
Drain the pineapple chunks, reserving one-half cup of the juice for the sauce.
Mix together the pineapple juice, soy sauce, one-quarter cup of the water, the sugar and the vinegar. Set aside until needed.
Heat the oil in a (separate) frying pan.
Add the onion, pepper and carrots and stir-fry for one minute.
Add the reserved liquid to the pan and simmer for two minutes.
Add the pineapple chunks.
Mix the cornstarch with the remaining quarter cup of water and add, stirring. Cook just until the sauce thickens.
Drain the pork and place onto a serving plate.
Pour the sauce over the meat and serve immediately.
Serves four as a main course or more if served with other dishes as part of a Chinese meal.
Alternates:
Sweet and Pungent Shrimp.
Marinate one pound of peeled and cleaned raw shrimp in one teaspoon oil, one teaspoon cornstarch and a pinch of salt and sugar.
Saute in three tablespoons oil for about three minutes, or until cooked. Drain well and serve with the sauce.
Sweet and Pungent Chicken.
Marinate one pound julienned chicken breast with a pinch of sugar and pepper, one-half teaspoon salt, one teaspoon Sherry and a teaspoon of egg white.
Before cooking, mix in two teaspoons of cornstarch.
Stir-fry in three tablespoons oil for three to four minutes. Drain well and serve with the sauce.

SAUSAGE STUFFED GREEN PEPPERS

4 large green peppers
1 pound sweet sausage
2 tablespoons oil
1 medium onion, chopped
2 large cloves garlic, minced
1/2 cup tomato juice
1 teaspoon dried thyme, or 1 tablespoon chopped fresh
1/2 teaspoon dried sage or about 6 fresh leaves, chopped
1/4 cup chopped fresh parsley
1 1/2 cups soft bread crumbs
1/4 cup grated Parmesan cheese
2 eggs
salt, pepper
1 recipe tomato sauce

Cut the tops off the peppers to form a lid and reserve. Remove the inner seeds, rinse and drain well.
Remove the casings from the sausage and crumble the meat.
Heat the oil in a frying pan and add the sausage.
Cook, stirring, until well broken apart and lightly browned.
Add the onions to the pan and continue to cook until they are lightly browned as well.
Stir in the garlic and cook for another minute.
If using dried herbs, add now.
Deglaze the pan with the tomato juice, scraping well to loosen any bits stuck to the bottom.
If using fresh herbs, stir in now. Cool the mixture a little.
Mix the bread crumbs, cheese and eggs into the cooked sausage to make the stuffing. Add salt and pepper to taste.
Stuff the four peppers evenly, placing the pepper lids back on top.
Pour the cooked tomato sauce into the bottom of a saucepan that is just large enough to hold all the peppers upright. Place the stuffed peppers into the pan and cover with a lid.
The peppers can be refrigerated at this point for a few hours.
Simmer the peppers for about thirty-five to forty minutes, or until they are tender. Serve with lots of sauce.
The peppers can be reheated, but they tend to get soggy and fall apart. Best when freshly cooked.
Serves four.

TOMATO SAUCE

2 tablespoons butter
1 large onion, chopped
1 clove garlic, minced
1/2 cup white wine
2 cups peeled and diced tomatoes†
2 teaspoons sugar
1 tablespoon chopped fresh basil or 1 teaspoon dried
1 tablespoon chopped fresh parsley
salt, pepper

Heat the butter in a saucepan. Add the onion and cook until golden.
Stir in the garlic and cook for another half minute.
If using dried basil, add now.
Add the wine, tomatoes, sugar and fresh herbs.
Season with a little salt and pepper.
Bring the sauce to a boil, cover and simmer for twenty minutes. Cool a little.
Puree the sauce, using a food processor or a blender. Taste to correct the seasonings. The sauce should be tart and spicy.
The sauce both reheats and freezes very well.
This recipe makes about two cups of sauce.

†Or use two cups of canned Italian plum tomatoes, coarsely chopped, along with any juice in the can.

OUTDOOR MARKET, INDIA

Accompaniments

BUTTERS

FENNEL BUTTER

4 tablespoons butter, softened
2 teaspoons finely chopped shallots
2 teaspoons chopped fresh fennel leaves
1 teaspoon chopped fresh chervil or parsley
1 teaspoon chopped fresh lemon balm or lemon verbena†
1 teaspoon chopped fresh chives
1/2 teaspoon salt
pepper to taste

Place all of the ingredients into a bowl and mix together until well blended.
Allow the butter to sit for a few hours in the refrigerator to mellow or leave at room temperature for one hour.
The butter will keep for two or three days in the refrigerator or it can be frozen for a few months. Slice and use while still frozen.
Place a slice on top of grilled fish. Fennel butter is especially good with grilled or broiled swordfish.

†One-half teaspoon lemon juice can be substituted. Serves four.

JUNIPER BERRY BUTTER

4 juniper berries
3 tablespoons butter, softened
1/4 teaspoon dried savory
1/2 teaspoon dried oregano
1/2 teaspoon lemon juice
salt, pepper

Crush the juniper berries by using a large chefs knife or the bottom of a heavy pot. Then chop well.
Place the chopped juniper berries into a bowl and mix with the butter, herbs and lemon juice.
Add salt and pepper to taste.
Allow the butter to mellow for a few hours in the refrigerator, or for an hour at room temperature.
The butter will keep for several days in the refrigerator or it can be frozen for a month or two.
Slice and use while frozen.
Serve on grilled meats. Also great on string beans.
Serves approximately four portions.

STEAMED SHRIMP AND CRAB CLAW S WITH CHILI TOMATO SAUCE AND CREAMY MUSTARD DILL SAUCE

MINT BUTTER

3 tablespoons butter, softened
2 teaspoons chopped fresh mint or 1/3 teaspoon dried
1 teaspoon chopped fresh lemon verbena or lemon balm†
1 tablespoon chopped fresh parsley
1 tablespoon finely chopped shallots
1/2 teaspoon salt
pepper to taste

Place all of the ingredients into a bowl and mix together until well blended.
Allow the butter to mellow for a few hours in the refrigerator or leave at room temperature for one hour.
The mint butter will keep well in the refrigerator for a few days.
Or freeze for a month or two. Slice and use while frozen.
Place a slice over grilled lamb chops or cooked vegetables.
Enough butter for four servings of vegetables or six lamb chops.

†One-half teaspoon lemon juice can be substituted.

MUSTARD BUTTER

1/4 cup butter, softened
1 tablespoon chopped shallots
1 small clove garlic, minced fine
2 teaspoons chopped fresh chives
1 tablespoon chopped fresh parsley
1 teaspoon Dijon mustard
pinch grated nutmeg
1 teaspoon lemon juice
1/2 teaspoon salt
pepper to taste

Place all of the ingredients into a bowl and mix together until well blended.
Refrigerate for several hours before serving to allow the flavors time to mellow.
Store in the refrigerator for a few days or freeze for a month or two. Slice and use while frozen.
Serve a slice on grilled fish, such as swordfish, salmon or halibut.
Also good on beef or lamb.
Four to six portions.

SAUCES

COLD

CHILI TOMATO SAUCE

Sauce:
1 to 2 tablespoons oil
1 small onion, chopped
1/2 hot pepper, seeded and chopped
white of 1 scallion, chopped
1 small clove garlic, chopped
1/2 teaspoon chopped ginger root
1/2 teaspoon salt
2 tomatoes, peeled and chopped†
1 tablespoon Sherry
1 teaspoon sugar
1/2 tablespoon wine vinegar
1 tablespoon ketchup

Heat the oil in a small frying pan. Add the onion, fresh hot pepper and scallion.
Saute for two minutes, then add the garlic and the ginger. Cook for another half a minute.
Add the salt, tomatoes and Sherry.
Bring the sauce to a boil, then lower the heat and simmer for ten minutes, stirring occasionally.
Cool a little, then puree the sauce in a blender or food processor, adding the sugar, vinegar and the ketchup. Taste to correct the seasonings.
Chill the sauce until serving time. The sauce can be refrigerated for three or four days or it can be frozen.
This recipe makes one cup of sauce, enough to serve with one pound of steamed shrimp.

†Or substitute one cup (one small can) of Italian plum tomatoes, diced.

STEAMED SHRIMP

1 pound raw shrimp, in the shell
1/2 cup white wine
1/2 cup water

You will need a pot that has a steamer rack and a tight-fitting lid.
Arrange the shrimp on the rack in a single layer and set aside.
Pour the wine and the water into the bottom of the pan and bring it to a boil.
Place the shrimp-lined rack into the pan and cover with the lid.
Steam for two minutes.
Remove the lid and turn the shrimp over (carefully). Cover and continue to steam for another two and one-half minutes.
Remove the rack from the pan and allow the shrimp to cool. Once they can be handled, peel and remove the veins.
Serve cold with the chili tomato sauce.

The shrimp will be very succulent when steamed this way. They can be kept, once cooked, in the refrigerator for two days. Leave the shells on until the day they are to be served to keep them from drying out.
Serves four as an appetizer, or more when served with other dishes.

CREAMY MUSTARD DILL SAUCE

1 egg yolk
2 tablespoons Dijon mustard
1 tablespoon white wine vinegar
1/2 cup salad oil
1/4 cup chopped fresh dill weed
1/4 cup heavy cream
salt, pepper

Place the egg yolk, mustard and vinegar into a blender or a food processor fitted with a steel blade.
Process for one minute.
With the motor running, slowly add the oil.
Add the chopped dill, the heavy cream and a little salt and pepper and process only until blended.
Taste to correct the seasonings and remove the sauce from the machine.
This is a thick sauce. If you prefer it thinner, whisk in a tablespoon or two of warm water.
Serve with smoked or Scotch salmon or gravadlox. Also good with cold poached salmon.
This recipe makes one cup of sauce.

PESTO

1 1/2 cups tightly packed fresh basil leaves
1/2 cup tightly packed fresh parsley leaves
1 large clove garlic, sliced
1 1/2 tablespoons pine nuts
1 tablespoon walnuts
2 tablespoons olive oil
2 tablespoons salad oil
salt, pepper

Place all of the ingredients into a food processor or blender and process until a coarse puree is formed, stirring down often.
If using a blender, you may have to do this in two batches.
Add salt and pepper to taste.
Store the sauce in the refrigerator covered with a thin layer of oil to keep the pesto from turning color.
Or freeze. I like to do this in packages of two tablespoons each. (One ice cube is two tablespoons.)
I purposely do not add cheese to my basic pesto sauce, since it freezes better without the cheese. I prefer to make a large quantity of sauce when fresh basil is in season. Also, a basic pesto sauce is more versatile for use in other recipes without the cheese.
This recipe makes about three-quarters cup of sauce.

HOT BARBEQUE SAUCE

1 large onion
2 large cloves garlic
3/4 cup A-1 sauce
3/4 cup ketchup
3/4 cup orange juice
3 tablespoons brown sugar
1/2 teaspoon Tabasco sauce
1 teaspoon salt
1/4 teaspoon cayenne pepper
1 tablespoon vinegar
1/2 cup beef stock

Chop the onion coarsely and slice the garlic.
Place them into a food processor or blender and add the rest of the ingredients.
Puree until the mixture is well blended.
You may have to do this in two batches.
Remove the puree from the machine and pour it into a saucepan.
Heat the sauce to the boiling point then simmer for fifteen to twenty minutes, stirring occasionally to keep it from sticking to the bottom of the pan.
Taste and correct the seasonings.
If you prefer a spicier sauce, add more cayenne pepper.
This sauce is excellent for spareribs.
There is enough for three racks of ribs with a little left over for dipping.
Use the sauce to baste the ribs during the last half-hour of cooking time, either in an oven or on a barbeque.
This sauce will keep in the refrigerator for up to a week. It also freezes very well.
Makes one and one-half cups sauce.

HOT CHILI SAUCE

1 eight ounce can Italian plum tomatoes
6 canned Tuscan peppers†
2 to 3 tablespoons butter or olive oil
1 small onion, chopped
salt
1 clove garlic, chopped

Drain the tomatoes and chop them, reserving the liquid.
Remove the seeds from the peppers if you like your sauce with a little less fire. Chop the peppers.
Heat the butter or oil in a frying pan.
Add the onions and a pinch of salt and cook until they are soft.
Add the garlic, tomatoes and peppers to the pan.
Simmer for ten or fifteen minutes, stirring occasionally.
Cool the sauce a little.
Puree in a food processor or blender, adding all or some of the reserved tomato liquid, depending on how thick you want your sauce.
Taste to correct the seasonings.
This sauce can be used for many things. Try it

RHUBARB CONSERVE

BASIC MEAT SAUCE FOR SPAGHETTI

with meat loaf or plain grilled hamburgers or hot dogs. Or mix with baked beans.
The sauce can be refrigerated or frozen and reheated.
This recipe makes a scant cup of chili sauce.
Alternate:
Chili sauce also makes an excellent cold spread for bread or crackers when combined with grated cheese. I like to use one recipe of the sauce mixed with one pound of grated cheddar cheese and about four tablespoons of softened butter.
You can, however, use almost any combination of cheeses you prefer.

†If Tuscan peppers are unavailable, use canned serrano peppers.

MINT SAUCE

2 tablespoons butter
2 tablespoons sugar
1/4 cup wine vinegar
1 cup white wine
2 tablespoons chopped fresh peppermint leaves
1 1/2 teaspoons cornstarch
2 tablespoons water

Place the butter, sugar and vinegar into a small saucepan.
Bring them to a boil and cook, shaking the pan often, until the mixture is well reduced and just begins to turn light brown in color.
Pour in the wine, stirring well to mix.
Cook until the liquid is reduced by one-third.
Add the fresh mint to the pan.
Mix the cornstarch with the water and stir into the boiling liquid.
Continue to cook for a minute or two, just until the sauce thickens and the color turns clear.
Serve immediately with broiled or grilled lamb.
This recipe makes about three-quarters cup of sauce, enough for four portions.

BASIC MEAT SAUCE FOR SPAGHETTI

1 or 2 tablespoons oil
1 large onion, chopped
2 cloves garlic, minced
1 pound ground beef (chuck)
salt, pepper
1 cup beef or chicken stock
4 cups Italian plum tomatoes, peeled and coarsely chopped
1 1/2 tablespoons tomato paste
1/2 to 1 teaspoon sugar
2 tablespoons chopped fresh parsley
1 tablespoon chopped fresh basil or 1 teaspoon dried
1/2 tablespoon chopped fresh oregano or 1/2 teaspoon dried

Heat the oil in a large saucepan.
Add the onion and saute for a few minutes, until golden.
Stir in the garlic, ground meat and some salt and pepper.
Cook, stirring to separate the meat, until it is nicely browned.
Pour in the stock and scrape well to loosen any bits of meat that may be stuck to the bottom of the pan.
Add the tomatoes (if using canned, add the liquid as well), tomato paste, sugar, cayenne pepper, parsley, basil and oregano. Stir well and bring the sauce to a boil.
Cover and simmer for one to one and a half hours, stirring occasionally.
If you prefer a very thick sauce, remove the lid and boil hard for a few minutes.
Taste to correct the seasonings and serve over cooked pasta. Pass a bowl of freshly grated Parmesan cheese on the side.
This sauce reheats well and freezes beautifully.
Enough sauce for six portions.
Alternates:
Mushroom: Add twelve sliced mushrooms to the pan before adding the meat. Cook for a few minutes, then continue with the recipe. Or mix in some cooked sliced mushrooms before serving.
Sausage: Cut one-half pound of either sweet or hot sausage into rings. Saute until browned and add to the sauce before serving.
Peperoni: Saute one quarter pound peperoni until browned. Add to the sauce before serving.
Cream: For a very rich tasting sauce, stir in one-quarter cup of heavy cream after the sauce is cooked. Heat and serve.

BOLOGNESE SAUCE

2 tablespoons butter or oil
4 slices boiled ham, diced fine
1 large onion, chopped fine
1 carrot, chopped fine
1 stalk celery, chopped fine
2 cloves garlic, minced
8 mushrooms, chopped fine
1 pound ground beef (chuck)
salt, pepper
pinch grated nutmeg
1/2 cup white wine
1 cup chicken or beef stock
3 cups peeled and chopped Italian plum tomatoes, fresh or canned
1 tablespoon tomato paste
1/2 teaspoon sugar
2 tablespoons chopped fresh parsley
2 chicken livers, diced
1/4 cup light cream

Heat the butter or oil in a large saucepan.
Add the diced ham, onion, carrot and celery. Cook for three or four minutes.
Add the garlic and mushrooms and continue to cook, stirring often, until the mixture is almost dry.

Stir in the ground meat, breaking it apart with a spoon as it cooks. Sprinkle with salt, pepper and the nutmeg.
Continue to cook until all the meat is lightly browned.
Pour in the wine and the stock, scraping well to deglaze the pan.
Add the chopped tomatoes (if using canned, add the liquid as well), tomato paste, sugar and parsley.
Bring the sauce to a boil, cover and simmer for one and one-half to two hours, stirring occasionally.
When finished, the sauce should be a fairly dry mixture.
The sauce can be completed to this point and refrigerated for a day or two or it can be frozen.
When ready to serve, heat the sauce to the boiling point.
Add the diced livers and the cream and mix well.
Cook without a lid for about seven or eight minutes, stirring often. Taste to correct the seasonings.
Serve with any thick pasta such as ziti, rigatoni or fettuccine.
The finished sauce can be refrigerated or frozen. It will lose some of its delicacy, but be quite tasty, nonetheless. Reheat just to the boiling point and serve.
This recipe makes enough sauce for six portions.

MARINARA SAUCE

2 tablespoons butter or oil
1 large onion, chopped
salt, pepper
2 cloves garlic, minced
4 cups Italian plum tomatoes, peeled and coarsely chopped
1 1/2 tablespoons tomato paste
1/2 teaspoon sugar
pinch cayenne pepper
1 tablespoon chopped fresh basil or 1 teaspoon dried
1/2 tablespoon chopped fresh oregano or 1/2 teaspoon dried
1 tablespoon chopped fresh parsley

Heat the butter or oil in a large saucepan. Add the onion, sprinkle with salt and pepper and cook until golden.
Stir in the garlic, cook for a half a minute, then stir in the tomatoes (if using canned, add the liquid as well), tomato paste, sugar, cayenne pepper and all of the herbs.
Bring the sauce to a boil. Add salt and pepper to taste. Cover and simmer for thirty minutes, stirring occasionally.
The sauce should be thick by the end of this time.
Taste to correct the seasonings.
Serve as is, or if you prefer a smooth sauce, allow it to cool a little then puree in a blender or food processor.
Serve over pasta or use a part of another recipe (great for making Eggplant Parmesan).
Makes about two and one-half cups sauce.

SPANISH SAUCE

2 tablespoons olive oil
1 large onion, chopped
salt, pepper
8 to 10 mushrooms, sliced
2 cloves garlic, minced
1 green pepper, diced
1 bay leaf
1/4 teaspoon dried thyme
pinch cayenne pepper
pinch sugar
1/4 cup white wine
2 cups canned Italian plum tomatoes
2 tablespoons tomato paste
1 tablespoon chopped fresh parsley

Heat the oil in a frying pan. Add the onions, sprinkle with salt and pepper and saute until golden.
Add the mushrooms to the pan and continue to cook until they are dry, stirring often.
Stir in the garlic and the green pepper, then add the bay leaf, thyme, cayenne pepper and the sugar.
Pour in the white wine and scrape the bottom of the pan well.
Dice the tomatoes and stir them in along with any liquid from the can.
Stir in the tomato paste and bring the sauce to a boil.
Cover the pan and simmer for twenty to thirty minutes, or until the sauce is thick.
Taste to correct the seasonings, mix in the parsley and serve. Excellent with an omelette or on sauteed or broiled fish.
The sauce can be reheated and also frozen.
This recipe makes about two cups of sauce.

RELISHES

APPLE AND RAISIN CONSERVE

5 tart apples
1/3 cup raisins
1/3 cup sugar
1/4 cup orange juice
strip of orange rind
strip of lemon rind
1/4 teaspoon ground cinnamon
1/4 teaspoon ground ginger
pinch salt
1 tablespoon butter
1 tablespoon Calvados or apple jack
1/4 cup chopped walnuts

Peel, core and slice the apples thinly.
Place them in a saucepan along with the raisins, sugar, orange juice, orange and lemon rinds, cinnamon, ginger and salt.
Cover and cook over a low heat, stirring occasionally, until the apples are very tender. This should take about thirty minutes.
Remove the orange and lemon rinds.
Stir in the butter, Calvados and walnuts.
Cool and store in jars in the refrigerator. It will keep for several weeks.
The conserve can also be frozen.
Serve cold as a relish with meat.
Makes three cups of conserve.

PRUNES WITH SOUR CREAM AND WALNUTS

16 extra-large prunes
2 inch piece of cinnamon stick
8 cardamom pods, lightly crushed
4 whole cloves
1 cup water
1 tablespoon sugar
1 teaspoon lemon juice
1/4 cup sour cream
1 tablespoon chopped walnuts

Place the prunes in a saucepan with the cinnamon stick, cardamom and cloves.
Pour in the water and bring the liquid to a boil.
Simmer the prunes until they are tender and the liquid has reduced to about two tablespoons.
Set aside until the prunes are cool enough to handle, then remove and discard the pits, if there are any.
Place the prunes into a small buttered casserole.
Mix together the sugar, lemon juice and the sour cream.
Strain the cooking liquid from the prunes (to remove the spices). Add this liquid to the sour cream.
Mix in the walnuts.
Pour this mixture evenly over the prunes.
The casserole can be readied to this point and refrigerated until serving time. It will keep overnight in the refrigerator, if covered.
Bake (uncovered) in a preheated 350 degree oven for twenty minutes, or until the sauce is bubbling and the prunes are hot.
Serve hot as an accompaniment to meat or fowl.
Serves four.

QUINCE AND APPLE COMPOTE

3 tart apples
3 quinces
1 tablespoon lemon juice
water, as needed
1/3 cup sugar, or more to taste
1/2 teaspoon ground cinnamon

Peel, core and dice the apples and the quinces.
Place them in a saucepan with the lemon juice and one-quarter cup of water.
Cover and simmer slowly until the fruit is tender, stirring frequently.
Add more water if the fruit begins to stick.
When done, the apples should be totally disintegrated, but the quinces will still remain in pieces.
Cooking time is usually about an hour. It can take even longer, depending on the ripeness of the quinces.
Stir the sugar and the cinnamon into the cooked fruit and remove the pan from the heat.
Taste and add additional sugar if needed.
Chill and serve the compote cold with meat or fowl.
This sauce will keep for a week or two in the refrigerator. It can also be frozen.
Makes two to three cups of compote.

RHUBARB CONSERVE

1 1/2 pounds fresh rhubarb
1/2 lemon
1 orange
1 cup walnuts
1 cup raisins
3 cups sugar
1 three inch cinnamon stick
6 whole cloves
1 whole star anise

Wash the rhubarb and cut it into small dice.
Chop the lemon and orange into small dice, leaving on the rind, but removing any seeds.
Break or chop the walnuts into fairly large pieces.
Place all of the above into a heavy saucepan along with the raisins and the sugar.
Wrap the spices in a small piece of cheesecloth and tie securely (for easy removal).
Place the spice bag into the pot.
Do not add any water, the fruit will give off enough liquid to cook the conserve.
Cover the pot and simmer the ingredients slowly for one hour. Stir occasionally to keep the mixture from sticking.
Remove the spice bag. If there is a lot of liquid in

the pan, boil hard without a cover for a few minutes.
Allow the conserve to cool to room temperature, then cover and chill.
Serve cold with meat or fowl.
This conserve will keep for several weeks in the refrigerator. It can also be frozen.
Makes about four cups of conserve.

GREEN TOMATO CHUTNEY

8 to 10 large green or yellow tomatoes, chopped
1 large sweet onion, chopped
1 stalk celery, chopped
1 or 2 large cloves garlic, minced
1 1/4 cups cider vinegar
3/4 cup raisins
1 tablespoon salt
1/2 teaspoon cayenne pepper
1/4 teaspoon grated nutmeg
1 inch piece ginger root, chopped fine
3 inch piece cinnamon stick

Place all of the ingredients into a large saucepan.
Cover and simmer for one hour, stirring occasionally.
Remove the lid and continue to simmer for another two hours, stirring often to keep from sticking.
Allow the chutney to cool, then pack into jars and refrigerate.
This relish, if sealed and refrigerated, will keep for a year.
Makes four cups chutney.

HOT PEPPER RELISH

1 large or 2 small tomatoes
1/2 green pepper
1/4 red pepper
1 carrot
1 cucumber, peeled and seeded
1 small onion
1 hot pepper
2 tablespoons wine vinegar
1/4 teaspoon toasted cumin seeds†
salt

Seed and dice the tomatoes.
All of the vegetables for this relish have to be cut into very fine dice.
Dice the green pepper, red pepper, carrot, cucumber and onion.
Remove the seeds and the pulp of the hot pepper and dice.
Combine the vegetables in a bowl and mix with the vinegar and the toasted cumin seed.
Add salt to taste.
Serve along with other dishes as an appetizer or use as a relish.
The relish will keep for two to three days in the refrigerator.
Makes two cups.

†Toast the cumin seeds in a 350 degree oven for about five minutes or in a microwave for one minute at high power.

GINGERED ORANGE BEETS

ACORN SQUASH STUFFED WITH PEARS

2 small acorn squash
1 large or two small pears
2 tablespoons brown sugar
1/2 teaspoon ground cinnamon
1/4 teaspoon ground ginger
1 tablespoon butter
water, as needed

Cut the acorn squash in half lengthwise and remove the seeds.
Peel, core and dice the pears.
Mix with the sugar, cinnamon and ginger.
Fill the cavity of each squash with a quarter of the pear mixture. Dot with the butter.
Place the squash, filled side up, into a casserole and pour about one inch of water into the bottom of the pan.
Bake them in a 375 degree oven for about forty-five minutes, or until they are tender.
The squash can be cooked in a microwave oven. Add only a tablespoon or two of water to the pan. Cover and cook at high power for fourteen minutes. Serve hot.
Serves four.
Alternate filling:
Cran-Apple Squash.
Peel and dice one small apple (1 cup).
Mix with one-half cup raw cranberries, two tablespoons brown sugar and one-half teaspoon ground cinnamon.
Fill the squash, dot with butter (1/2 tablespoon) and cook as in the above recipe.

STUFFED ARTICHOKES

4 artichokes
1 lemon, cut in half
1/2 cup butter, divided
1 medium onion, chopped
2 large cloves garlic, minced
2 cups fresh whole wheat bread crumbs
1/4 cup grated Parmesan cheese
1/4 cup chopped fresh parsley
1 tablespoon chopped fresh oregano, or 1 teaspoon dried
salt, pepper

Work with one artichoke at a time. Cut off the bottom stem and reserve. Rub the exposed bottom with the lemon.
Slice off about one-third of the top leaves, then trim off the sharp points from the remaining leaves with a scissors. Rub the exposed top with the lemon.
Place all of the trimmed artichokes, along with the stems into a saucepan so that they fit tightly. Squeeze the lemon over the top, fill the pan with water to cover and add about a tablespoon of salt. Cover with a lid and bring the water to a boil. Boil the artichokes for fifteen to twenty minutes, just until the stem ends are barely tender (they will cook again).
Refresh under cold water and drain well. When cool enough to handle remove the center choke portion that is inedible.
Peel the cooked stems and chop them finely to use for the filling.
Heat five tablespoons of the butter in a frying pan. Add the onion and saute until golden.

STUFFED ARTICHOKES

Add the garlic and cook for another minute.
Place the crumbs into a bowl and add the cooked onions and garlic, along with any butter remaining in the pan.
Stir in the cheese, parsley, oregano and the chopped stems. Add salt and pepper to taste.
Divide the stuffing into four parts for easy handling. Place the stuffing between the outer leaves of the artichokes, working your way in towards the center. Fill in the centers last.
Set the stuffed artichokes into a baking pan.
Melt the remaining butter and spoon it over the tops of the artichokes.
The artichokes can be covered and refrigerated at this point for a day or two. Bring to room temperature before heating or allow an extra five to ten minutes in the oven.
Uncover and add about a quarter inch of water to the pan.
Bake in a preheated 425 degree oven for twenty to twenty-five minutes, or until the stuffing is lightly browned. Serve hot.
Serves four as an appetizer or lunch course.

GINGERED ORANGE BEETS

1 bunch fresh beets (4)
1 tablespoon butter
1/4 cup orange juice
1 tablespoon sugar
pinch salt
2 tablespoons wine vinegar
1 teaspoon minced ginger root†

Wash and trim the beets, leaving about one inch of the top and root ends attached.
Place the beets in a pot and cover them with water.
Bring the water to a boil, then lower the heat and simmer until the beets are tender. This usually takes about one hour.
Add water to the pot, as needed, to keep the beets covered as they cook.
Or cook in a microwave oven for fifteen to twenty minutes at high power. Use less water and turn the beets over once while cooking.
Drain and rinse the beets under cold water.
Slip off the skins as soon as they are cool enough to handle.
The beets can be cooked to this point and stored, covered, in the refrigerator for a few days.
When ready to serve, cut the beets into slices, about a quarter-inch thick.
If they are very large, cut them in half first, then into slices.
Heat the butter, orange juice, sugar, salt, vinegar and ginger in a frying pan.
Simmer for three to four minutes, or until the sauce thickens a little.
Add the sliced beets and stir to coat well.
Simmer for five to six minutes, stirring occasionally, until the beets have absorbed most of the sauce. Serve hot.
These beets can be reheated. Add a little more orange juice or a few spoons of water to keep them from sticking.
Serves four.

†One-half teaspoon of ground ginger can be used instead of the fresh, but the taste will not be the same, as fresh ginger has a more pungent flavor.

BEETS IN A MUSTARD CREAM SAUCE

1 bunch fresh beets (4)
1/2 cup sour cream
1 teaspoon flour
1 teaspoon Dijon mustard
2 teaspoons lemon juice
1 teaspoon chopped fresh chives
2 tablespoons butter
1 medium onion, chopped
salt, pepper

Cook the beets as in the previous recipe.
Cut them into julienne strips. You will need about three cups of julienned beets.
Mix together the sour cream, flour, mustard, lemon juice and chives in a small bowl and reserve.
Heat the butter in a frying pan.
Add the onion, sprinkle with salt and pepper and cook until golden.
Add the beets and cook, tossing, until they are hot.
Stir in the sour cream mixture.
Continue to cook and stir for a minute or two longer, just until the mixture is hot.
Taste to correct the seasonings and serve.
Serves four to six.

BROCCOLI CASSEROLE

1 tablespoon butter
2 tablespoons chopped shallots
1 small clove garlic, minced
1/8 teaspoon ground cardamom
1 tablespoon flour
1/3 cup milk
2 tablespoons chopped fresh parsley
1 1/2 cups cooked broccoli, chopped†
salt, pepper
2 tablespoons chopped pistachios
1/3 cup sour cream
2 tablespoons grated cheddar cheese
1/3 cup sour cream
2 tablespoons grated cheddar cheese

Heat the butter in a small saucepan. Add the shallots and cook for a minute or two.
Add the garlic to the pan and cook for a half a minute.
Mix in the cardamom and the flour. Continue to cook, stirring, for one minute.
Slowly stir in the milk and bring the mixture to a boil, then continue to cook for one minute. The sauce base will be very thick.
Remove the pan from the heat.

This casserole can be assembled in a food processor or by hand.
To make in a processor, first chop the parsley. Leave it in the machine and add the broccoli. Chop to a coarse puree.
Add the cooked sauce and some salt and pepper, turning the machine on and off to mix.
Taste to correct the seasonings.
Add the chopped pistachios and briefly mix.
Or chop the broccoli finely and place it into a bowl. Add the chopped parsley, the sauce and the chopped pistachios.
Mix well and season to taste with salt and pepper.
Spoon the finished mixture into a well buttered casserole.
Spread a thin layer of sour cream on top and sprinkle with the cheese.
The dish can be baked immediately or refrigerated at this point for several hours or overnight.
Bake in a preheated 375 degree oven for twenty-five minutes, or until hot. If refrigerated, allow an extra five to ten minutes.
Serves four.

†About one-half bunch fresh broccoli (two large stalks).

BROCCOLI GRATIN

1/2 bunch fresh broccoli (2 large stalks)
1 tablespoon chopped shallots
1/2 cup half and half
3/4 cup + 2 tablespoons soft bread crumbs
1 egg yolk
2 tablespoons butter
1/2 teaspoon lemon juice
1/4 teaspoon dried savory
salt, pepper
2 tablespoons grated Swiss cheese

Cook the broccoli in a pot of salted boiling water until tender. Refresh under cold water and drain well.
Chop the broccoli into coarse pieces and reserve.
Place the shallots and the half and half into a small saucepan and heat slowly until the mixture comes to a boil.
Or heat in a microwave oven at a low setting for two or three minutes.
Pour this mixture over the three-quarters cup of bread crumbs, stir and let sit until fairly cool.
Place the broccoli into a food processor fitted with a steel knife and process only until it is fairly well chopped, you do not want a puree.
Add the bread crumb mixture, egg yolk, one and one-half tablespoons of the butter, lemon juice, savory and some salt and pepper.
Process, turning the machine on and off just until the ingredients are mixed.
Taste to correct the seasonings.
If you do not have a processor, the broccoli can be chopped in a food mill or by hand. Place into a bowl and mix with the rest of the ingredients.
Pour the broccoli mixture into a well buttered gratin dish or casserole (two and one-half cup).
Smooth the top and sprinkle evenly with the two tablespoons of bread crumbs and the grated cheese. Dot with the remaining half tablespoon of butter.
The recipe can be prepared to this point early in the day, covered and refrigerated. Allow it to come to room temperature before baking.
Bake in a preheated 375 degree oven for fifty minutes, or until the casserole is firm and the topping lightly browned.
Serves five to six portions.

BRUSSELS SPROUTS WITH BACON

1 box Brussels sprouts
2 slices bacon, diced
1 medium onion, chopped
1/2 teaspoon dried marjoram
salt, pepper
1/4 cup water
1 tablespoon butter

Wash and trim the Brussels sprouts. Using the slicing blade of a food processor, cut them into thin slices.
Or use a knife and slice the sprouts into thin rounds.
Place the bacon into a frying pan. Cook for one minute, then add the onion.
Saute until the bacon is crisp and the onion golden.
Stir in the marjoram.
Add the shredded sprouts, sprinkle with salt and pepper and mix well.
Pour in the water and immediately place a tight fitting lid over the pan.
Cook for three to four minutes without removing the lid, shaking the pan a few times to keep the sprouts from sticking.
The Brussels sprouts should steam enough to be cooked crisp-tender in this amount of time.
Stir in the butter and taste to correct the seasonings. Serve immediately.
Serves four to six.

JULIENNE OF CARROTS WITH MINT

6 carrots
1/4 cup water
1 tablespoon lemon juice
1/2 teaspoon sugar
2 tablespoons butter
salt, pepper
pinch ground cardamom
pinch ground mace or nutmeg
1/2 teaspoon dried mint†

Peel the carrots and cut them into julienne strips. A food processor is excellent for this.
Mix together the water, lemon juice and sugar in a small bowl and set aside.

BROCCOLI GRATIN

Melt the butter in a frying pan.
Add the carrots and stir to coat them with the butter.
Stir in the salt, pepper, cardamom, mace and dried mint.
Add the liquid and immediately cover the pot with a tight fitting lid.
Steam the carrots for five minutes, shaking the pot occasionally without removing the lid.
Taste to correct the seasonings and serve immediately.
Serves four.

†If fresh mint is in season, use about two teaspoons chopped and do not add until the end of the cooking time.

CARROTS a LA VARENNE

6 carrots, sliced thin
water, as needed
salt, pepper
1 1/2 tablespoons butter
1 small onion, diced
1 1/2 teaspoons wine vinegar
pinch nutmeg

Cook the carrots in a little water with a pinch of salt added until they are tender.
The water should be evaporated by the time the carrots are cooked. If not, boil down.
Heat the butter in a medium-sized frying pan.
Add the onions and saute for a few minutes, until they are golden.
Stir in the carrots, vinegar and nutmeg.
Add salt and pepper to taste.
Cook just until hot and serve immediately.
Serves four.

CURRIED CAULIFLOWER

2 tablespoons butter
1 large onion, chopped
1/4 teaspoon cumin seeds
1/2 teaspoon white mustard seeds
1 teaspoon minced ginger root
1/4 teaspoon ground turmeric
1 teaspoon salt
1/2 teaspoon pepper
1/2 cup water
4 to 5 cups cauliflower florets, about one-half of a large head
1/2 cup peas

Heat the butter in a medium-sized saucepan and add the onions.
Cook for a few minutes, until golden.
Add the cumin and mustard seeds to the pan along with the ginger root.
Cook over low heat for a few minutes, until the seeds begin to pop.
Add the turmeric, salt and pepper to the pan.
Continue to cook for another five minutes, stirring often.
Pour in the water and mix well.
Add the cauliflower and the peas (if fresh) and mix well.
Allow the vegetables to simmer for about ten minutes, stirring occasionally.
If using frozen peas, defrost and add two or three minutes before the cooking time is up.
This dish can be reheated, just be careful not to cook too long the first time or the cauliflower will fall apart.
Serves four to six.

CORN FRITTERS

1 cup cooked corn (1 large ear)
2/3 cup flour
1/2 teaspoon baking powder
2/3 teaspoon salt
1 to 2 teaspoons sugar
pepper to taste
2 eggs
2 tablespoons milk
1 tablespoon chopped fresh parsley
2 tablespoons butter
2 tablespoons oil

Cut the corn off the cob and reserve.
Mix together the flour, baking powder, salt, sugar and a little pepper.
Beat the eggs with the milk in a bowl just until mixed.
Add the dry ingredients to the eggs and mix until smooth.
Stir in the corn and the parsley.
Heat the butter and the oil in a large frying pan.
When hot, drop in the batter, a tablespoon at a time.
Lower the heat to medium and cook until the fritters are browned on the bottom.
Then turn and brown the other side.
The fritters should take about fifteen minutes to cook, seven to eight minutes per side.
Serve immediately, while hot.
This recipe will make approximately sixteen small corn fritters.
Serves four.

CORN PUDDING

1 1/2 cups cooked corn
1/2 cup flour
1/2 teaspoon salt
1 tablespoon sugar
1/2 teaspoon chili powder†
1/2 teaspoon baking powder
1 egg
2 tablespoons butter, melted
1/2 cup milk
1 tablespoon dried bread crumbs

Remove the cooked corn from the cob.
Although better with fresh corn, this recipe can be made with canned corn.
Mix together the flour, salt, sugar, chili powder and the baking powder and reserve.
In a bowl, mix the egg with the cooled melted butter.
Add the dry ingredients to the bowl and mix well.
Gradually stir in the milk. This is best done with a whisk.
Stir in the corn.
Pour the pudding into a well buttered shallow casserole.
Sprinkle the top with the crumbs.
Place the casserole into a pan filled with about a half inch of hot water (bain marie).
Bake in a preheated 350 degree oven for about fifty minutes, or until the pudding is set and the top is lightly browned.
Serve immediately.
Serves four.

†Up to one teaspoon of chili powder can be added if you prefer a spicier tasting pudding.

CURRIED CAULIFLOWER

EGGPLANT WITH SCALLIONS

1 small eggplant
4 tablespoons butter
4 scallions, chopped
1/3 cup water
2 teaspoons chopped fresh basil
1 1/2 tablespoons chopped fresh parsley

Peel the eggplant and cut into large dice, about one inch square by one-quarter inch thick.
The eggplant does not need to be degorged for this recipe.
Heat three tablespoons of the butter in a frying pan.
Add the scallions and cook for one minute.
Add the eggplant, sprinkle with salt and pepper and stir to coat well with the butter.
Add the water to the pan and immediately cover with a tight fitting lid.
Steam the eggplant for three minutes, or just until tender.
Stir in the chopped fresh herbs and the remaining tablespoon of butter.
Taste to correct the seasonings and serve immediately.
Serves four.

SWEET AND SOUR EGGPLANT

1 large eggplant
1 green pepper
1 medium onion
1/2 cup chicken stock
2 tablespoons soy sauce
2 tablespoons rice wine vinegar
2 tablespoons sugar
1 to 2 tablespoons oil
1 teaspoon cornstarch
2 tablespoons water
12 cherry tomatoes (optional)

Peel and cut the eggplant into one inch dice.
Steam just until barely tender.
Use a microwave oven at high power for two minutes or a conventional steamer.
Be careful not to overcook, you want the eggplant to remain firm for this dish.
Cut the green pepper and the onion into one inch chunks and reserve.
Mix together the stock, soy sauce, vinegar and sugar and set this sauce aside.
Heat the oil in a frying pan and add the onion and the green pepper. Stir-fry for one minute.
Add the reserved sauce and continue to cook for one minute.
Mix the cornstarch with the water.
Bring the sauce to a fast boil and stir in the cornstarch.
Cook, stirring, for about fifteen seconds, just until the sauce thickens.
Add the eggplant and the tomatoes.
Cook for one minute just to heat. Serve immediately.
If you plan to reheat this dish, turn off the heat as soon as you have added the eggplant. Reheat briefly, just until hot.
Serves four as a vegetable course.

STUFFED EGGPLANT

2 medium eggplants
salt, pepper
1/2 cup butter
1 large onion, chopped
1/2 pound mushrooms, sliced
2 tomatoes, peeled, seeded and diced
1 tablespoon chopped fresh parsley
2 tablespoons flour
1 cup half and half
1/4 cup + 2 tablespoons grated Swiss cheese
1 teaspoon Dijon mustard
1/4 cup dry bread crumbs

Cut the eggplants in half, lengthwise. Score the flesh diagonally and sprinkle with a little salt.
Let sit for thirty minutes, then wipe the eggplants dry.
For this dish, the eggplants have to be partially cooked. There are several ways to do this.
You can either bake them in a 350 degree oven in a pan filled with about a half inch of water for about thirty minutes or steam them for ten to fifteen minutes in a conventional steamer. Or cook in a microwave oven (check the manual for the time needed).
You can also dredge the halves in a little flour and saute them in a few spoons of oil in a covered pan for five minutes on each side.
Allow the eggplants to cool enough to be handled, then scoop out the pulp, reserving the skins for stuffing. Chop the pulp.
Heat four tablespoons of the butter in a frying pan. Add the onion, sprinkle with salt and pepper and cook until golden.
Add the mushrooms and continue to cook for about five minutes, or until they are dry.
Stir in the tomatoes, parsley and the chopped eggplant pulp. Cook for a few minutes, then set aside.
Heat two tablespoons of butter in a saucepan and stir in the flour. Cook for a minute or two and remove the pan from the heat.
Slowly mix the half and half into the roux. Return the pan to the heat and bring the sauce to a boil, stirring often.
Mix a quarter cup of the grated cheese into the sauce along with the mustard.
Season with salt and pepper to taste.
Stir this sauce into the eggplant mixture.
Stuff the eggplant shells with the filling and place them in a buttered baking dish.
Sprinkle the tops with the two tablespoons of cheese and the bread crumbs. Dot with the remaining butter.
The dish can be prepared to this point early in the

day and refrigerated until baking time.
Bake in a preheated 375 degree oven for twenty to twenty-five minutes or until hot and browned.
Allow an extra five to ten minutes if the eggplant is cold.
Serves four as a main course.
Alternate:
Four slices of diced ham can be added along with the mushrooms.

SNOW PEA PODS WITH WATER CHESTNUTS

1/2 pound snow pea pods
1 tablespoon oil
2 scallions, minced
1/3 cup chicken stock
1 tablespoon soy sauce
6 water chestnuts, sliced†
1/2 teaspoon cornstarch
2 tablespoons water

Remove the tips and the strings from the snow pea pods.
Heat the oil in a frying pan.
Add the scallions and cook for one minute.
Add the snow pea pods and stir-fry for just one minute.
Pour in the chicken stock and the soy sauce.
Add the water chestnuts and continue to stir-fry for two minutes.
Dissolve the cornstarch in the water and add, stirring constantly.
Cook for a half a minute and serve immediately.
Serves four.

†A quarter cup of sliced fresh jicama can be substituted for the water chestnuts.

SNOW PEA PODS WITH ALMONDS

1/2 pound snow pea pods
1 to 2 tablespoons butter
2 tablespoons slivered almonds
salt, pepper
pinch ground allspice

Remove the strings and tips from the snow pea pods.
Rinse well and drain.
Melt the butter in a frying pan.
Add the almonds and cook, stirring often, until they are lightly browned.
They burn easily, so be careful.
Add the snow pea pods, sprinkle with salt, pepper and the allspice.
Stir-fry for just a minute or two. You want the pea pods to remain very crisp.
Serve immediately.
Serves four.

SPINACH CASSEROLE

1 pound fresh spinach leaves†
1 to 2 tablespoons water
1 tablespoon butter
1 slice bacon, diced fine
1 tablespoon chopped shallots
1/2 tablespoon flour
2/3 cup milk
salt, pepper
pinch grated nutmeg
2 tablespoons grated Swiss cheese
2 tablespoons grated Parmesan cheese
1 tablespoon dried bread crumbs

Cook the spinach with a few spoons of water in a frying pan (covered) just until the leaves are wilted and barely tender.
Or use a microwave oven for three to four minutes at high power.
Refresh under cold water, squeeze dry and chop.
Place two teaspoons of the butter along with the bacon and the shallots into a small saucepan.
Cook for a few minutes, until the bacon is lightly browned and the shallots are golden.
Stir in the flour and continue to cook for another minute.
Gradually add the milk, stirring well.
Season the sauce with salt, pepper and the nutmeg.
Continue to cook for two to three minutes, then mix with the spinach.
Taste to correct the seasonings.
Spoon into a small buttered casserole, smoothing the top.
Sprinkle with the grated cheeses and the bread crumbs.
Dot with the remaining teaspoon of butter.
The recipe can be completed to this point and refrigerated until needed.
Allow the casserole to come to room temperature before baking.
Bake in a preheated 400 degree oven for twenty to twenty-five minutes, or until the spinach is hot and the topping browned.
Serves four.

†Or use one ten-ounce package of frozen spinach leaves. Cook only until the leaves are separated. Refresh and drain very well.

STRING BEANS WITH SHALLOTS AND HAM

1 pound string beans
2 tablespoons butter
2 tablespoons chopped shallots
2 slices boiled ham, diced
1 teaspoon chopped fresh savory or a pinch dried
salt, pepper

Cook the string beans in a large pot of salted boiling water until they are just tender.

Refresh under cold water and drain well.
The beans can be cooked and kept refrigerated for a few days.
Heat the butter in a frying pan.
Add the shallots and the ham and saute for a few minutes, until the shallots are golden and the ham is lightly browned.
Add the cooked beans, savory and salt and pepper to taste.
Mix well and cook only until the beans are hot.
Serves four.

STRING BEANS WITH SAVORY AND MUSTARD

2 tablespoons butter
1 small onion, chopped fine
1 clove garlic, minced
1 teaspoon chopped fresh savory or 1/3 teaspoon dried
salt, pepper
1/4 cup water
1 teaspoon Dijon mustard
1 pound string beans, cooked

Heat the butter in a frying pan.
Add the onion and saute for a few minutes, until golden.
Add the garlic, savory and some salt and pepper.
Cook for a half a minute, then pour in the water and mix well.
Stir in the mustard, then add the string beans.
Cook until the beans are hot and the sauce is reduced to just a coating.
This should take only a few minutes.
The beans can be reheated. Add a spoon or two of water to keep them from sticking.
Serves four.

STRING BEANS WITH SPICED TOMATOES

1 pound string beans, cooked
3 large tomatoes†
1 or 2 tablespoons oil
1 medium onion, chopped
salt, pepper
1 large clove garlic, minced
1 tablespoon tomato paste
pinch sugar
pinch cayenne pepper or hot pepper flakes

Cut the cooked string beans into one inch lengths.
Peel, seed and dice the tomatoes and reserve.
Heat the oil in a frying pan.
Add the onion, sprinkle with salt and pepper and cook until golden.
Add the garlic, tomatoes, tomato paste, sugar and hot pepper flakes or cayenne pepper to the pan.
Be cautious with the hot pepper, you can always add more later.
Cook for five minutes, stirring occasionally.
Add the string beans to the pan, cover and heat the beans in the sauce for a few minutes.
Taste to correct the seasonings and serve.
These beans reheat well.
Serves four.

†A small can of Italian plum tomatoes can be substituted for the fresh tomatoes. Drain and chop before adding them to the pan.

STRING BEANS WITH MUSHROOMS AND ALMONDS

STRING BEANS WITH MUSHROOMS AND ALMONDS

1 pound string beans
2 tablespoons butter
2 tablespoons chopped shallots
4 large mushrooms, sliced
salt, pepper
1/2 teaspoon dried thyme†
2 tablespoons toasted almond slices

Cook the string beans in a large pot of boiling salted water until they are just tender.
Refresh under cold water and drain well.
The string beans can be cooked ahead and refrigerated, covered, for a day or two.
Heat the butter in a frying pan. Add the shallots and cook for a minute or two.
Add the mushrooms, sprinkle with salt and pepper and continue to cook until they are dry, stirring occasionally.
Add the thyme to the pan, then stir in the string beans. Cook, stirring, until the beans are hot.
Add the toasted almonds and cook for another half a minute.
Taste to correct the seasonings and serve.
Serves four.

†Or use dried savory.

SUMMER VEGETABLE COMBINATION

1 small eggplant
1 medium zucchini
4 large plum tomatoes
2 tablespoons butter
1 medium onion, chopped
1 clove garlic, minced
salt, pepper
2 teaspoons chopped fresh basil
1/2 teaspoon lemon juice

Peel and cut the eggplant into one-inch dice.
Scrub but do not peel the zucchini. Trim off the ends and cut into one-quarter inch rounds.
You can remove the seeds from the tomatoes, if you wish, but it is not necessary when using plum tomatoes for this dish. Cut the tomatoes into dice.
Heat the butter in a frying pan.
Add the onion and cook until golden.
Add the garlic, cook for a half a minute, then stir in the eggplant.
Sprinkle with salt and pepper.
Cover the pan and cook for two or three minutes.
Add the zucchini and the tomatoes.
Cover and continue to cook for about two minutes, or until the eggplant and the zucchini are tender, but still crisp.
Stir in the basil and the lemon juice.
Taste to correct the seasonings and serve immediately.
Serves four.

SUMMER VEGETABLE COMBINATION

CHEESE STUFFED TOMATOES

2 tomatoes
2 tablespoons grated Swiss or Parmesan cheese
2 1/2 tablespoons sour cream
2 tablespoons dried bread crumbs
1 tablespoon chopped fresh parsley
1 tablespoon chopped fresh basil
salt, pepper

Remove the cores and cut the tomatoes in half, crosswise.
Place the rest of the ingredients into a small bowl and mix well.
Divide the topping into four portions.
Spoon a dollup on each tomato half and spread evenly to cover.
Butter or oil an ovenproof pan. Place the tomatoes into the pan.
The tomatoes can be covered and refrigerated for several hours at this point.
Bake in a preheated 375 degree oven for twenty-five to thirty minutes, until the tomatoes are tender (not falling apart) and the topping is lightly browned.
Serve immediately. Do not reheat.
Serves four.

CURRY-RICE TOMATOES

2 large tomatoes
1/2 cup cooked rice
1/4 teaspoon curry powder
2 tablespoons yogurt or sour cream
1 tablespoon raisins
1 tablespoon toasted almond slices†
1 tablespoon chopped fresh dill
salt, pepper
1 teaspoon dried bread crumbs
1 teaspoon butter

Core, then cut the tomatoes in half, crosswise.
Using a melon ball scoop or a spoon, scoop out the pulp and the seeds, leaving the center stem intact.
Dice the pulp and reserve.
Discard the seeds and juice or save for stock.
In a bowl, mix together the rice, tomato pulp, curry powder, yogurt, raisins, almonds and dill.
Add salt and pepper to taste.
Fill each tomato half with one-quarter of the mixture and place them into an oiled baking pan.
Sprinkle the tops of the tomatoes with the bread crumbs and dot with butter.
The tomatoes can be prepared to this point early in the day and refrigerated until baking time.
Bake in a preheated 375 degree oven for twenty-five to thirty minutes, or until the stuffing is hot and the tomatoes are cooked, but still firm.
Serve immediately.
Serves four.

†Toasted pine nuts can be substituted for the almonds.

TOMATO CASSEROLE

1 tablespoon butter
1 small onion, chopped
salt, pepper
1 clove garlic, minced
1/4 teaspoon curry powder
1/4 cup sour cream
1 teaspoon flour
2 tablespoons heavy cream
4 tomatoes, sliced 1/4 inch thick
1/2 cup grated Swiss cheese
1 tablespoon dried bread crumbs

Heat the butter in a small frying pan.
Add the onion, sprinkle with a little salt and pepper and cook until golden.
Add the garlic and cook, stirring, for about a half a minute.
Stir in the curry powder and remove the pan from the heat.
Mix together in a small bowl the sour cream, flour and the heavy cream.
Add this mixture to the cooked onion, stir well and taste to correct the seasonings. Set aside for a few minutes.
You can prepare this dish individually in four small gratin dishes or use one shallow casserole.
Butter the baking dishes well and line with the tomatoes in overlapping slices.
Spread the curry mixture evenly over the tomatoes.
Sprinkle the top (or tops) with the grated cheese and the bread crumbs.
The casserole can be prepared to this point and refrigerated for several hours.
Bake in a preheated 425 degree oven for twenty minutes (a few minutes longer, if cold). The topping should be golden and the tomatoes tender.
Serve immediately.
Serves four.

ZUCCHINI WITH BASIL

4 small zucchini
salt, pepper
2 tablespoons butter
1 small onion, chopped
1/2 teaspoon lemon juice
1/2 tablespoon chopped fresh basil

Scrub the zucchini and trim off the ends but do not peel.
Cut into julienne. A food processor is excellent for this.
Place the zucchini into a colander and sprinkle with about a teaspoon of salt. Mix well with your hands and allow it to sit for twenty to thirty minutes.
Rinse with cold water and drain very well.
Heat the butter in a frying pan.
Add the onion and cook for a few minutes, until

golden.
Add the zucchini to the pan, sprinkle with pepper (no salt) and saute for two to three minutes over high heat, tossing constantly.
You want the zucchini to be barely tender.
Add the lemon juice and the basil. Taste to correct the seasonings and serve immediately.
Serves four.
Alternate:
Substitute one yellow squash for one of the zucchini for added color.

STUFFED ZUCCHINI

3 medium zucchini
1 yellow squash
salt,pepper
1 tablespoon butter
1 1/2 teaspoons chopped shallots
1/2 teaspoon chopped fresh marjoram or pinch dried
1/2 teaspoon flour
1 tablespoon sour cream
1/2 teaspoon lemon juice
2 tablespoons grated Swiss cheese
1 to 2 tablespoons grated Parmesan cheese

Scrub, then trim the stem ends off the squash.
Cut two of the zucchini in half, lengthwise, then into quarters.
With a melon ball scoop, hollow out the shells carefully, leaving a rim around all four sides of each piece.
Julienne the remaining zucchini along with the yellow squash. A food processor is good for this.
The zucchini pulp removed from the shells can be chopped and added to this as well.
Sprinkle a spoon or two of salt on the julienned squash and mix well.
Allow to sit for thirty minutes, then rinse well and squeeze very dry.
Heat the butter in a medium-sized frying pan.
Add the shallots and saute for a minute or two.
Add the julienned zucchini and yellow squash to the pan and cook, stirring often, for just a few minutes, until all the moisture is gone.
Stir in the marjoram and the flour.
Continue to cook, stirring, for another minute, then remove the pan from the heat.
Add the sour cream, lemon juice and the Swiss cheese. Mix well and add salt and pepper to taste.
Stuff the zucchini shells with this mixture.
Sprinkle with grated Parmesan cheese and place into a buttered baking pan.
The dish can be prepared to this point and allowed to sit at room temperature for an hour or two before cooking. Or it can be covered and refrigerated overnight, if necessary.
Bake in a preheated 425 degree oven for twenty minutes, or until hot and bubbling. Allow an extra five minutes or so if refrigerated.
Serves four, two shells per person.

STARCHES

NEW POTATOES WITH SOUR CREAM

12 small new potatoes
1/2 cup sour cream
1 tablespoon chopped fresh chives
1 teaspoon chopped fresh dill weed
salt, pepper

Scrub the potatoes well.
Cook them in boiling salted water just until they are tender. This should take about twenty-five to thirty minutes.
Drain well.
The potatoes can be peeled or not, as you like. I prefer them with their skins on.
If they are large, you can cut them in half.
Mix the remaining ingredients together and toss with the potatoes while still hot. Serve immediately.
Serves four.

MASHED POTATOES WITH ONIONS AND CHIVES

2 large potatoes
1 medium onion, chopped
2 1/2 to 3 tablespoons butter
1/2 cup hot milk
2 tablespoons chopped fresh chives
salt, pepper

Bake or boil the potatoes until they are tender.
If boiling, peel first and drain very well.
The potatoes can be baked in a microwave oven for eight minutes, turning once. Or bake in a 425 degree oven for one hour.
Let cool for a few minutes, then peel.
While the potatoes are cooking, saute the onion slowly in two tablespoons of the butter until very soft and reserve.
Put the hot potatoes through a potato ricer or food mill or mash them very well (do not use a food processor).
Stir the hot milk into the potatoes, then mix in the cooked onions and the chives.
Add salt and pepper to taste.
Add the rest of the butter if the mixture seems too dry.
Serve immediately, if possible.
The potatoes can be held for up to one hour before serving. Hold at room temperature, do not refrigerate.
Dot the top with extra butter and reheat briefly in the oven. They can also be reheated in a microwave oven.
They are best, however, when fresh.
Serves four.

STUFFED ZUCCHINI

BAKED STUFFED POTATOES

2 large baking potatoes
2 tablespoons butter
2 tablespoons cream cheese
1/4 cup milk
2 tablespoons chopped chives
salt, pepper
2 tablespoons grated Swiss cheese

Scrub and dry the potatoes. Prick and bake in a preheated 400 degree oven for one hour.
Remove and allow the potatoes to cool for ten minutes.
Cut the potatoes in half, lengthwise. Remove the pulp with a spoon, being careful not to break the shells.
Mash the pulp using a food mill, a potato ricer or a masher, or even a mixer fitted with a flat blade. Do not use a food processor, it will make potato soup.
Stir the butter and the cream cheese into the hot potatoes. Mix until they are melted.
Stir in the milk and the chives. Add salt and pepper to taste.
Mound the potatoes back into the shells and sprinkle each with a half tablespoon of the grated cheese.
The potatoes can be prepared to this point and refrigerated for a few hours or even overnight.
Bake for twenty minutes (about five minutes longer if cold) in a preheated 425 degree oven, until the potatoes are puffed and hot and the cheese is melted and browned.
Serve immediately.
Serves four.

OVEN BROWNED POTATO SLICES

2 large baking potatoes
4 tablespoons butter
salt, pepper
1/2 teaspoon paprika

Scrub the potatoes well, but do not peel them.
Cut the potatoes into halves, lengthwise, then into half-inch wide wedges.
Melt the butter in an ovenproof pan large enough to hold all of the potatoes in one layer, if possible.
Add a little salt and pepper and stir in the paprika.
Place the potato wedges into the pan, turning to coat both sides with the butter.
Bake in a preheated 400 degree oven for one hour, turning once, or until the potatoes are tender inside and nice and brown and crunchy on the outside.
Serve immediately.
Serves four.

OVEN ROASTED POTATOES WITH ROSEMARY

2 Idaho baking potatoes
2 tablespoons butter
salt, pepper
1/2 teaspoon chopped fresh rosemary or pinch dried
2 teaspoons chopped fresh parsley

Scrub the potatoes, dry and slice them in half, lengthwise.
Score the tops of the potatoes on the diagonal in

OVEN ROASTED POTATOES WITH ROSEMARY

both directions, cutting in about a quarter of an inch. Be careful not to cut too deeply, or the potato will fall apart.
Melt the butter in an ovenproof pan.
Place the potatoes in the pan cut side down, to coat them with butter, then turn them cut side up.
Sprinkle the tops with salt, pepper, the rosemary and the parsley.
Bake in a 400 degree oven for fifty to fifty-five minutes. The potatoes should be fork tender and nicely browned on top.
Serves four.

BAKED HERBED POTATOES

2 large potatoes, cooked and peeled
2 1/2 tablespoons butter
1 tablespoon chopped shallots
salt, pepper
1 teaspoon chopped fresh chives
1/2 teaspoon chopped fresh dill weed
4 teaspoons chopped fresh parsley
1/2 cup milk
2 tablespoons heavy cream
1/2 cup grated Swiss cheese
1/4 cup grated Parmesan cheese
1 tablespoon dried bread crumbs

You can use leftover cooked potatoes for this dish. Baked potatoes are excellent, as are those cooked in a microwave.
Peel and cut into one-quarter inch slices.
Using a medium-sized ovenproof casserole, add two tablespoons of the butter.
Heat until melted, then add the shallots.
Sprinkle with salt and pepper and saute for a minute or two.
Remove the pan from the heat and add the herbs, milk, cream and the Swiss cheese.
Carefully mix in the potatoes.
Taste to correct the seasonings and pat the potatoes down in an even layer.
Sprinkle the top of the casserole with the grated Parmesan cheese and the bread crumbs. Dot with the remaining half tablespoon of butter.
The casserole can be prepared to this point and refrigerated for several hours, if necessary. Remove from the refrigerator about a half hour before baking.
Bake the casserole in a preheated 375 degree oven for about twenty to twenty-five minutes, or until the potatoes are hot and the topping is lightly browned.
Serves four.

POTATOES WITH DILL

2 large Idaho potatoes
1 clove garlic, minced
1/2 teaspoon salt
pepper to taste
1/2 teaspoon dill seed
1 1/2 cups milk
2 tablespoons sour cream
1 1/2 teaspoons chopped fresh dill weed
2 tablespoons grated Swiss cheese
1 tablespoon dried bread crumbs
1 teaspoon butter

Peel the potatoes. Cut them in half, lengthwise, then slice into one-quarter inch rounds.
Place the potatoes into a medium-sized saucepan.

Add the garlic, salt, pepper, dill seed and the milk.
Bring to a boil, then lower the heat and simmer the potatoes for about twenty minutes, until they are just about tender. Stir a few times while cooking.
Once cooked, the potatoes should have absorbed most of the milk.
Let cool for a few minutes, then stir in the sour cream and the dill weed.
Taste to correct the seasonings.
Spoon this mixture, including any liquid, into a gratin dish or casserole.
Smooth down the top then sprinkle with the grated cheese and the bread crumbs. Dot with the butter.
The potatoes can be completed to this point and allowed to sit at room temperature for about an hour before continuing. Or they can be refrigerated overnight. Allow the casserole to come to room temperature before baking.
Bake the potatoes in a preheated 425 degree oven for twenty to twenty-five minutes, or until they are hot and the topping is lightly browned.
Serves four.

HUNGARIAN POTATOES

2 tablespoons butter
1 medium onion, sliced thin
salt, pepper
1 clove garlic, minced
1 teaspoon paprika†
1/2 teaspoon dried marjoram
1 tomato, peeled, seeded and diced
2 large potatoes
1 cup chicken stock
1 tablespoon dried bread crumbs

Use a large shallow ovenproof pan, big enough to hold all the potatoes in a single layer, if possible.
Heat the butter in the pan, add the onions and saute them for a few minutes.
Sprinkle with a little salt and pepper.
Add the garlic, paprika, marjoram and the tomato.
Cook, stirring, for one minute, then remove the pan from the heat.
Peel and cut the potatoes into slices about one-quarter inch thick.
Layer the potato slices on top of the onion mixture. Sprinkle with a little salt and pepper.
Pour the stock into the casserole and sprinkle the tops of the potatoes lightly with the crumbs.
Bake in a preheated 425 degree oven for fifty-five minutes to one hour. The potatoes should be tender and the tops crunchy.
Serves four.

†If your paprika is very bland, add a pinch of cayenne pepper also. This dish should be somewhat spicy.

JULIENNED POTATO CASSEROLE

2 large baking potatoes
1/2 cup sour cream
1 cup milk
2 tablespoons chopped fresh chives
salt, pepper
1 tablespoon dried bread crumbs
2 tablespoons grated Parmesan cheese
1 teaspoon butter

Peel and julienne the potatoes. A food processor is excellent for this.
Immediately mix them with the sour cream, milk, chives and some salt and pepper.
Spoon the mixture into a well buttered casserole and pat down evenly.
Sprinkle the top of the casserole with the bread crumbs and the cheese. Dot with the butter.
Bake in a preheated 375 degree oven for one hour, or until the potatoes are tender and the topping is browned.
Serves four.

POTATO PANCAKES

2 tablespoons butter
3 tablespoons oil
2 large baking potatoes, peeled and diced
1 egg
3 tablespoons flour
1 tablespoon onion (1 slice)
1 tablespoon sour cream
1 teaspoon salt
pepper to taste
1 tablespoon chopped fresh parsley

This is a food processor recipe. The pancakes must be cooked as soon as they are made or the batter will turn brown.
Peel the potatoes and get everything ready before you begin to use the processor.
Begin to heat the butter and the oil in a large frying pan.
Place the potatoes, egg, flour, onion, sour cream, salt and pepper into a food processor fitted with a steel blade.
Blend, turning the machine on and off until the mixture has the consistency of grated potatoes. It will not be completely smooth.
Add the chopped parsley and turn on just to mix (if you add the parsley sooner, your mixture will be green).
Spoon the batter, by tablespoonfuls, into the hot butter-oil mixture.
Cook on a medium heat until the pancakes are nicely browned on one side.
Then turn to brown the other side.
The pancakes should take about ten to fifteen minutes to cook.
Remove from the pan and drain on paper towels.
Serve hot.
The pancakes can be reheated. I find the easiest

way to do this is to place them (in a single layer) onto aluminum foil broiling pans.
Heat in a 425 degree oven for about ten minutes. Drain again on paper towels and serve.
The pancakes can also be frozen. Do not thaw, but reheat as above, allowing an extra five to ten minutes.
Serve with apple sauce or a dollop of sour cream. Great as a vegetable or as an appetizer.
This recipe makes about twenty-four small pancakes.
Serves four.

SWEET POTATOES WITH A PECAN TOPPING

2 sweet potatoes
1 tablespoon melted butter
2 tablespoons chopped pecans
1/4 teaspoon ground cinnamon
1 teaspoon sugar

Scrub and dry the potatoes. Cut them in half, lengthwise.
Score the tops of the potatoes, cutting in about one-quarter of an inch on the diagonal in both directions.
Melt half of the butter in a shallow baking pan. Place the potatoes in the pan, turning them to coat the tops with the butter.
Bake, scored side up, in a preheated 425 degree oven for forty to forty-five minutes.
Mix the ground pecans with the cinnamon and sugar in a small bowl and reserve.
Remove the potatoes from the oven and sprinkle the pecan mixture evenly over the scored tops. Spoon the remaining melted butter on top.
The potatoes can remain at room temperature for an hour or two, if necessary, at this point.
Place the potatoes back into the oven and bake for another fifteen to twenty minutes, or until the topping is browned and the potatoes are tender.
Serves four.

RICE WITH COCONUT AND RAISINS

1/4 cup raisins†
1 1/2 cups water
2 tablespoons butter
1 teaspoon sugar
1/4 teaspoon salt
1/4 teaspoon ground allspice
1/4 cup shredded coconut
1 cup rice

Soak the raisins in the water for about thirty minutes.
Heat the butter in a saucepan.
Stir in the sugar, salt, allspice and the coconut and cook for a few minutes.
Add the rice and mix well to coat all the grains with the butter.
Pour in the water, along with the raisins.
Bring the liquid to a boil and stir again.
Cover the pan with a tight fitting lid and bake in a preheated 375 degree oven for twenty minutes.
Remove the pan from the oven and allow the rice to sit with the lid on for five minutes. Then mix well and serve.
Serves four.

†Currants can be substituted for the raisins.

CURRIED RICE

1 tablespoon butter
1 small onion, chopped fine
1/2 green pepper, finely diced
1/2 red pepper, finely diced
1 cup rice
1 teaspoon curry powder
1 cup pineapple, finely diced
1 tablespoon raisins
1 1/2 cups chicken stock
2 tablespoons yogurt or sour cream
salt, pepper
1 tablespoon toasted almond slices

You can use fresh or canned pineapple for this dish.
Heat the butter in a saucepan.
Add the onion and saute for a minute or two, until golden.
Add the green and red peppers and continue to cook for another minute.
Stir in the rice, mixing well to coat all the grains with the butter.
Mix in the curry powder, then add the pineapple, raisins and stock.
Bring the liquid to a boil and stir again.
Cover the pan with a tight fitting lid and bake in a preheated 375 degree oven for twenty minutes.
Remove from the oven and let the pan sit with the lid on for five minutes.
Then stir in the yogurt. Taste and add salt and pepper as needed.
Serve garnished with the toasted almonds.
Serves four.

HERBED RICE WITH PINE NUTS

2 tablespoons butter
1/4 cup pine nuts
1 small onion, chopped
1 cup rice
1/2 teaspoon dried thyme
1/2 teaspoon dried marjoram
1 1/2 cups chicken stock
2 tablespoons chopped fresh parsley
1/4 cup grated Parmesan cheese
salt, pepper

Heat the butter in a saucepan.
Add the pine nuts and the onion and saute over a moderate heat until the onions are golden and the pine nuts are lightly toasted. This should take

about five minutes.
Add the rice and stir well to coat all the grains with the butter.
Stir in the dried herbs, then the chicken stock.
Bring the liquid to a boil, then cover the pan and bake in a preheated 375 degree oven for twenty minutes.
Allow the pan to sit for five minutes without removing the lid.
Stir in the parsley and the cheese.
Taste to correct the seasonings and serve.
Serves four.
Alternate: Substitute tarragon for the marjoram for a more aromatic combination.

MEXICAN RICE

2 1/2 tablespoons butter
1 medium onion, chopped fine
1 large clove garlic, minced
1 cup rice
1/2 green pepper, diced fine†
1 large tomato, peeled, seeded and diced
1 1/2 cups chicken stock
1 tablespoon chopped fresh cilitrano††

Heat the butter in a saucepan.
Add the onion and cook for a few minutes, until golden.
Stir in the garlic and continue to cook for another minute.
Add the rice and stir to coat all the grains with the butter.
Mix in the green pepper and the tomato, then pour in the stock.
Bring the liquid to a boil, stir well and cover with a tight fitting lid.
Bake the rice in a preheated 375 degree oven for twenty minutes.
Remove from the oven and allow the rice to sit with the lid on for five minutes.
Stir in the cilitrano, taste to correct the seasonings and serve.
Serves four.

†Substitute one-quarter cup of diced hot peppers for the green pepper if you prefer spicy rice.
††Or use two tablespoons of chopped parsley.

ORANGE PECAN RICE

1 orange
1 1/2 tablespoons butter
1/4 cup coarsely chopped pecans
1 cup rice
pinch dried thyme
pinch salt
1 1/2 cups orange juice

Peel and cut the orange into segments, being careful to remove all the pith and the membrane surrounding the segments.
Cut into dice and reserve until needed.
Heat the butter in a saucepan.
Add the pecan pieces and cook and stir for a few minutes, to toast lightly.
Add the rice, thyme and salt, mixing well to coat all the grains of rice with the butter.
Pour in the orange juice and bring the liquid to a boil.

POTATO PANCAKES

CURRIED RICE

Stir, then cover the pan with a tight fitting lid.
Bake in a preheated 375 degree oven for twenty minutes.
Remove the pan from the oven and allow it to remain with the lid on for five minutes.
Mix in the reserved orange segments, taste to correct the seasonings and serve.
Serves four.

PINEAPPLE RICE

1 cup diced pineapple, fresh or canned
1 1/2 tablespoons butter
1 small onion, chopped fine
pinch salt
1/2 teaspoon curry powder
1 cup rice
1 1/2 cups unsweetened pineapple juice

Cut the pineapple into small dice. Fresh is better for this dish, but canned (well drained) will do.
Heat the butter in a saucepan.
Add the onion and cook for a few minutes, until golden.
Mix in a pinch of salt and the curry powder.
Add the rice and stir to coat all the grains with the butter.
Mix in the diced pineapple, then pour in the pineapple juice.
Bring the liquid to a boil and stir well.
Cover the pan with a tight fitting lid and bake in a preheated 375 degree oven for twenty minutes.
Remove from the oven and allow the pan to sit with the lid on for five minutes.
Mix well and serve.
Serves four.

SESAME RICE

1 tablespoon butter
1 small onion, chopped fine
1/4 cup sesame seeds
2 teaspoons sesame oil
1 cup rice
pinch ground cardamom
1/2 teaspoon salt
1 1/2 cups water

Heat the butter in a saucepan.
Add the onion and the sesame seeds and cook, stirring, until the onion is golden and the seeds are toasted and lightly browned.
Add the sesame oil and the rice. Mix well to coat all the grains of rice in the butter and the oil.
Mix in the cardamom and the salt, then pour in the water.
Bring the liquid to a boil, stir and cover with a tight fitting lid.
Bake the rice in a preheated 375 degree oven for twenty minutes.
Remove from the oven and allow the pan to sit with the lid on for five minutes.
Stir the rice and serve.
Serves four.

BASMATI RICE WITH CUMIN

1 cup basmati rice
2 cups water
3 tablespoons butter
1 large onion, chopped fine
2 tablespoons pine nuts
1 teaspoon cumin seeds

1 teaspoon salt
1/2 teaspoon ground pepper
1 carrot, peeled and grated

Pick over the rice for impurities and wash it well.
Soak the rice in the two cups of water for thirty minutes.
Drain, reserving the water.
Heat the butter in a frying pan.
Add the onion and cook for a few minutes, until golden.
Add the pine nuts and the cumin seeds to the pan.
Cook, stirring, for a few minutes until the nuts are lightly toasted.
Mix in the rice and stir to coat all the grains with the butter.
Add the salt and pepper and the reserved water.
Bring the liquid to a boil, mix well and cover with a tight fitting lid.
Simmer over low heat for fifteen minutes.
Remove the pan from the heat and let the rice sit undisturbed for five to ten minutes.
Then remove the lid, stir in the grated carrot and serve.
Serves four.

BASMATI RICE WITH SAFFRON

1/4 teaspoon saffron threads
2 tablespoons milk
1 cup basmati rice
2 cups water
2 tablespoons butter
1 medium onion, chopped fine
1 teaspoon chopped ginger root
1 teaspoon ground coriander
2 tablespoons currants
1/2 teaspoon salt

Soak the saffron threads in the milk for thirty to forty minutes.
Pick over the rice for impurities. Wash the rice well and then soak it in the two cups of water for thirty minutes. Drain, reserving the water.
Heat the butter in a frying pan.
Add the onion and the ginger root and cook for a few minutes.
Stir in the ground coriander and cook for another minute or two.
Add the rice, mixing well to coat all the grains with the butter.
Mix in the currants, salt and reserved water.
Bring the liquid to a boil, then drizzle the saffron and milk over the surface of the rice.
Cover with a tight fitting lid and simmer the rice for fifteen minutes.
Remove from the heat and allow the rice to sit undisturbed for five minutes.
Then stir well with a fork and serve.
Especially good with the Indian Braised Lamb, page 134.
Serves four.
If using coriander seeds, toast them first in a 375 degree oven for ten minutes or for two minutes in a microwave on high power. Cool, then grind.

HERBED NOODLES

3 tablespoons butter
1/4 cup chopped shallots
salt, pepper
2 tablespoons chopped fresh parsley
1 tablespoon chopped fresh oregano or 1 teaspoon dried
1 tablespoon chopped fresh basil or 1 teaspoon dried
1/2 cup milk
1/4 cup sour cream
2 to 2 1/2 cups cooked broad noodles

Heat the butter in a frying pan.
Add the shallots, sprinkle with salt and pepper and saute for a few minutes.
Add the dried herbs and stir.
Then add the fresh herbs and the milk.
Cook until the milk is hot.
Add the sour cream and stir until smooth.
Add the noodles and cook, stirring often, until everything is hot and the sauce has thickened. This will take only a few minutes.
Taste to correct the seasonings and serve.
Serves four.

POPPY SEED NOODLES WITH COTTAGE CHEESE

3 tablespoons butter
2 tablespoons ground poppy seeds
8 ounces broad noodles, cooked
salt, pepper
1/4 cup cottage cheese
1/4 cup sour cream

Heat two tablespoons of the butter in a frying pan.
Add the poppy seeds and toast them for a few minutes.
Add the noodles, sprinkle with salt and pepper and cook, stirring, until they are hot.
Add the rest of the butter to the pan.
Mix the cottage cheese with the sour cream and stir into the noodles.
Continue to cook for a minute or two, just until hot.
Taste to correct the seasonings and serve.
Serves four.

SESAME NOODLES

4 tablespoons butter
2 tablespoons sesame seeds
1/4 cup dried bread crumbs
2 cups cooked noodles
salt, pepper

Melt the butter in a frying pan.
Add the sesame seeds and the bread crumbs.

Cook over a low heat, stirring often, until both are lightly toasted.
Mix in the cooked noodles and sprinkle with salt and pepper.
Cook, stirring, until the noodles are hot, then serve.
Serves four.

FUSILLI WITH PESTO

8 ounces fusilli
2 tablespoons butter
1 1/2 tablespoons walnuts, coarsely chopped
1 1/2 tablespoons pine nuts
salt, pepper
3 tablespoons pesto sauce, page 143†
freshly grated Parmesan cheese

Cook the noodles in lots of boiling salted water until they are just al dente. Rinse with hot water and drain well.
Heat the butter in a large frying pan.
Add the walnuts and the pine nuts and cook, stirring, until they are lightly colored.
Add the noodles and mix well to coat with the butter.
Continue to cook until they are nice and hot.
Stir in the pesto, add some grated cheese and freshly ground pepper.
Cook for just a minute until hot and serve.
Pass a bowl of grated Parmesan cheese and a peppermill with the pasta.
Serves two as a main course or four as a side dish or appetizer.

†If frozen, thaw before using.

PASTA WITH MUSHROOMS AND TOMATOES

8 dried mushrooms
1/2 cup warm water
3 to 4 tablespoons butter
1 large onion, chopped
2 dozen mushrooms, sliced
salt, pepper
2 cloves garlic, minced
4 cups plum tomatoes, peeled and chopped
2 tablespoons tomato paste
pinch sugar
2 tablespoons chopped fresh basil
2 tablespoons chopped fresh parsley
10 to 12 ounces pasta

Soak the dried mushrooms in the warm water for thirty minutes.
Squeeze dry and chop the mushrooms. Save the liquid for soups or sauces.
Begin to heat a large pot of salted water for the pasta.
Heat the butter in a large frying pan.
Add the onion and saute for a few minutes.
Add the fresh and dried mushrooms to the pan.
Sprinkle with a little salt and pepper and continue to cook until the mushrooms have released their liquid and are dry.
Add the garlic, cook for a half a minute, then stir in the plum tomatoes, the tomato paste, a pinch of sugar and the herbs.
Continue to cook, stirring occasionally, for about ten minutes.
While the sauce is simmering, cook the pasta in lots of boiling salted water until just al dente. Rinse under hot water and drain well.
Taste the sauce to correct the seasonings. Mix with the pasta and serve immediately with a large bowl of grated Parmesan cheese and some fresh pepper.
Serves four as a main course.

KASHA WITH BOWTIES

4 tablespoons butter
1 cup kasha (buckwheat groats)
1 egg
2 cups water, or more as needed
salt, pepper
1 medium onion, chopped
1/4 teaspoon paprika
1/4 cup dried bread crumbs
2 cups cooked bowtie noodles

Heat two tablespoons of the butter in a large frying pan that has a lid.
Add the kasha and cook, stirring often, until the groats are lightly toasted and begin to give off a strong nutty aroma.
Reduce the heat to low.
Mix the egg with a tablespoon of water and add to the kasha, stirring constantly with a fork to scramble them into very small pieces.
Sprinkle with salt and pepper and gradually stir in the two cups of water.
Cover with a lid and simmer for thirty minutes, stirring a few times, until the kasha is tender.
Add more water, if needed, to keep the groats from sticking. There should be no water left by the time the groats are done.
While the groats are cooking, slowly saute the onion in a separate frying pan in the remaining two tablespoons of butter, until tender and golden.
Sprinkle with salt and pepper and stir in the bread crumbs.
Continue to cook until the crumbs are lightly toasted, stirring often.
Mix in the paprika and cook for another minute.
Mix together the cooked kasha, the onion and crumb mixture and the cooked noodles.
Taste to correct the seasonings. Heat and serve.
This dish can be kept in the refrigerator for several days. It also freezes very well.
Serves four to six.

HERBED NOODLES

KASHA WITH BOWTIES

Desserts

CAKES

CHOCOLATE CHERRY CAKE

1 3/4 cups flour
1/2 cup cocoa powder (2 ounces)
1 teaspoon baking powder
1/2 teaspoon baking soda
1/4 teaspoon salt
1/2 teaspoon ground ginger
16 ounce can pitted dark sweet cherries
10 tablespoons butter
1 cup sugar
4 eggs
2/3 cup sour cream
3 tablespoons Kirschwasser

Butter the bottom of two nine-inch baking pans. Line them with parchment or waxed paper. Then butter and flour the pans and the paper. Preheat the oven to 375 degrees.
Sift together the flour, cocoa powder, baking soda, salt and the ginger. Set aside until needed.
Drain the cherries well. Reserve twelve (or more) for decoration.
Using a mixer, cream the butter with the sugar until light and fluffy.
Beat in the eggs, two at a time.
Mix half the dry ingredients into the batter.
Add the sour cream and the Kirsch and mix well, then beat in the rest of the dry ingredients.
Stir in the cherries.
Spoon the batter evenly into the prepared pans.
Bake for thirty minutes, or until the cakes test done.
Let cool for about ten minutes, then turn the cakes out of the pans onto a rack to finish cooling.
The cake layers can be refrigerated for two or three days before they are frosted, if wrapped well. Or they can be frozen.
Ice with the Chocolate Kirsch Frosting, page 170.
Or use the buttercream recipe found on page 170,

CHOCOLATE CHERRY CAKE

substituting Kirschwasser for the brandy and omitting the coffee extract.
Decorate the top of the cake with the reserved cherries.
I like to press a layer of dark chocolate shavings around the sides of the cake, as well.
This cake will taste even better the day after it is made. Serve at room temperature.
Serves twelve or more.

CHOCOLATE KIRSCH FROSTING

3 ounces semi-sweet chocolate
1/4 cup butter
1 egg
1 tablespoon Kirschwasser
2 cups sifted confectioners sugar (8 ounces)

Coarsely chop the chocolate.
Melt the chocolate with the butter, then cool.
Once cool, whip in the egg and the Kirschwasser.
Gradually add the sugar, beating well.
Enough frosting for two nine-inch cake layers.

COCOA SPICE CAKE

1 1/2 cups flour
1/2 cup unsweetened cocoa powder
2 teaspoons baking powder
1/4 teaspoon salt
1/4 teaspoon ground ginger
1/8 teaspoon ground allspice
1/4 teaspoon grated nutmeg
1/2 teaspoon ground cinnamon
3/4 cup butter
1 cup sugar
4 eggs
1/2 cup milk (or water)
1/2 teaspoon vanilla extract
2 tablespoons brandy

Butter a nine inch springform pan. Line the bottom with parchment paper, then butter and flour the paper and the pan.
Or bake in a buttered and floured (unlined) eight by twelve inch baking pan.
Preheat the oven to 375 degrees.
Sift together the flour, cocoa powder, baking powder, salt and the spices and reserve.
Using a mixer, cream the butter with the sugar until light and fluffy. Then beat in the eggs, two at a time.
Mix the dry ingredients into the batter alternately with the liquids. Begin and end with the dry ingredients.
Pour the batter into the prepared pan and bake about sixty-five minutes for the springform pan, or about forty minutes for the flat pan, or until the cake tests done.
Allow the flat cake to cool in the pan.
Turn the cake baked in the springform pan out of the pan to cool on a rack (leave the cake upside down so that the top will flatten, and make it easier to ice).
The cake base can be wrapped and refrigerated for a day or two before frosting or it can be frozen.
When cool, cut the round cake in half. If you prefer a moist cake, sprinkle the layers with a little extra brandy.
Or spoon on a brandy syrup. Boil a tablespoon and a half of water with a tablespoon of sugar for a minute or two, then add a tablespoon of brandy and cool a little.
Prepare the Chocolate Buttercream frosting on this page, using the alternate spice cream version found below the recipe. Use the spice cream to frost between the layers, covering the top and sides with the chocolate cream.
For the flat cake, frost the top with the Mocha Frosting recipe.
Both versions of this cake will serve twelve.

MOCHA FROSTING

3 ounces semi-sweet chocolate
1/4 cup heavy cream
1/4 teaspoon instant coffee powder
1/4 teaspoon vanilla extract

Chop the chocolate into small pieces.
Place the chocolate along with the cream and the coffee powder into a small saucepan.
Melt over low heat, stirring constantly. Or use a microwave oven on a low setting, stirring every two minutes, until melted.
Stir in the vanilla and allow the frosting to cool to room temperature.
Spread over the top of the flat version of the Cocoa Spice Cake.
Enough frosting to ice an eight by twelve inch cake.

CHOCOLATE BUTTERCREAM

1 1/2 tablespoons cornstarch
2 egg yolks
3/4 cup milk
1/3 cup + 1 tablespoon sugar
1 1/2 cups butter, room temperature
2 tablespoons brandy
3 ounces semi-sweet chocolate, melted
1/4 teaspoon coffee extract, optional

Mix the cornstarch, egg yolks and a few spoons of the milk together until they are smooth.
Heat the rest of the milk in a small saucepan.
Whisk a spoon or two of the hot milk into the egg yolk mixture, then stir this mixture back into the saucepan.
Cook, stirring constantly, until thick.
Remove the pan from the heat and scrape the pastry cream mixture out onto a plate.
Sprinkle the top of the cream with the tablespoon of sugar to prevent a skin from forming as the cream cools.
Allow it to cool to room temperature.
If your cream is lumpy (it should not be), you can

save it by placing it in a food processor and pureeing until smooth.
Using a mixer, beat the butter with the one-third cup of sugar until light and fluffy.
Whip the cooled cream, the chocolate, brandy and the coffee extract into the butter.
Continue to beat until smooth.
This recipe makes enough frosting to ice two nine inch cake layers.
Alternate: **Spice cream layer:**
Follow the above recipe until the point where you combine the whipped butter and sugar with the rest of the ingredients.
Add just the cooled pastry cream and the brandy to the butter and beat well.
Remove three quarters cup of this mixture and reserve.
Add the chocolate and the coffee extract to the buttercream remaining in the mixer and beat well. Use this to frost the top and sides of the cake.
Add one-eighth teaspoon each ground cinnamon and ginger and a pinch of grated nutmeg to the reserved three-quarters cup of frosting and mix well. Use this to frost between the layers.

CHRISTMAS CAKE

1 1/2 cups flour
1/2 cup ground almonds (2 ounces)
1/2 teaspoon salt
1 teaspoon ground cinnamon
1/2 teaspoon ground allspice
1/2 teaspoon ground ginger
1/2 teaspoon grated nutmeg
1 teaspoon baking powder
grated rind and juice of 1 lemon
1 cup pitted dried prunes (6 ounces)
1 cup dried pears (5 ounces)
1 cup dried apricots (6 ounces)
1 cup currants (4 ounces)
1 cup dark raisins (4 ounces)
1 cup white raisins (4 ounces)
1 cup pecans (5 ounces)
1 1/2 cups butter
1 1/2 cups sugar
6 eggs
1/3 cup brandy

Butter the bottom of a ten inch springform pan. Line with parchment or waxed paper, then butter and flour the paper and the pan. Preheat the oven to 325 degrees.
Mix together the flour, ground almonds, salt, spices, baking powder and the lemon rind. Set aside.
Dice the dried prunes, pears and apricots and mix them with the currants and the dark and white raisins.
Coarsely chop the pecans. Add them to the dried fruit and reserve until needed.
Using a mixer, cream the butter with the sugar until light and fluffy.
Add the eggs, two at a time and beat until well incorporated.
Stir in the lemon juice and the brandy.
Add the dry ingredients and mix until smooth, then stir in the dried fruits and nuts.
Pour the batter into the prepared pan and bake for two hours and forty-five minutes to three hours, or until the cake tests done.
Place on a wire rack and allow the cake to cool until it reaches room temperature.
Then remove from the pan and peel off the paper lining.
Wrap well and refrigerate for at least a day or two to allow the flavors to mellow before icing. The cake keeps well for a week or longer, it just seems to get better with age. It can also be frozen for several months.
Ice with the Almond Frosting.
Decorate with glazed cherries and nuts.
This is a large rich cake and will serve sixteen or more portions.
Alternate:
Two eight ounce bags of mixed dried fruits can be substituted for the prunes, pears and apricots in this recipe.

ALMOND FROSTING

4 ounces butter
4 ounces cream cheese
7 ounces marzipan or almond paste
1 egg yolk
1/2 teaspoon lemon juice
1/4 teaspoon almond extract
3/4 cup sifted confectioners sugar (3 ounces)

In a mixer fitted with a flat blade, whip the butter, cream cheese and almond paste together, until very smooth and creamy.
Do not use a food processor, it will make the frosting too soft.
Blend in the egg yolk, lemon juice and the almond extract.
Gradually beat in the confectioners sugar.
Continue to whip the frosting until it is smooth.
If it is too soft to handle easily, refrigerate for about a half hour.
Enough frosting to ice the top and sides of a ten inch Christmas Cake.

GRATED CHOCOLATE CAKE

1 cup flour
1/2 cup ground almonds (2 ounces)
1/2 cup ground hazelnuts (2 ounces)
1 teaspoon baking powder
1 teaspoon baking soda
pinch salt
1/4 teaspoon grated nutmeg
1 cup grated semi-sweet chocolate (4 ounces)
1/2 cup butter
1/2 cup sugar
2 eggs
1 cup sour cream
1/2 teaspoon coffee extract
1 teaspoon vanilla extract

COCOA SPICE CAKE, layer

COCOA SPICE CAKE, flat

GRATED CHOCOLATE CAKE

MARJOLAINE

Butter and flour a nine by thirteen inch baking pan. Preheat the oven to 350 degrees.
Mix together the flour, almonds, hazelnuts, baking powder, baking soda, salt, nutmeg and grated chocolate. Reserve.
Cream the butter with the sugar until light and fluffy, then add the eggs and beat well.
Stir in half the dry ingredients.
Then mix in the sour cream and the coffee and vanilla extracts.
Add the rest of the dry ingredients and beat until smooth.
Spread (it is thick) the batter into the prepared pan and bake for about forty to forty-five minutes, or until the cake tests done.
Cool the cake in the pan.
Spread the top of the cake with the Chocolate Honey Frosting.
Serves twelve.
Alternate:
To make a layer cake, bake in two nine-inch round cake pans that have been lined with parchment or waxed paper, buttered and floured. Baking time will be about the same. Turn out of the pans to cool.
Substitute the Chocolate Buttercream on page 170, for the Chocolate Honey Frosting recipe.
Decorate with toasted almond slices or chocolate shavings or both.

CHOCOLATE HONEY FROSTING

4 ounces semi-sweet chocolate
6 tablespoons butter
2 tablespoons honey

Chop the chocolate into fairly small pieces.
Place the chocolate, along with the butter, into a double boiler or a metal bowl set over a pan of hot water and heat until melted. Or use a microwave oven on a low setting.
Stir in the honey and chill the frosting just until it is thick enough to spread.
This recipe makes enough frosting for a nine by thirteen inch cake.

MARJOLAINE

This is a somewhat complicated cake in that the next three recipes make up the complete 'Gateau Marjolaine'.

5 ounces ground almonds
5 ounces ground hazelnuts
1 ounce flour
10 ounces sugar
1/8 teaspoon ground nutmeg
1 1/4 cups egg whites (8 to 10)
pinch salt

For best results, the ingredients for this cake should be weighed, rather than measured.
Preheat the oven to 350 degrees.
Line two baking sheets with parchment paper. Draw two rectangles on each of the sheets, about twelve by four and one-half inches (use a pencil).
Mix together the almonds, hazelnuts, flour, sugar and nutmeg and set aside.
Beat the egg whites until they are foamy. Add a pinch of salt and continue to beat until they are stiff.
Quickly fold in the reserved dry ingredients.
Fill a large pastry bag fitted with a plain half-inch round tip and pipe the outline of the four rectangles onto the baking sheets.
Then fill in the centers, using a metal spatula to even and smooth the tops.
Place the cakes into the oven and bake for about forty-five minutes.
Shift the pans from top to bottom halfway through the baking time, unless you are using two ovens (then bake in the center).
The cakes should be light brown in color and firm to the touch when they are done.
Remove the parchment paper, with the cakes still attached, from the baking sheets.
When cool, peel off the parchment paper.
The cake layers can be used immediately or wrapped in a plastic wrap or aluminum foil and refrigerated for a few days. Or they can be frozen for up to six weeks.
Makes four rectangular cake layers.
Assembly of the cake is described in the Triple Frosting recipe.

TRIPLE FROSTING

1 1/2 cups milk
2 inch piece of a vanilla bean, or 1 teaspoon extract
1/2 cup + 1/2 tablespoon sugar
1/4 cup cornstarch
4 egg yolks
1 1/4 pounds butter, room temperature
1/4 cup praline powder, recipe page 175
1 tablespoon Kirschwasser
1/3 cup heavy cream, lightly whipped
4 ounces semi-sweet chocolate, melted and cooled
2 tablespoons Cognac or brandy

Heat one and one-quarter cups of the milk with the vanilla bean (if using).
In a small bowl, mix one-quarter cup of the sugar with the cornstarch. Add the egg yolks and the remaining milk and stir until smooth.
When the milk is hot, whisk a few spoonfuls into the egg yolks, then stir the yolk mixture back into the pan.
Cook, stirring constantly, until the mixture is very thick.
If using vanilla extract, stir in at this point.
Pour the cooked cream onto a plate and sprinkle with the half tablespoon of sugar. Allow it to cool

to room temperature before proceeding.
Cream the butter with the remaining quarter cup of sugar until very light and fluffy.
If the cooled pastry cream is at all lumpy, smooth by pureeing in a food processor or blender before continuing.
Add the cooled pastry cream mixture to the butter and beat until light and smooth.
Measure off one cup of this frosting and stir in the praline powder.
Measure off another one-half cup of the frosting and fold the Kirschwasser and the whipped cream into it.
Add the melted chocolate and the Cognac to the remaining frosting.
To ice the marjolaine, place one cake layer on a rectangular board or platter.
Frost with a thin layer of the chocolate frosting.
Place a second cake layer on top. Frost with all of the cream and Kirsch mixture.
Place a third cake layer on top and frost with all of the praline mixture.
Top with the fourth cake layer.
Ice the top and sides of the cake with the chocolate frosting. Pipe a decorative edge around the bottom, sides and top of the cake.
Refrigerate the cake overnight to allow the flavors time to mellow before serving.
This cake will keep well for a few days if covered and refrigerated.
Serves sixteen slices, each about three-quarters inch thick.

PRALINE POWDER

1/3 cup skinned hazelnuts (1 ounce)
1/3 cup blanched almonds (1 1/2 ounces)
1 cup sugar

Line a baking sheet with a piece of heavy duty aluminum foil. Spread a few drops of oil on the surface of the foil.
Place the almonds and the hazelnuts in a single layer in the center of the sheet.
Using a small frying pan, heat the sugar until it becomes liquid and has turned light brown in color. Be careful not to burn the caramel.
Stir with a wooden spoon once the sugar begins to melt so that it will brown evenly.
Pour the caramel over the nuts and allow it to cool to room temperature.
Be very careful not to touch the hot liquid as it can cause a nasty burn.
Once cool, remove the praline from the foil.
Break into pieces and grind into a fine powder using a food processor or a blender.
Store the powder in an airtight container in the refrigerator. The powder will keep for a few months. Use to flavor desserts and cakes.
Makes two cups praline powder.

PUMPKIN CHIFFON CAKE

2 cups flour
1/2 cup brown sugar
1 cup sugar
1 tablespoon baking powder
1 teaspoon salt
1 teaspoon ground cinnamon
1/4 teaspoon grated nutmeg
1/2 teaspoon ground ginger
1/2 cup oil
5 egg yolks
2/3 cup cooked or canned pumpkin
1/3 cup water
1 cup egg whites (about 7)
Brandy Buttercream†
1 to 1 1/2 cups chopped walnuts or pecans

You will need a nine or ten inch ungreased tube pan. Preheat the oven to 325 degrees.
Using a large bowl, mix together the flour, brown sugar, one-half cup of the granulated sugar, baking powder, salt, cinnamon, nutmeg and ginger.
Make a well in the center and add the oil, egg yolks, pumpkin and water.
Beat until smooth.
In a separate bowl, whip the egg whites until they turn white and soft peaks begin to form.
Gradually add the remaining half cup of sugar and continue to beat until the whites are stiff and glossy.
Stir one-quarter of the beaten whites into the pumpkin mixture, then fold in the rest.
Pour the batter into the pan and bake for one hour and fifteen minutes, or until the cake tests done.
Invert the cake to cool.
Remove from the pan when it reaches room temperature.
The cake can be wrapped and refrigerated for a few days at this point, or it can be frozen.
Frost the top and sides of the cake with the Brandy Buttercream.
Press the chopped nuts onto the sides of the cake.
Decorate the top with rosettes of buttercream, if desired.
The finished cake can be refrigerated overnight.
Allow to sit at room temperature for one hour before serving.
Serves twelve or more.

†Use the Chocolate Buttercream recipe on page 170. Omit the chocolate and the coffee extract. Instead, add one-quarter teaspoon each of cinnamon and ginger and a pinch of nutmeg into the entire frosting recipe when you add the cooled cream to the butter.

PUMPKIN CHIFFON CAKE

POPPY SEED CAKE

BANANA RAISIN CAKE

1 1/4 cups flour
2 teaspoons baking powder
1/2 teaspoon baking soda
1/2 teaspoon salt
1 teaspoon ground cinnamon
1/4 teaspoon grated nutmeg
1 cup oatmeal (not instant)
2 eggs
2/3 cup sugar
2/3 cup oil
2 large bananas, mashed
1/2 cup raisins
1/2 cup chopped walnuts or pecans
Topping:
2 tablespoons sugar
1/4 teaspoon ground cinnamon

Butter and flour a nine inch square pan. Preheat the oven to 350 degrees.
Mix together the flour, baking powder, baking soda, salt, cinnamon, nutmeg and the oatmeal and reserve.
Using a mixer, beat the eggs with the sugar until light and fluffy.
Slowly beat in the oil.
Stir in the mashed bananas.
Add the dry ingredients and mix until well blended.
Stir in the raisins and the nuts.
This batter will be very liquid. Pour the batter into the prepared pan.
Mix the sugar and cinnamon for the topping and sprinkle evenly over the batter.
Bake for forty-five to fifty minutes, or until the cake tests done.
Serve warm or cool.
This cake keeps well for a week if wrapped and refrigerated. It can also be frozen.
Serves twelve.
Alternate: Fold in one-half cup of chocolate chips along with the raisins and the nuts.

BERRY CRUMBLE

Crust:
1 cup quick cooking oatmeal
1/2 cup chopped walnuts
1/3 cup brown sugar
1/4 teaspoon ground cinnamon
1/3 cup melted butter
Fruit Filling:
1/4 cup sugar
1 1/2 teaspoons cornstarch
1 teaspoon lemon juice
2 cups blueberries†
Topping:
1/2 cup heavy cream
1/2 teaspoon vanilla extract
1/2 cup sour cream
1 tablespoon sugar

Preheat the oven to 375 degrees. Butter a nine inch square pan or a nine or ten inch pie tin.
Spread the oatmeal in a thin layer in a baking pan. Toast in the oven for ten minutes. Remove and place into a bowl.
Add the nuts, cinnamon and sugar to the oatmeal.
Stir in the melted butter.
Press this crust into an even layer on the bottom and sides of the pie tin, or just the bottom of a square pan.
Bake for fifteen minutes (375 degrees), then remove from the oven.
While the crust is baking, prepare the filling.
Place the sugar, cornstarch and lemon juice into a medium-sized saucepan.
Mix well, then stir in the berries.
Cook, stirring often, for about five minutes.
The berries will have released some of their juice and the sauce should be nice and thick.
Spread this warm filling into the crust and allow it to cool a little.
Whip the cream lightly with the sugar.
Stir in the sour cream and the vanilla.
Store the cream in the refrigerator until the crumble reaches room temperature, then spread evenly over the berries.
This dessert tastes even better the day after it is made. It will keep well for three or four days if covered and refrigerated—if it lasts that long.
Serves ten to twelve.

†Fresh blackberries work equally well for this recipe.
You can also use frozen blueberries. Thaw first, adding any juice accumulated to the pan when cooking.

FIVE SPICE CAKE WITH WATER CHESTNUTS

1 eight ounce can water chestnuts
2 cups crushed pineapple†
2 cups flour
2 teaspoons baking powder
1 teaspoon baking soda
1 teaspoon salt
1 1/2 teaspoons five spice powder
1 1/2 cups sugar
4 eggs
1 cup oil
2 tablespoons Cognac or brandy

Butter and flour a nine inch tube pan or two nine-inch bread pans. Preheat the oven to 350 degrees.
The cake can be made in a mixer or a food processor.
When using a mixer: Drain and finely chop the water chestnuts. Drain the crushed pineapple, saving the juice for the glaze or frosting.
In a bowl, mix together the flour, baking powder, baking soda, salt and the five spice powder and reserve.

Using the mixer, beat the eggs with the sugar until they are light and fluffy.
Gradually add the oil, beating well.
Stir the drained pineapple, water chestnuts and the Cognac into the egg mixture.
Add the dry ingredients and mix well.
When using a food processor: Drain the water chestnuts and the pineapple, reserving the pineapple juice for the glaze or frosting.
Mix together the dry ingredients as above and reserve.
Place the eggs and the sugar into the bowl of a processor fitted with a steel knife. Process for about fifteen seconds, until light and fluffy.
Add the oil and the Cognac and process until well mixed.
Add the dry ingredients and mix, turning the machine on and off just until blended.
Add the drained water chestnuts and process just until they are chopped into small pieces. Add the drained pineapple and mix.
Pour the completed batter into the prepared pan or pans and bake for one hour and ten minutes, or until the cake tests done. It will take the same amount of time in either pan.
When cool, turn the cake out of the pan. You can leave it plain, ice it with the Pineapple Frosting, or the Pineapple Glaze.
The cake will keep well for several days, if wrapped and refrigerated. It also freezes very well.
Serves twelve to sixteen portions.

†If using a food processor, you can substitute a can of pineapple chunks. Add along with the water chestnuts.

PINEAPPLE FROSTING

1/2 cup pineapple juice†
1/3 cup sugar
2 tablespoons butter
8 ounces cream cheese, softened

Place the pineapple juice and the sugar into a small saucepan. Heat to the boiling point.
Then simmer the juice for five to ten minutes, until thickened, stirring occasionally. Cool a little.
Whip the butter and the cream cheese together until they are light and fluffy.
Gradually beat in the syrup. Continue to beat until very smooth.
This makes enough frosting to ice the top and sides of a nine-inch tube cake.
Or use for the loaf cakes.

†Use the juice drained from the crushed pineapple or pineapple chunks.

PINEAPPLE GLAZE

1/2 cup pineapple juice†
2 tablespoons sugar
1 teaspoon cornstarch
1 tablespoon water

Place the pineapple juice and the sugar into a small saucepan.
Bring to a boil and continue to boil hard for three minutes.
Mix the cornstarch and the water together. Add this mixture to the boiling liquid, stirring constantly.
Cook until the color of the liquid turns clear. This should only take a minute.
Let cool and pour over the warm tube or loaf cakes.

†Use the juice drained from the canned pineapple.

OATMEAL GINGER CAKE

1 cup quick cooking oatmeal
1/2 cup raisins
1 1/4 cups boiling water
1 1/2 cups flour
1 teaspoon baking powder
1 teaspoon baking soda
1/2 teaspoon salt
1 teaspoon ground cinnamon
2 teaspoons ground ginger
1/4 teaspoon grated nutmeg
1/2 cup butter
1 cup brown sugar
2 eggs
2 tablespoons blackstrap molasses
1 teaspoon vanilla extract

Butter and flour a nine by thirteen inch baking pan. Preheat the oven to 350 degrees.
Place the oatmeal and the raisins into a bowl. Pour in the boiling water, stir and allow the mixture to stand for twenty minutes.
Mix together the flour, baking powder, baking soda, salt, cinnamon, ginger and nutmeg and reserve.
Using a mixer, cream the butter with the brown sugar until light.
Beat in the eggs, then stir in the molasses to form a batter.
Stir the dry ingredients into the batter.
Mix in the oatmeal and the vanilla. The batter will be very liquid.
Pour into the prepared pan and bake for about thirty-five minutes, or until the cake tests done.
Allow the cake to cool in the pan.
This cake stores well in the refrigerator for several days. It also freezes beautifully.
Serves twelve to fifteen portions.

PEACH PRALINE DESSERT

4 cups sliced peaches
3 tablespoons flour
1/2 cup sugar
2 teaspoons lemon juice
Topping:
1/2 cup brown sugar

1/2 cup flour
2 teaspoons ground cinnamon
1 cup chopped pecans
6 tablespoons butter

Butter a nine-inch glass baking pan. Preheat the oven to 400 degrees.
Prepare the topping. Mix together the brown sugar, flour, cinnamon and the pecans.
Work in the butter until small crumbs are formed. You can either use your hands or a food processor.
Peel and slice the peaches. Mix them with the flour, sugar and the lemon juice.
Sprinkle about one-third of the topping mixture evenly into the bottom of the pan.
Spoon in the peach mixture, then sprinkle the rest of the topping over the peaches.
Bake for thirty-five minutes, or until the peaches are tender and the topping browned.
Serve while still warm.
Serves nine or more portions.

PINEAPPLE COCONUT CAKE

1 1/2 cups flour
1 1/2 teaspoons baking powder
1/2 teaspoon baking soda
1/2 teaspoon ground cinnamon
pinch salt
1/2 cup butter
1/4 cup sugar
2 eggs
1 small can cream of coconut (8.5 oz.)
1/2 teaspoon vanilla extract
1 teaspoon lemon juice
1 eight ounce can crushed pineapple, drained
Topping:
1/3 cup brown sugar
1/3 cup coconut
1/4 teaspoon ground cinnamon
pinch grated nutmeg

Butter and flour a seven and one-half by eleven inch baking pan. Preheat the oven to 350 degrees.
Mix together the topping ingredients and reserve.
Mix the flour with the baking powder, baking soda, cinnamon and salt and set aside.
Using a mixer, cream the butter with the sugar until light and fluffy.
Beat in the eggs, one at a time.
Stir in the cream of coconut, vanilla and lemon juice.
Mix in the dry ingredients, beating until smooth.
Fold in the drained pineapple.
Pour the batter into the prepared pan and smooth the top.
Cover with the topping, sprinkling it over the surface as evenly as possible.
Bake for one hour, or until the cake tests done.
Good warm or cold.
This cake will keep well for several days if wrapped and refrigerated.
It can also be frozen.
Serves approximately ten portions.

PLUM CAKE

Crust:
1 1/2 cups flour
pinch salt
1/2 teaspoon baking soda
1/4 cup sugar
1/2 cup butter
1 egg
1/3 cup sour cream
1/2 teaspoon vanilla
Filling:
1 cup prune butter†
Streusel:
1/4 cup flour
1/4 cup sugar
1 teaspoon ground cinnamon
1/2 cup chopped walnuts
3 tablespoons butter

Butter and flour a nine-inch springform pan or a nine or ten inch pie pan.
Preheat the oven to 400 degrees.
To make the crust, place the flour, salt, baking soda and sugar into the bowl of a food processor fitted with a steel blade.
Process for a few seconds to mix.
Mix the egg with the sour cream and the vanilla.
Add this mixture to the machine and process until a dough is formed.
Press the dough into the prepared pan using your fingers (floured). If you are using a springform pan, press it up to form a rim about a half of an inch high around the edges.
Fill the crust with an even layer of the prune butter.
Mix all the streusel ingredients together until small crumbs are formed. A processor is fine for this, just add the nuts last.
Sprinkle in an even layer over the prune filling.
Bake the cake for forty-five to fifty minutes, or until the crust is browned.
Serve warm or cool.
This cake can be refrigerated for several days. It can also be frozen.
Serves ten or more.

†Apricot butter can be substituted for the prune butter.

POPPY SEED CAKE

2 cups flour
1 teaspoon baking soda
pinch salt
1/2 cup ground poppy seeds
1 cup butter
1 cup sugar
2 eggs
1/4 cup Sherry
grated rind of 1 lemon
1 cup sour cream
1 cup chopped walnuts or macadamia nuts

Butter and flour a nine-inch tube pan or two bread loaf pans. Preheat the oven to 350 degrees.
Mix the flour, baking soda, salt and poppy seeds together and reserve.
Using a mixer, cream the butter with the sugar until light and fluffy.
Add the eggs and beat well.
Mix in half the dry ingredients.
Then stir in the Sherry, lemon rind and the sour cream.
Add the rest of the dry ingredients and mix well.
Fold in the nuts.
Pour the batter into the prepared pan or pans and bake for one hour and ten minutes, or until the cake tests done. It will take the same amount of time in either type pan.
Allow the cake to remain in the pan until it is cool enough to handle.
Then turn out onto a rack to finish cooling.
The cooled cake can be topped with a chocolate glaze or dusted with confectioners sugar. I prefer it absolutely plain.
Serves twelve to sixteen.

ROMAN SEED CAKE

1/2 teaspoon anise seeds
1/2 teaspoon fennel seeds
1/4 teaspoon cumin seeds
1 1/2 cups flour
pinch salt
3/4 cup butter
3/4 cup sugar
3 eggs
1 tablespoon brandy
4 or 5 bay leaves

This is my own version of the ancient Roman 'mustaeceous' customarily served at the end of a meal to prevent indigestion. See page 26 for details.
Butter and flour a nine-inch loaf pan. Preheat the oven to 350 degrees.
Mix the anise, fennel and cumin seeds with the flour and the salt and reserve.
Using a mixer, cream the butter with the sugar until light and fluffy.
Add the eggs, one at a time, beating well between each addition.
Stir in the brandy, then add the dry ingredients to the batter, mixing well.
Spoon the batter into the prepared pan, smoothing the top.
Place the bay leaves in a row, on top of the cake.
Bake for forty-five minutes, or until the cake tests done.
Cool for ten minutes, then turn the cake out of the pan to finish cooling on a rack.
Remove the bay leaves when ready to slice. They are not good to eat, but flavor the cake nicely.
This loaf will keep for a week or longer, and is even better tasting after a few days. Wrap and refrigerate. It also freezes well.
Serves ten to twelve.
Alternate:
The recipe can be doubled and the cake baked in a tube pan. Use enough bay leaves to form a ring pattern around the top. The baking time is about the same.

ROMAN SEED CAKE

PIES AND TARTS

APPLE CREAM TART

Crust:
1 1/3 cups flour
1/4 teaspoon salt
1/2 teaspoon ground cinnamon
1 1/2 tablespoons sugar
1/2 cup butter
2 1/2 tablespoons Calvados
Filling:
6 apples
1/4 cup water†
1 teaspoon lemon juice
1/4 cup + 1 tablespoon sugar
1/2 teaspoon ground cinnamon
pinch grated nutmeg
pinch ground ginger
2 tablespoons heavy cream
1 tablespoon butter, melted
Apricot glaze††

To make the crust, mix the flour, salt, cinnamon and sugar together in a small bowl or a food processor.
Work in the butter until small crumbs are formed.
Add the Calvados and mix just until a dough is formed.
Wrap and chill for at least thirty minutes.
Roll out the dough and line a nine-inch square baking form placed on a buttered baking sheet.
Or use a buttered nine inch round tart pan with a removable bottom.
Cover with a piece of aluminum foil and line the pan with metal baking weights (or rice or beans).
Chill for another thirty minutes.
Preheat the oven to 400 degrees.
Bake the crust blind for fifteen minutes.
Then remove the foil and the weights and continue to bake the crust for another eight minutes.
Remove from the oven and cool for fifteen to twenty minutes before continuing.
While the crust is baking (or earlier), peel and core four of the apples. Cut into thin slices and cook with the water and lemon juice until the mixture is very soft and dry, stirring often.
Mix one-quarter cup of the sugar into the applesauce along with the cinnamon, ginger, nutmeg and heavy cream.
Taste and add more sugar and/or lemon juice, if needed. The mixture should be fairly tart. Chill.
The filling can be made a day or two ahead of time and chilled until needed.
It can also be frozen. Thaw before using.
Spread the cooled filling evenly into the partially baked shell.
Peel and core the remaining two apples. Cut into halves and slice thinly.
Place the apple slices in overlapping rows on top of the filling.
Sprinkle with the remaining tablespoon of sugar

PEAR AND ALMOND TART

and drizzle with the melted butter.
Return the tart to the oven (400 degrees) and bake for one hour, or until the apples are tender and the crust is nicely browned.
Cool for about ten minutes, then paint the top of the apple slices with the apricot glaze.
Remove from the pan when cool enough to handle. Serve warm.
Serves eight to nine portions.

†To cook the apples in a microwave oven, reduce the water to one tablespoon and cook for six minutes at high power, stirring once or twice.
††An apricot glaze is made from apricot preserves that have been heated with a spoon or two of water or brandy, just to melt. If there are large pieces of apricots present, then strain the glaze before using.

BANANA CREAM PIE

Crust:
1 cup flour
1/4 cup ground almonds
1 tablespoon sugar
pinch salt
1/4 teaspoon ground cinnamon
pinch grated nutmeg
1/2 cup butter
2 tablespoons cold water
Filling:
1 tablespoon gelatin (1 packet)
1/4 cup water
1 cup mashed bananas (2 or 3)
1 tablespoon lemon juice
1/4 teaspoon ground ginger
pinch grated nutmeg
6 tablespoons sugar
2 eggs, separated
1/4 cup sour cream
1 tablespoon rum
1 teaspoon vanilla extract
1/2 cup heavy cream, whipped

First make the crust. Mix the flour, ground almonds, sugar, salt, cinnamon and nutmeg together in a bowl or a food processor.
Work in the butter until small crumbs are formed.
Add the water and work until the mixture forms a dough.
Roll into a ball, flatten, wrap and chill for at least thirty minutes.
Roll out the dough and line a nine or ten inch pie tin, crimping the edges decoratively.
Chill the formed crust for another ten to fifteen minutes.
Cover with a piece of aluminum foil and weight the bottom with baking weights.
Bake (blind) in a preheated 400 degree oven for fifteen to eighteen minutes.
Remove the weights and the foil and continue to bake the crust until nicely browned, another twenty to twenty-five minutes.
Cool the crust a little before filling.
Sprinkle the gelatin over the water to soften.
Add to a saucepan along with the mashed bananas, lemon juice, ginger, nutmeg and three tablespoons of the sugar. Stir in the egg yolks.
Cook over a moderate heat, stirring, until the mixture thickens.
Remove from the heat and stir in the sour cream, rum and vanilla.
Cool a little.
Whip the cream separately and refrigerate until needed.
Once the filling has cooled, beat the egg whites until they are foamy and begin to turn white.
Gradually add the remaining three tablespoons of sugar and continue to beat until the whites are firm and glossy.
Fold half the whites into the cooled banana mixture.
Fold in the whipped cream, then the rest of the whites.
Pour the filling into the crust and refrigerate for a few hours until set.
This pie will keep well in the refrigerator for a few days.
Serve garnished with sweetened whipped cream.
Serves twelve.

PEAR CUSTARD TART

Shortcrust:
1 1/4 cups flour
2 tablespoons sugar
pinch salt
6 ounces butter
1 egg
1 1/2 teaspoons water
Filling:
1/2 cup cake or bread crumbs
5 or 6 pears
2/3 cup sugar
1 tablespoon cornstarch
1 egg
3/4 cup sour cream
3/4 cup heavy cream
juice of 1/2 lemon
1/2 teaspoon vanilla extract

You will need a nine inch tart pan with a removable bottom. Preheat the oven to 375 degrees.
First make the crust. Mix the flour, sugar and salt together.
Work in the butter until small crumbs are formed.
Mix the egg with the water. Add and work together just until a dough is formed.
Shape the dough into a ball, flatten a little, wrap and chill for at least thirty minutes.
Roll out the dough and fit it into the tart pan, cutting off any excess from around the edges.
Chill the crust for ten minutes.
Sprinkle the bread or cake crumbs in an even layer over the bottom of the crust, they will keep it from

becoming soggy.
Peel, core and cut the pears into one-half inch thick slices. Place the pears into the prepared crust.
Mix the sugar and the cornstarch together in a bowl.
Beat in the egg.
Then stir in the sour cream, heavy cream, lemon juice and the vanilla. Beat until smooth.
Pour the custard over the pears and place the tart in the oven.
Bake for one hour and fifteen minutes, or until the crust is browned, the filling set and the pears tender.
Serve the tart at room temperature or chilled.
This tart is best the day it is made, but will keep well in the refrigerator for a day or two. Do not freeze.
Serves ten to twelve.

PEAR AND ALMOND TART

Crust:
1 1/4 cups flour
dash salt
1 tablespoon sugar
1/2 cup butter
1 egg yolk
4 teaspoons ice water
Almond Filling:
1/3 cup butter
1/3 cup sugar
1 egg
2 ounces ground almonds (1/2 cup)
2 ounces ground hazelnuts (1/2 cup)
1 ounce flour (2 tablespoons)
1/2 teaspoon ground cinnamon
1 teaspoon lemon juice

4 pears
2 teaspoons sugar
apricot glaze, page 182

Butter a shallow ten-inch tart pan with a removable bottom. Preheat the oven to 400 degrees.
Make the crust. Combine the flour, salt and sugar in a bowl or a food processor.
Cut the butter into the mixture and work until small crumbs are formed.
Mix the egg yolk and the water. Add and work until a dough is formed.
Wrap and chill the dough for at least thirty minutes.
Roll out the crust and fit it into the pan. Prick the bottom with a fork and chill for at least ten minutes.
To make the almond filling, use a mixer and cream the butter with the sugar until light and fluffy.
Add the egg and beat well.
Combine the nuts, flour and cinnamon and stir them into the butter mixture.
Mix in the lemon juice.
This filling can be made up to a day ahead of time and refrigerated until needed.
Spread the almond cream evenly in the bottom of the chilled crust.
Peel the pears and cut them in half, lengthwise.
Cut out the cores, using a melon ball scoop and remove the stems.
Cut the pears, crosswise, into very thin slices.
Arrange the pears (use a palette knife to lift them so that the halves remain intact) on top of the filling.
Seven pear halves will fit into a ten inch pan. Cut the remaining pear half into shreds and use it to fill the spaces between the halves.
Press the pears down gently, and sprinkle the tops with the two teaspoons of sugar.
Bake for one hour and twenty to thirty minutes, or until the pears are tender and the crust is nicely browned.
Cool before removing the tart from the pan.
When room temperature, paint the top of the tart with the apricot glaze.
This tart tastes best when served at room temperature.
The pear tart will keep well for several days if covered and refrigerated.
Serves eight to ten portions.

NECTARINE CRUMB PIE

Filling:
10 nectarines (5 cups, sliced)†
1/3 cup flour
1/2 teaspoon ground cinnamon
2/3 cup sugar
1/2 cup sour cream
Crust:
1 cup flour
1/2 cup ground walnuts or pecans
1 tablespoon sugar
pinch salt
1/2 cup butter
2 tablespoons ice water
Topping:
1/4 cup flour
1/4 cup coarsely ground walnuts or pecans
1/4 cup sugar
1/4 teaspoon ground cinnamon
1/4 cup butter

You will need a nine and one-half or ten inch pie tin. Preheat the oven to 400 degrees.
Make the crust. Mix together the flour, ground nuts, sugar and salt in a bowl or a food processor.
Cut in the butter and work until small crumbs are formed.
Add enough ice water to form a dough.
Wrap and chill for at least thirty minutes.
Roll out the crust and place it into the pie tin. Flute the edges.
Chill for at least ten more minutes.
For the topping, mix together the flour, sugar,

PEAR CUSTARD TART

RICOTTA AMARETTI TART

nuts and cinnamon in a bowl or a food processor. Work in the butter until small crumbs are formed. The topping can be prepared a day or two ahead of time and refrigerated until needed.
Peel and slice the nectarines. Mix with the flour, cinnamon, sugar and the sour cream.
Spoon the fruit filling into the crust and smooth evenly.
Sprinkle the prepared topping over the fruit.
Bake for one hour and fifteen to twenty minutes, or until the crust and the topping are browned and the fruit is tender.
Allow to cool a little before slicing.
This pie is best when fresh, but will keep well for a few days if covered and refrigerated.
Serves twelve.

†Peaches can be substituted for the nectarines.

RICOTTA AMARETTI TART

Crust:
12 amaretti cookies (1/2 cup ground)
10 chocolate icebox cookies (1/2 cup ground)
1/2 cup unblanched almonds, ground
6 tablespoons butter, melted
Filling:
1/4 cup white raisins
1/4 cup Amaretto liqueur
1/4 cup water
1 packet gelatin (1 tablespoon)
1 fifteen ounce container whole milk ricotta cheese
1/2 cup sugar
1/2 teaspoon vanilla extract
2 tablespoons chopped walnuts
2 ounces grated semi-sweet chocolate

To make the crust, place the two kinds of cookies and the nuts into a food processor or blender and grind until fine.
Add the butter and process until the crumbs are moist.
Remove the crumbs from the machine and spread them evenly (with your fingers) into a nine inch pie tin or a nine inch tart pan with a removable bottom.
Chill in the refrigerator for at least thirty minutes or place in the freezer for ten to fifteen minutes before filling.
The crust can be prepared a day ahead of time and refrigerated, covered. It can also be frozen.
Soak the raisins in the liqueur for one hour or longer.
Pour the water into a small saucepan. Sprinkle the gelatin on top and allow it to soften for a few minutes.
Heat, stirring, to dissolve. Cool for a few minutes.
Place the cheese, sugar, vanilla and the gelatin into a food processor fitted with a steel knife and process until smooth.
Remove the cheese mixture from the machine and stir in the raisins, Amaretto, nuts and the chocolate.
Spoon the mixture into the crust, smooth and refrigerate for an hour or two, until set.
If using a pan with a removable bottom, the tart can be taken out once it is firm.
This tart will keep well for several days in the refrigerator. Wrap well.
Serves ten.

ANISE TOAST

COOKIES

ANISE TOAST

3 cups flour
1 1/2 teaspoons baking powder
1/4 teaspoon salt
1 teaspoon ground cinnamon
1/2 teaspoon anise seed
grated rind of one lemon
1/2 cup butter
1 cup sugar
3 eggs
1 tablespoon Pernod
1/2 teaspoon vanilla extract
1 cup almond slivers

Butter and flour a baking sheet. Preheat the oven to 375 degrees.
Mix together in a small bowl the flour, baking powder, salt, cinnamon, anise seed and grated lemon rind. Set aside.
Using a mixer, cream the butter with the sugar until light.
Beat in the eggs, one at a time.
Then stir in the Pernod and the vanilla.
Add the dry ingredients and mix well.
Mix in the almond slices. The dough should be very thick.
Turn the dough out onto a floured board and separate into three even pieces.
Shape each piece into a log, about nine or ten inches long by two inches wide and one inch thick.
Place the logs onto the baking sheet and bake for forty minutes.
They should be browned on the bottom and fairly firm.
Remove the logs from the oven and place them on a wire rack to cool for five to ten minutes.
Turn the oven up to 400 degrees.
Cut the logs into slices about one-half inch thick.
Place these slices back onto the baking sheet, on their sides. You can use a second baking sheet or do this in two batches.
Return the slices to the oven for six minutes.
Turn over and continue to bake for six more minutes. The slices should be lightly browned.
Remove and cool on a wire rack.
These cookies will keep well for a very long time.
Makes fifty-four to sixty cookies, depending on how thickly they are sliced.

BAKLAVA COOKIES

3/4 cup chopped pistachios
3/4 cup walnuts
1/2 cup sugar
1 teaspoon ground cinnamon
10 filo leaves
1/2 cup butter, melted
Syrup:
1 1/2 cups sugar
3/4 cup water
3 inch piece cinnamon stick
juice of 1 lemon

Shell and peel the pistachios. I find the easiest way to peel them is to dip them into boiling water for just one minute.
Drain, peel and allow the nuts to either air dry, or place in a warm oven for a few minutes before chopping.
Butter two baking sheets. Preheat the oven to 400 degrees.
Mix together the pistachios, walnuts, sugar and ground cinnamon.
Place all the syrup ingredients together in a saucepan so that they will be ready to cook once you put the cookies in the oven.
Spread out one filo leaf vertically. Keep the rest of the dough covered while working.
Brush the filo leaf with melted butter and sprinkle with some of the filling (one to two tablespoons).
Fold in half from top to bottom.
Brush again with the butter and sprinkle with a little more filling.
Roll into a cylinder, starting at the bottom.
Cut the roll into five or six pieces (about two inches each) and place them onto the buttered baking sheet as soon as they are finished.
Brush the tops of the cookies with the melted butter.
Repeat until all the filling is used. You can make from fifty to sixty cookies, depending on how generous you are with the filling.
Bake the cookies for fifteen minutes, just until lightly browned.
As soon as you have placed the cookies in the oven, bring the syrup to a quick boil.
Then cook over a moderate heat until thickened. Large bubbles should begin to form.
The cookies should be done at about the same time as the syrup.
If not, remove the syrup from the heat and reheat just before using.
Place the cookies onto a wire rack, with a drip pan underneath and spoon the syrup generously over the tops, coating all of them.
Allow to cool to room temperature before serving.
Best when fresh, they can be stored in the refrigerator overnight. Allow them to reach room temperature before serving. The cookies can be frozen.
Makes fifty to sixty cookies.

GEBACHENES

2 cups flour
1/2 teaspoon baking powder
1/4 teaspoon ground cinnamon
1/2 pound butter
7/8 cup sugar
1 egg plus 1 egg yolk
1/4 cup heavy cream
1/2 tablespoon apricot brandy
1/4 teaspoon vanilla

Decorations—Use any or all of the following:
1/2 cup cinnamon-sugar
1/2 cup chopped nuts
colored sprinkles
chocolate jimmies

Mix together the flour, baking powder and the cinnamon and reserve.
Using a mixer, cream the butter with the sugar until light and fluffy.
Blend in the whole egg.
Mix in the heavy cream, brandy and vanilla.
Gradually add the flour mixture, blending well.
Wrap the dough and chill overnight.
Remove the dough from the refrigerator an hour before baking.
Butter several baking sheets or line them with parchment paper.
Preheat the oven to 375 degrees.
Roll the dough out to about one-quarter inch thickness on a lightly floured board.
Cut into whatever shapes you like and place the cookies onto the baking sheets.
The extra dough can be rolled again and cut until it is all used.
Beat the yolk just to mix and lightly brush onto the tops of the cookies using a pastry brush.
Top with the cinnamon sugar and the nuts or the sprinkles.
Bake the cookies for about ten minutes, or until they are lightly browned.
Remove to a rack to cool.
These cookies will keep well for several days. They can also be frozen.
Makes six dozen or more cookies, depending on how they are cut.

GINGERBREAD MEN

2 cups flour
1 teaspoon baking soda
pinch salt
1 1/2 teaspoons ground ginger
1 teaspoon ground cinnamon
1/3 cup butter
1/3 cup brown sugar
1 egg yolk
2 tablespoons black strap molasses
1/4 cup dark corn syrup

Mix the flour, baking soda, salt, ginger and cinnamon and reserve.
Using a mixer, cream the butter with the sugar until light.
Stir in the egg yolk, molasses and the corn syrup.
Mix in the dry ingredients.
Form the dough into a ball, wrap and refrigerate for twenty to thirty minutes if you have the time. The dough will then be easier to roll out.
Roll the dough onto a lightly floured surface until it is about a quarter inch thick.
Cut with a small gingerbread cookie cutter and place onto baking sheets lined with aluminum foil.
The extra dough can be rolled out several times and cut until it is used up.
Bake in a preheated 325 degree oven just until the cookies are lightly browned on the bottom.
Cool on a wire rack and decorate once cold.
The cookies will keep well for at least a week. They can also be frozen.
Makes one hundred and twenty to thirty miniature gingerbread men.

DECORATORS ICING

1/2 egg white
1 cup or more sifted confectioners sugar
few drops lemon juice

Place the egg white and the lemon juice into a small bowl.
Gradually beat in the sifted sugar until a thick, but still liquid paste if formed. This is easiest done with a spoon.
Pipe the icing onto the cookies using a small paper coronet or a small pastry bag fitted with a number one or two round tip.
This icing dries out quickly, so use as soon as it is made. Cover tightly if you wish to keep it for a while.

LEMON HEARTS

1 cup butter
4 ounces cream cheese
1/2 cup sugar
1 tablespoon grated lemon rind
1/8 teaspoon lemon extract
2 1/2 cups flour
pinch salt
1/2 teaspoon grated nutmeg

Using a mixer, whip the butter with the cream cheese until the mixture is light and fluffy.
Blend in the sugar, lemon rind and lemon extract.
Mix the flour with the salt and add, working to form a dough.
Roll into a ball, flatten, wrap and refrigerate for at least one hour before rolling.
The dough can be refrigerated for a day or two at this point.
Lightly butter a few baking sheets. Preheat the oven to 350 degrees.
Roll out half the dough to a quarter-inch thickness on a lightly floured board.
Cut into small heart shapes and place the cookies on the baking sheets.
Repeat with the other half of the dough.
Sprinkle the tops of the cookies with a little nutmeg.
Bake for about twenty minutes, or until the cookies are lightly browned at the edges.
Remove and cool on a wire rack.
The cookies can be stored for a few days in an airtight container. They also freeze beautifully.
Makes about fifty small cookies.

SESAME PEANUT COOKIES

2 tablespoons toasted sesame seeds
1 cup flour
1 teaspoon baking powder
pinch salt
1/4 teaspoon grated nutmeg
2/3 cup butter
1/2 cup brown sugar
2 eggs
2/3 cup chunky peanut butter

Butter two baking sheets. Preheat the oven to 350 degrees.
Toast the sesame seeds for about ten to fifteen minutes in the oven or for two minutes on high power in a microwave oven.
Mix together the flour, baking powder, salt, nutmeg and sesame seeds and reserve.
Using a mixer, cream the butter with the sugar until light and fluffy.
Add the eggs and beat well.
Stir in the peanut butter and the dry ingredients.
Drop by heaping teaspoonfuls onto the prepared baking sheets. Leave room between the cookies, as they will spread when baked.
Bake for eighteen to twenty minutes. The cookies should be lightly browned around the edges.
Leave on the baking sheets for a few minutes, then remove the cookies to a rack to finish cooling.
Serve when cool.
These cookies will keep for several days. Store in an open container at room temperature, do not refrigerate.
They can also be frozen.
Makes about forty cookies.

LEMON HEARTS

CREAMS, MOUSSES, AND FRUIT DESSERTS

APPLE MOUSSE

4 baking apples
1 1/2 teaspoons gelatin (1/2 packet)
2 tablespoons lemon juice
3 tablespoons sugar
1/4 teaspoon ground cinnamon
1/8 teaspoon ground ginger
2 egg whites

Wash the apples. Do not core or peel them.
At the stem end, about three-quarters inch from the top, make a cut around the apples about one-half inch in depth.
Place the apples into a baking dish.
Add a quarter inch of water to the pan and bake the apples in a preheated 400 degree oven for thirty to thirty-five minutes.
The apples will still be firm.
Or bake in a microwave oven with only a spoon or two of water on high power for about eight minutes.
Remove the apples and allow them to cool a little.
Pour the lemon juice into a small saucepan. Sprinkle the gelatin over the lemon juice and let soften.
Heat to dissolve. This can also be done in a microwave.
Slice the pre-cut caps off the apples and reserve.
Using a sharp spoon or a melon ball cutter, scoop most of the pulp out of the apples.
Leave about a quarter-inch of pulp attached to the skin so the apples will retain their shape.
Discard the core and the seeds.
Place the pulp in a blender or food processor.
Add the lemon juice and gelatin, half the sugar, the cinnamon and the ginger.
Puree and remove from the machine.
Whip the egg whites until they turn white in color.
Gradually beat in the remaining sugar.
Continue to beat until the whites are stiff.
Fold the egg whites into the apple mixture.
Spoon into the apple shells and refrigerate until serving time.
The mousse will need an hour or two to set.
It will hold for about six hours, but should be served the day it is made.
At serving time, place the caps back onto the apples at an angle.
Decorate with a mint leaf, if desired.
Serves four.

APPLE MOUSSE, PINEAPPLE MINT CREME, TROPICAL FRUIT CREAM, ORANGE BAVARIAN CREAM

GINGER PEARS

2 pieces orange rind
2 pieces lemon rind
3 inch piece cinnamon stick
12 whole peppercorns
1 thick slice ginger root
2 cups sugar
juice of 1 lemon
4 to 6 cups water, or more to cover
6 firm pears

Place all the ingredients (except for the pears) into a pot just large enough to hold all the pears upright.
Bring to a boil and simmer for about ten minutes.
While the syrup is cooking, peel the pears. Core them through the bottom, leaving the top stems attached. I find a zucchini corer works well for this.
If you are not cooking the pears immediately, keep them in a bowl of water with some lemon juice added so that they will not darken.
Place the pears into the hot syrup. If there is not enough liquid to cover the pears, add more water.
Bring the liquid to a boil, cover the pan with a lid and simmer just until tender.
The amount of time this will take depends on the ripeness of the pears. Firm pears usually take about twenty minutes, but if yours are ripe, start checking after ten minutes.
Allow the pears to cool in the syrup. Once they reach room temperature, they can be refrigerated. Store in the syrup so that the pears do not dry out.
When ready to serve, drain well. Spoon on some ginger or chocolate sauce and top with toasted almond slices, if desired.
The pears will keep well if covered and refrigerated for three days.
The poaching liquid can be used again for another batch of pears. Store in the refrigerator for a week or so.
Serves six.
Alternate: Use whole peaches instead of pears.

GINGER SAUCE

1 inch slice ginger root
1 piece vanilla bean†
1/4 cup sugar
1 1/2 cups milk
1/2 cup heavy cream
3 egg yolks
2 slices crystallized ginger††

Crush the ginger root lightly with the back of a knife.
Place it, along with the vanilla bean and the sugar into a saucepan with one and one-quarter cups of the milk.
Heat slowly, so that the flavors of the ginger and the vanilla will infuse the milk.
Place the heavy cream into a bowl large enough to hold the sauce.
Set a strainer on top and refrigerate until needed.
Mix the egg yolks with the remaining quarter cup of milk.
When the ginger milk is very hot, stir a few spoons into the egg yolks.
Then whisk the yolks back into the pan.
Cook until the yolks have thickened the sauce, stirring constantly.
Do not boil, the sauce should just coat the back of a spoon.
Pour the sauce into the strainer (the cold cream in the bowl will stop the cooking).
Press well on the ginger root and discard.
The vanilla bean can be rinsed, dried and used again.
Chill the sauce.
Slice the crystallized ginger into thin slivers.
When ready to serve, stir the ginger into the sauce.
Excellent over poached fruit, such as pears or peaches. Serve with a sprinkling of toasted almond slices on the top.
Store, covered, in the refrigerator for a day or two. Do not freeze.
This recipe makes two cups of sauce, enough for six or more servings.

†Vanilla extract can be substituted. Add a quarter teaspoon to the finished sauce.
††Preserved ginger can be substituted.

KIRSCH CHARLOTTE RUSSE

1 package ladyfingers
1 tablespoon gelatin (1 packet)
1/4 cup water
1/3 cup sugar
1 cup milk
3 egg yolks
1/2 teaspoon vanilla extract
2 tablespoons Kirschwasser
3/4 cup heavy cream
Cherry Sauce, page 191

Line a five cup charlotte mold with plastic wrap.
Place a layer of the ladyfingers along the sides of the mold, brown side out.
Leave them in one piece if possible, they will be easier to handle.
Cover and reserve until needed.
Soften the gelatin in the water for a few minutes.
Place the softened gelatin into a saucepan along with the sugar and the milk.
Heat until very warm, stirring occasionally.
Stir the egg yolks just to mix. Add a few spoons of the hot milk mixture to the yolks, beating well.
Then whisk the yolks back into the hot milk.
Continue to cook just until the mixture thickens, stirring constantly. Do not allow the mixture to come to a boil.
Remove from the heat and pour into a bowl to

cool. Stir in the vanilla and the Kirsch.
Whip the cream lightly and refrigerate until needed.
When the charlotte base is cool but not set, fold in the whipped cream.
Pour this mixture into the prepared mold.
Place a layer of ladyfingers on top of the mold, covering it completely. Do not worry about how this looks, it will not show when the dessert is finished.
Cover and refrigerate for at least four hours. The charlotte will keep up to three days in the refrigerator.
To unmold, turn out onto a serving plate and remove the plastic wrap.
Serve with the Cherry Sauce on the side.
Serves eight.

CHERRY SAUCE

1 package frozen dark sweet pitted cherries (12 ounces)
1/4 cup sugar
1/2 tablespoon currant jelly
1 teaspoon lemon juice
1/2 teaspoon cornstarch
1/2 tablespoon water
1 tablespoon Kirschwasser

Thaw the frozen cherries. Remove one-half cup and reserve.
Puree the rest of the cherries along with any juice from the package using a food mill. If you use a food processor or blender, you will have to strain the puree to remove the skins.
Place the puree into a saucepan and add the sugar, currant jelly and the lemon juice.
Heat, stirring often, until the sauce is boiling and the sugar and jelly are dissolved.
Mix the cornstarch with the water. Stir this into the boiling liquid.
Continue to cook for two or three minutes.
Remove the sauce from the heat and stir in the Kirsch.
Chop the reserved cherries coarsely and add them to the sauce.
Once the sauce is cool, cover and refrigerate until serving time.
The sauce can be refrigerated for up to three days or it can be frozen.
This recipe makes about two cups of sauce, enough for one charlotte recipe.

MANGO AND COCONUT SNOW

1/2 tablespoon gelatin (1/2 packet)
1/4 cup water
1 cup crushed mango pulp
1 cup plain yogurt
2 teaspoons sugar
1/2 teaspoon ground cinnamon
4 teaspoons unsweetened coconut
4 teaspoons chopped toasted cashews

Sprinkle the gelatin over the water and allow to sit for a few minutes to soften. Heat, stirring, to dissolve.
This can be done in a small saucepan on top of the stove or in a dish in a microwave oven.
Mix the dissolved gelatin with the mango and the yogurt.
Stir in the sugar and the cinnamon.
Pour into four individual serving dishes and chill for a few hours until set.
The cream will keep for a day or two in the refrigerator, if covered.
Sprinkle each dessert with a teaspoon of the unsweetened (sometimes called dessicated) coconut and the nuts (no salt) and serve.
Excellent after an Indian dinner.
Serves four.

MOCHA PARFAIT

1 tablespoon gelatin (1 packet)
1/3 cup water
2 tablespoons instant coffee powder
1 tablespoon dark cocoa powder
1/8 teaspoon ground ginger
1 1/2 cups heavy cream
3 eggs
1/2 cup sugar
2 tablespoons brandy†
1/3 cup grated chocolate

Using a small saucepan, sprinkle the gelatin over the water to soften.
Heat, stirring, until the gelatin is dissolved.
Add the coffee powder, cocoa and ginger to the hot liquid. Mix well and set aside to cool a little.
Whip the cream and refrigerate until needed.
Using a mixer, beat the eggs with the sugar until they are very light in color and have doubled in volume.
Stir in the coffee mixture along with the brandy.
Fold in the whipped cream and the grated chocolate.
Pour the parfait into individual serving dishes or wine glasses and refrigerate for a few hours.
At serving time, you can decorate the tops of the parfaits with a little sweetened whipped cream and chocolate coffee beans, if desired.
The parfait will keep well in the refrigerator for two days. Keep covered.
Serves eight.

†Or use a coffee flavored liqueur, such as Tia Maria.

ORANGE BAVARIAN CREAM

4 egg yolks
1 1/2 cups milk
1/2 cup sugar
pinch salt
1 tablespoon Grand Marnier
1/2 teaspoon vanilla extract

GINGER PEARS, GINGER SAUCE

MANGO AND COCONUT SNOW

1 teaspoon grated orange rind
1/2 cup orange juice
1 tablespoon gelatin (1 packet)
1 cup heavy cream
1/4 teaspoon ground cinnamon
pinch grated nutmeg

Mix the egg yolks with a few spoons of the milk and reserve.
In a saucepan, heat the remaining milk with the sugar and the salt until very hot.
Mix a few spoons of the hot milk into the yolks, then add the yolks back to the pan, stirring constantly.
Cook just until the sauce has thickened, stirring constantly. Do not allow the egg yolks to boil.
Remove from the heat and pour into a bowl.
Stir in the Grand Marnier, vanilla and orange rind. Allow the cream to cool a little.
Pour the orange juice into a small saucepan. Sprinkle the gelatin on top and allow it to soften for a few minutes.
Heat to dissolve, then cool a little.
Whip the heavy cream with the cinnamon and nutmeg until thick.
Combine the cooled egg base with the gelatin mixture.
Fold in the whipped cream.
Pour into individual serving dishes or wine glasses and refrigerate for a few hours until set.
This dessert will keep well for a day or two in the refrigerator if well covered. Do not garnish until the day it is to be served.
Serve garnished with a little sweetened whipped cream and a fresh orange segment.
Serves six.

PINEAPPLE MINT CREME

1 tablespoon dried mint leaves
1/4 cup lime juice (2 limes)†
2/3 cup sugar
1 cup water
1 eight ounce can crushed pineapple
1 tablespoon gelatin (1 packet)
2 tablespoons Creme de Menthe
1 1/4 cups heavy cream

Place the mint leaves into a small saucepan along with the lime juice, sugar and water.
Bring to a boil and simmer for ten minutes.
Allow the mixture to cool to room temperature, then strain, pressing the leaves well to extract all the liquid.
Reserve the liquid and discard the leaves.
Drain the crushed pineapple, reserving the liquid.
Pour this pineapple juice into a small saucepan and sprinkle the gelatin on top.
Heat, stirring, to dissolve the gelatin.
Combine the mint extract with the gelatin and cool the combination in the refrigerator until it just begins to set.
Whip the heavy cream until stiff.
Stir the crushed pineapple and the Creme de Menthe into the cooled base, then fold in the whipped cream.
Spoon into serving dishes or a bowl and chill for a few hours until set.
Serve garnished with fresh mint leaves, if available.
The creme can be refrigerated for a few days, keep well covered.
It will taste even better the day after it is made.
Serves six.

†Lemon juice can be substituted, but this dessert is better if made with lime juice.

TROPICAL FRUIT CREAM

1 tablespoon gelatin (1 packet)
1/4 cup water
1 cup sour cream
1/2 cup sugar
1/2 teaspoon grated ginger root
1/2 teaspoon vanilla extract
1/2 cup mango pulp or puree†
3 cups diced fruits or berries††
1 cup heavy cream

Using a small saucepan, sprinkle the gelatin over the water and allow it to sit for a few minutes to soften.
Heat, stirring until it is dissolved.
Place the dissolved gelatin, along with the sour cream, sugar, grated ginger, vanilla and the half cup of mango puree into a food processor fitted with a steel knife. Or use a blender.
Puree well, then remove from the machine.
Whip the cream lightly. Stir one-third of the whipped cream into the fruit mixture, then fold in the rest.
Drain the diced fruits well, then fold them into the cream.
Pour the fruit cream into individual serving dishes or wine glasses and refrigerate for a few hours until firm.
The cream can also be poured into a bowl, but looks better if served individually.
Garnish with a little sweetened whipped cream and a whole berry or slice of fruit.
The fruit cream will keep well for a day or two if covered and refrigerated.
Serves eight.

†The puree lends both color and flavor to the basic cream. If mango is not available, then substitute strawberries, blueberries, peaches, etc. Almost any summer fruit will do.
††Several combinations of fruits can be used for this dessert.
Lychee nuts, green seedless grapes, strawberries, blueberries, blackberries and raspberries are all excellent.
Or try diced peaches, nectarines or even apricots.
Use only canned pineapple, not fresh.

MEASUREMENTS

WEIGHTS

1 ounce	= 30 grams (approximate)
8 ounces (1/2 pound)	= 225 grams
16 ounces (1 pound)	= 450 grams
1 gram	= 0.035 ounces
100 grams	= 3 1/3 ounces
1 kilogram (1000 grams)	= 2.2 pounds

To convert ounces to grams, multiply the number of ounces by 28.35.
To convert grams to ounces, multiply the number of grams by 0.035.

COMPARATIVE OVEN TEMPERATURES

DEGREES FAHRENHEIT	DEGREES CELSIUS
225	110
250	120
275	135
300	150
325	165
350	180
375	190
400	205
425	220
450	230
475	245
500	260
525	275
550	290

LIQUID MEASUREMENTS

	CUPS	FLUID OUNCES	MILLILITERS (approximate)
1 teaspoon	= 60 drops	= 1/6	= 5
3 teaspoons	= 1 Tablespoon	- 1/2	= 15
4 Tablespoons	= 1/4	= 2	= 60
8 Tablespoons	= 1/2	= 4	= 120
16 Tablespoons	= 1	= 8	= 240
1 pint	= 2	= 16	= 480
1 quart	= 4	= 32	= 960
1 American cup		= 8	
1 English cup		= 10	

INCHES TO CENTIMETERS

1 inch	= 2 1/2 centimeters
12 inches = 1 foot	= 30 centimeters
24 inches = 2 feet	= 60 centimeters

To convert inches to centimeters, multiply the number of inches by 2.54.
To convert centimeters to inches, multiply the number of centimeters by 0.39.

GLOSSARY

A listing of useful terms as they relate to herbs and spices.

ABSORB. To suck up or take in. Plant cells absorb materials that are in solution.
ACHENE. A dry, hard, one-seeded fruit.
ADAPTATION. The adjustment of an organism to its environment.
ANNUAL. A plant which completes its life cycle within one year.
ARIL. An auxiliary covering or appendage present on some seeds (example, mace).
BARK. The external covering of a woody plant or tree.
BERRY. A simple, fleshy fruit in which one or more seeds are embedded.
BIENNIAL. A plant which takes two years to complete its life cycle.
BOLT. A condition referred to when a plant produces seeds prematurely, usually caused by dry, hot weather.
BOTANNICAL NAME. A Latin name in two parts given to all plants. The first name represents the genus of the plant, the second is for the species.
BUD. A small protuberance which contains an undeveloped stem or branch on a plant.
BULB. A modified leaf bud consisting of a fleshy underground stem which acts as a storage unit, enabling the plant to survive the winter.
BUSH. A low thick shrub that does not have a distinct trunk.
CAPSULE. A dry fruit that splits open when ripe.
CHLOROPHYLL. A green pigment necessary for the absorption of light energy in the process of photosynthesis.
CONDIMENT. A seasoning used to give flavor to food.
CORM. An enlarged underground stem of a plant in which food is stored.
COTYLEDON. The first leaf developed by the embryo of a seed plant.
CUTTING. A section of stem or root used for plant propagation.
DECIDUOUS. Trees and shrubs which lose their leaves in the winter.
DECOCTION. An extract obtained by boiling a solid material, such as bark, roots or seeds in water.
DORMANT. A state of reduced activity.
ESSENTIAL OIL. See volatile oil.
EXTRACT. A substance which contains the true essence or flavor of an herb or spice.
FAMILY. A group of related plants. For botannical purposes, a family would be classified below order and above genus.
FRUIT. The developed ovary, usually edible, of a seed plant.
GENUS. A group of plants, having a common ancestor, that are similar in structure. The plural is genera.
GERMINATION. The earliest stage in the growth of a seed or bud.
HABITAT. The natural home of a plant.
HARDEN OFF. The gradual exposure of indoor plants to outdoor conditions.
HERB. A foliage plant grown in a temperate climate which is used to flavor foods.
HIP. The fruit of a rose that consists of a fleshy hollow floral cap with its enclosed seeds.
HULL. The outer covering of some fruits and seeds.
HUMUS. Decomposing organic matter found in the soil.
HYBRID. The result of a cross between two parents that are genetically unlike.
INFUSION. A liquid extract resulting from the steeping of a substance (such as leaves) in water.
LEAF BUD. An undeveloped leaf.
MULCH. A protective covering spread around plants to retain the soil moisture and to keep them from freezing.
NIP OFF. To remove the growing tip of a plant. Same as pinch back.
NODE. An enlarged portion of the stem from which branches, leaves and buds originate.
NUT. A dry, hard one-seeded fruit.
OFFICIAL. (Plant) A plant used in medicine, listed in the Pharmacopeia.
PERENNIAL. A plant with a life cycle of three years or more.
PHOTOSYNTHESIS. A process by which water and carbon dioxide are chemically brought together to form a carbohydrate, using the sun as a source of energy.
POD. An elongated vessel containing seeds.
RHIZOME. A large horizontal elongated underground root-like stem, which sends out roots

below and shoots above.

RUNNER. A stem that grows horizontally along the surface of the ground.

SEED. A ripened ovule which contains the embyronic plant and a reserve food supply.

SHRUB. A woody plant that remains relatively low in height and produces permanent stems which branch from or near to the ground.

SPECIES. A group of individual plants belonging to the same genus.

SPICE. A class of aromatic substances of vegetable origin grown in the tropics.

SPIKE. An elongated stem with flowers directly attached.

STEM. The main leaf and flower bearing support of a plant.

TAP ROOT. The primary root of a plant which grows downwards. Small branch-like roots can develop from a tap root.

TEA. A simple infusion.

TENDRIL. A slender, coiling, leafless shoot-like organ which attaches to an object to help support the plant.

TERMINAL BUD. The bud at the end of a stem.

THINNING OUT. The removal of extra seedlings so as to allow enough growing room for those remaining.

TINCTURE. A solution of a medicinal substance in alcohol.

TISANE. A medicinal tea prepared from a herb or spice. Originally prepared with barley water and fed to invalids.

TREE. A woody perennial plant that produces one main trunk and a more or less distinct and elevated crown or branches.

TUBER. A short thick (usually but not always) underground stem or branch which bears buds or eyes and serves as a storage organ for the plant.

UMBEL. A flower cluster arising from a single flower stalk or stem.

VARIETY. A category of distinct plants within a species.

VOLATILE OIL. A complex oil contained in plants which gives to each a characteristic and distinct scent and taste. Same as essential oil.

WHORL. A circle of three or more leaves or flower parts at a single node.

WILT. To become limp, usually because of heat and/or the lack of water.

BIBLIOGRAPHY

Albert, Virginia F. and George. *Fun With Growing Plants Indoors.* New York: Crown Publishers, Inc., 1974.

All You Need to Know About Herbs. London: Marshall Cavendish, Ltd., 1973.

Boxer, Arabella and Philippa Back. *The Herb Book.* London: Octopus Books, Ltd., 1980.

Brimer, John Burton. *Growing Herbs in Pots.* New York: Simon and Schuster, 1976.

Brownlow, Margaret. *Herbs and the Fragrant Garden.* New York: McGraw Hill, 1963.

Carter, Susannah. *The Frugal Housewife.* Philadelphia: James Carey, 1796.

Clarkson, Rosetta E. *The Golden Age of Herbs and Herbalists.* New York: Dover Publications, Inc., 1972.

Clarkson, Rosetta E. *Herbs, Their Culture and Uses.* New York: The MacMillian Co., 1942.

Clarkson, Rosetta E. *Magic Gardens.* New York: The MacMillian Co., 1939.

Dampney, Janet and Elizabeth Pomeroy. *All About Herbs.* New Jersey: Chartwell Books, Inc., 1977.

David, Elizabeth. *Spices, Salt and Aromatics in the English Kitchen.* New York: Penguin Books, 1970.

De Sounin, Leonie. *Magic in Herbs.* New York: M. Barrows and Co., 1941.

Dowden, Anne Ophilia. *A Chronicle of Herbs, This Noble Harvest.* New York: William Collins Publishers, Inc., 1979.

Foster, Gertrude B. *Herbs for Every Garden.* New York: E.P. Dutton And Co., 1973.

Fox, Helen Morgenthau. *Gardening with Herbs for Flavor and Fragrance.* New York: The MacMillian Co., 1933.

Freeman, Margaret B. *Herbs for the Mediaeval Household.* New York: Huxley House, 1943.

Garland, Sarah. *The Complete Book of Herbs and Spices.* London: Frances Lincoln Publishers, Ltd., 1979.

Glasse, Hannah. *The Art of Cookery.* London: Printed for the author, 1747.

Gilbertie, Sol with Larry Sheehan. *Herb Gardening at It's Best.* New York: Antheneum, 1978.

Grieve, M. *Culinary Herbs and Condiments.* New York: Harcourt, Brace and Co., 1934.

Hagner, Dorothy Childs. *A Fresh Herb Platter.* New York: Doubleday and Co., 1961.

Hall, Dorothy. *The Book of Herbs.* New York: Charles Scribner's Sons, 1972.

Harris, Ben Charles. *The Compleat Herbal.* New York: Larchmont Books, 1972.

Hatfield, Audrey Wayne. *Pleasures of Herbs.* New York: St. Martin's Press, 1964.

Healey, B.J. *A Gardener's Guide to Plant Names.* New York: Charles Scribner's Sons, 1972.

Hlava, Bohumir and Dagmar Lanska. *Kitchen Herbs and Spices.* London: Octopus Books, Ltd., 1980.

Hoffman, Irene Bosford. *The Book of Herb Cookery.* Boston: Houghton Mifflin Co., 1940.

Hortus Third. Staff of the L.H. Bailey Hortorium, Cornell University. New York: Macmillian Publishing Co., 1976.

How to Grow Herbs. Sunset Books and Sunset Magazines. California: Lane Books, 1972.

Jacobs, Betty E.M. *Growing and Using Herbs Successfully.* Vermont: Garden Way Publishing, 1976.

Jones, Dorothy Bovee. *The Herb Garden.* Philadelphia: Dorrance and Co., 1947.

Krutch, Joseph Wood. *Herbal.* Boston: David R. Godine, 1976.

Landry, Robert. *The Gentle Art of Flavoring.* New York: Abelard-Schuman, Ltd., 1970.

Lang, George. *The Cuisine of Hungary.* New York: Crown Publishers, Inc., 1972.

Lathrop, Norma Jean. *Herbs, How to Select, Grow and Enjoy.* Tucson: H.P. Books, Fisher Publishing, Inc., 1981.

La Varenne, Francois-Pierre de. *The French Cook.* London: Printed for Charles Adams, 1653.

Loewenfeld, Claire and Philippa Back. *The Complete Book of Herbs and Spices.* London: David and Charles, 1974.

Loewenfeld, Claire and Philippa Back. *Herb Gardening, Why and How to Grow Herbs.* London: Faber and Faber, Ltd., 1964.

Mazza, Irma Goodrich. *Herbs for the Kitchen.* Boston: Little, Brown and Co., 1939.

Miloradovitch, Milo. *The Home Garden Book of Herbs and Spices.* New York: Doubleday and Co., Inc., 1952.

The Rodale Herb Book. Emmaus: The Rodale Press, Inc., 1974.

Rosengarten, Frederic, Jr. *The Book of Spices.* Wynnewood: Livingston Publishing Co., 1969.

Rhode, Eleanor Sinclair. *A Garden of Herbs.* New York: Dover Publications, Inc., 1969.

Root, Waverly. *Herbs and Spices, The Pursuit of Flavor.* England: McGraw-Hill Book Co., 1980.

Sanecki, Kay N. *The Complete Book of Herbs.* New York: Macmillian Publishing Co., Inc., 1974.

Spices of the World Cookbook by McCormick. New York: McGraw-Hill Book Co., 1964.

Stevenson, Violet. *A Modern Herbal.* London: Ocotopus Books, Ltd., 1974.

Stuart, Malcolm. *The Encyclopedia of Herbs and Herbalism.* New York: Grosset and Dunlap, 1979.

Vehling, Joseph Dommers. *Apicius, Cookery and Dining in Imperial Rome.* New York: Dover Publications, Inc., 1977.

Webster, Helen Noyes. *Herbs, How to Grow Them and How to Use Them.* Boston: Hale, Cushman and Flint, 1939.

What You Need to Know to Preserve Herbs. Michigan: Fox Hill Farms, 1981.

INDEX

Italics indicate recipes
Boldface numbers indicate pictures